The Culture of Al Jazeera

The Culture of Al Jazeera

Inside an Arab Media Giant

MOHAMED ZAYANI
and
SOFIANE SAHRAOUI

McFarland & Company, Inc., Publishers
Jefferson, North Carolina, and London

LIBRARY OF CONGRESS CATALOGUING-IN-PUBLICATION DATA

Zayani, Mohamed, 1965–
    The culture of Al Jazeera : inside an Arab media giant / Mohamed
Zayani and Sofiane Sahraoui.
        p.   cm.
    Includes bibliographical references and index.

    ISBN-13: 978-0-7864-2961-5
    softcover : 50# alkaline paper ∞

    1. Al Jazeera (Television network)   I. Sahraoui, Sofiane.
II. Title.
PN1992.92.A39Z39   2007
384.55'23 — dc22   2007001363

British Library cataloguing data are available

©2007 Mohamed Zayani and Sofiane Sahraoui. All rights reserved

Cover image: From the documentary *Control Room,* 2004
(Al Jazeera/Magnolia Pictures)

Manufactured in the United States of America

*McFarland & Company, Inc., Publishers
  Box 611, Jefferson, North Carolina 28640
    www.mcfarlandpub.com*

Acknowledgments

This book would not have been possible without the support, help and input of a great many individuals. We appreciate the accessibility and openness shown by many of the people we interviewed over the course of this research, and we are especially grateful to those people for their willingness to share with us some of their innermost perspectives.

In this context, we would like to thank officials and personnel from Al Jazeera and Al Arabiya who agreed to be interviewed including those who asked to remain anonymous. In particular, we would like to thank Mahmoud Abbulhadi, Abdallah Al Dhaher, Sarah Al Dundaravy, Abed Al Jubeh, Abdelfatteh Al Maneie, Yousef M. Al Shouly, Ahmad Sheikh, Amal Wannas, Dana Al Suyyegh, Faisal Al Kasim, Habib Ghreibi, Jamal Demloj, Jihad Ballout, Kefah Salem, Khaled Al Hroub, Lamis Andoni, Leila Chaiebi, Maan Al Sheriti, Madawi Al Ansari, Malek Triki, Mekki Helal, Moftah Al Suwaidan, Mohamed Al Alami, Mohamed B. Al Sada, Mohammed Jassim Al Ali, Mohamed Krichene, Mohamed Madani, Montaha Al Ramhi, Tahani Sabbagh, Mostefa Souag, Osama Moustafa, Saeed A. Shouly, Salah Nejm, Ghassan bin Jeddou, Abdelwahhab Ali Mohamed, Mohammad Dawod, Abdullah Adam Hurbokanin, Manal El Hrisse, Ahmed Hesham El Deeb, Khuloud Amer, Atef Al Dalkamouni, Mohamaden Baba Ould Etfagha, Claire Talon, and Waddah Khanfar.

Particular thanks are also due to Abdellatif Kemakhem, Abdelkader Daghfous, Jihad Fakhreddine, Mohammed El Oifi, Naomi Sakr, Marwan Kraidy, Noureddine Miladi, Ihab Bessaiso, Donatella Della Ratta, and Muhammad I. Ayish for their insights. Finally, we are most grateful to Anthony Collins for his insightful conversations.

This research was partly formulated in the context of an International Collaborative Research Grant from the Social Science Research

Council's Program on the Middle East and North Africa. To both Craig Calhoun and Seteney Shami from the SSRC we express our appreciation. We also would like to thank the American University of Sharjah for partial support to this project through its FRG program.

Table of Contents

I'm perfectly aware of having continuously made shifts both in the things that have interested me and in what I have already thought. In addition, the books I write constitute an experience for me that I'd like to be as rich as possible. An experience is something you come out of changed. If I had to write a book to communicate what I have already thought, I'd never have the courage to begin it. I write precisely because I don't know yet what to think about a subject that attracts my interest. In so doing, the book transforms me, changes what I think. As a consequence, each new work profoundly changes the terms of thinking which I had reached with the previous work. In this sense I consider myself more an experimenter than a theorist. I don't develop deductive systems to apply uniformly in different fields of research. When I write, I do it above all to change myself and not to think the same thing as before.

— Michel Foucault, *Remarks on Marx*

Preface

This book is about Al Jazeera Satellite Channel, not so much as a news broadcaster but as an organization. It is an attempt to determine what explains Al Jazeera's prowess from an organizational perspective and whether Al Jazeera is a new breed of media organization whose "success" emanates from its organizational model. Motivating this study is a central question: why and how Al Jazeera managed to do what it did better than any other media outlet or competing media player in the Middle East region and to what extent Al Jazeera's experience in the field of broadcasting can be considered "successful" and lasting. It also opens the door for probing the question of the transferability of such an experience within the media sphere and beyond. Naturally, one would assume that for Al Jazeera's experience to be transferable to the rest of the media scene in the Arab world it has to have solid organizational underpinnings, without which the network would be little more than a fad born out of special circumstances, and maybe carrying the same propagandistic agenda which pervades Arab media, though of a different nature.

Besides serving as an inquiry into the structure of Al Jazeera, this study is also necessarily an attempt to map out the organizational culture of such an organization. When considering Al Jazeera, organizational culture is of utter importance as an analytical tool that is essential to understanding how the organization functions. As with any other organization, Al Jazeera's value orientation has a significant impact on its strategic options and decisions. Hence it becomes of the essence to explore Al Jazeera's distinct cultural beliefs which drive its *modus operandi*, define its strategic options and provide the emotional engine of its success.

Broadly speaking, organizational culture refers to those elements in an organization that are most stable and least malleable which provide meaning and motivation for members or employees to behave in a particular way. Within every organization, there is a set of unconscious

1

shared basic assumptions and beliefs which are unique to the organization and which shape the way the members of the organization think and act. For Edgar H. Schein, one of the prominent organizational culture theorists, "culture is for the organization what character is to the individual."[1] As a culture successfully solves problems and overcomes difficulties, the assumptions which contributed to this success become widespread and internalized, thus providing for a certain degree of consistency.[2]

Although the notion of culture is inherent to all organizations, some appear to have stronger, more deeply rooted cultures than others. Treating culture in the organization as a manageable competitive asset rather than a natural phenomenon goes a long way toward increasing the effectiveness of the organization and maximizing the value of its human capital. The culture of an organization can be managed, so to speak, to improve performance in such varied aspects as coordination and integration, product, strategy and process innovation, effective management of dispersed work units, management of workforce diversity and facilitation and support of teamwork. The need to pay attention to organizational culture in the increasingly competitive environment which marks the age of globalization is more acute than ever. Overall, the culture of an organization can provide an external identity, create a sense of commitment, serve as a source of high reliability, define an interpretative scheme and act as a social control mechanism — although when strong and imposing, it can also create barriers to change and lead to conflict within the organization. Culture is essentially the soul of the organization, and all formal and informal systems in place are the manifestation of that culture; as such, they are cultural artifacts. Abstracting values and norms as manifestations of culture from organizational analysis is like trying to understand human behavior without analyzing its underlying psyche.

As much as it is pervasive, culture is also elusive, which is tantamount to saying that culture may not be revealed in its entirety. For Schein, one can distinguish between the essence of culture and its manifestation. In his view, the culture of an organization is made up of three distinct layers or levels: assumptions, values and artifacts. The first level — which is the deepest and hardest to uncover — is that of underlying beliefs and basic assumptions. It constitutes shared assumptions (which are deep-rooted and therefore unquestioned) about the organization and its environment which form an interrelated system of beliefs. Because they are shared, and therefore mutually reinforced, these tacit or hidden assumptions create a sense of group identity which reduces uncertainty and promotes predictability. The second level, that of values, is less covert and includes the organization's official mission statement, corporate philosophy and goals; in other words, all that which dictates one's behavior. The third and overt level, which is easy to observe but difficult to decipher, is that of artifacts. These are the manifestation of a certain character or value and can be seen in such varied aspects as visible products (including architecture and physical environment) and communication style (including manner of address, dress and logo).[3]

While outlining the distinctive features of Al Jazeera's culture, it is important to emphasize that culture is far from being a cohesive, static or stable whole. Culture is more complex and more asymmetrical than some unitary theoretical frameworks often lead one to believe.[4] The description of a particular culture should take heed of the various subcultures within the organization that may be in conflict with each other or the subunits whose shared experience may not be long enough to form shared common assumptions. In the words of Schein, "culture as a state does not have to imply unanimity or absence of conflict. There can be some very strong shared assumptions and large areas of conflict and/or ambiguity within a given cultural state."[5] In exploring a particular organization, one should attempt to identity the unifying culture without being insensitive to the presence of idiosyncratic subcultures or incognizant of the effect of these subcultures on the organization. Indeed, there are subcultures and countercultures which exist alongside, challenge or even deny the cultural patterns and dominant values of the overall culture. Consequently, one needs to look at both how given cultural assumptions are reinforced and confirmed and possibly challenged and unsettled.[6]

The need to deconstruct an apparently seamless culture cannot be emphasized enough, as there is a common tendency among researchers to homogenize the culture of the organization when investigating it insofar as culture tends to be treated as given and unavoidable. In reality, neatly organized and well integrated cultural patterns do not fully reflect the complexity and dynamism of a culture. The preoccupation with cultural patterns and cultural systems is sometimes achieved at the expense of contradictions, inconsistencies and discrepancies — which are often dismissed as irrelevant or simply unworthy of investigation.[7] If we concede, along with Henri Lefebvre, that "all systems are incommensurable," then we need to take heed of asymmetries that exist within the organization and which may be integral to the culture. In order to avoid falling into a reductionist approach which looks at the media organization through the lenses of a normative model, special attention will be paid to contradiction, change and adaptability within the culture. The absence of a rigid structure, as was the case with Al Jazeera at least during its formative years, suggests that the culture which managed to seep in is one of flexibility, in which case improvisation — which marks some of the practices of the network — acquires a positive value. Since this is the case, identifying trends, even if these are sometimes asymmetrical or possibly conflictual, may be a worthwhile pursuit as it wards off the threat of petrifying the structures at work within the system.

Seeing the organizational culture of Al Jazeera for what it is has set us on an exciting course of discovery, at times bringing home simple truths that did not live up to the image we had of Al Jazeera, while at other times leaving us puzzled by the complexity of the organizational reality of this news network. The joys of discovery were there not only when we thought we had come close to understanding an important phenomenon in the Arab world in general and Middle East broadcasting in particular, but also when there was nothing to uncover and we knew it. That in itself was an insightful discovery. Being an eccentric organization which refuses typification has made Al Jazeera all the more interesting. If for nothing else, Al Jazeera begs for attention because it is an aberration in the Arab world. Regardless of the outcome and irrespective of the findings of this study, the elusive nature of Al Jazeera suggests that it is an organization that is worthy of investigation.

Before delving into the nitty-gritty of Al Jazeera's organizational culture, it is desirable to say a word about the methodology that informs this research. It is particularly useful at this point to provide a summary of the case study design, a description of the sources of evidence, a rationale for data collection procedures, and an explanation of the format for data analysis. A word is also in order about the difficulties with which research about Arab broadcasting is fraught and the spirit of collaboration which underpins this project.

In presenting the findings of this research, we have made extensive use of interviews and company documentation. We have relied to a great extent on impressions from the network staff — what they perceive and how they understand the culture of the organization. These impressions were largely conveyed in the interviews we conducted with employees during our visits to Al Jazeera. During our data collection trips to Al Jazeera headquarters in Doha over a period of 18 months (starting from the latter part of 2004 and extending throughout 2005), we observed the network staff at work, held in-depth discussions with key people in the organization, made formal interviews in accordance with scales that have been developed for that purpose, conducted informal interviews, and had phone conversations. The number of people who were interviewed or were associated in one way or another with our fact finding endeavors exceeds 50. Over the course of our research, we interacted with upper management and staff members, talked to old-timers and newcomers, interviewed on-screen figures and behind-the-scene figures. We also traced a number of former Al Jazeera staff members who moved on to competing media outlets in the region and beyond. Understandably, aside from published interviews and public statements, most of the interviews are uncredited to ensure anonymity.

While insightful, these interviews are not sufficient. People often take for granted the basic aspects of the culture of the organization. They perceive as culture those aspects that stand out when put in the context of general ideas, values and views. Mats Alvesson further points out the limits of such an approach: "People recognize as culture those aspects that they have experienced as relative compared to other settings, but not what is common to the overall managerial culture which provides the ground against which minor company-specific variations are perceived.... What we need are broader approaches whereby the overall cultural characteristics of organizations are not taken for granted in a way that allows for the exclusive concentration on performance-related norms and behavior patterns."[8] In order to delve even deeper into the culture of the organization, the employees' impressions of the culture of Al Jazeera are reinforced with the organization's own perception of what its own culture is all about. Such information provides a complementary perspective which highlights cultural patterns in more depth and exposes culture where people in the organization may not recognize the cultural element — whence the chapter on the values Al Jazeera upholds. In addition to interviews, this particular research relies on different sources of evidence, including artifacts, internal or official organization literature put out by Al Jazeera, literature available on and studies about Al Jazeera, and observations recorded in our researchers' log.

In much the same way the employees of an organization may take for granted the culture of their organization, the perspective of the inquirer can also prove constraining if it is close to the subject of inquiry to the extent that it takes certain practices for granted. Collaboration, which enables us to develop a perspective that can rise to the complexity and interdisciplinary nature of the issue at hand, goes a long way toward warding off the danger of falling into a normative perspective. In "The Cultural Perspective of Organizations," Mats Alvesson points out the value of merging management and organization research with an outsider's perspective:

> Management and organization researchers "know" what business and organizations are about; they have specific ideas about what to look for and are consequently unlikely to discover anything new in an anthropological sense. Their tradition overlaps that of organizations too much. These people cannot be expected to adopt the "naïve" and questioning perspective of a person unfamiliar with a particular culture to avoid falling into unquestioning assumptions about the culture concerned.[9]

This research project brings together two researchers from different though not unrelated fields of study: organizational studies and cultural studies. Such collaboration offers an informed business perspective while providing grounding in social sciences. The cultural environment of the research we have undertaken makes the marriage between the two approaches all the more appropriate. We are hoping that collaboration between someone from the field of business management who is well versed in organizational culture literature and someone who is steeped in media studies will reduce the risk of cultural blindness and afford us the opportunity to get out of our systems and to think differently and collectively about the issue under consideration. It will also allow for breaking areas of study monopoly and enlarging our findings beyond the formulations of an individual researcher constrained by a particular discipline. We believe that the insights which collaboration brings in can greatly enhance the quality and outcome of this project.

Naturally, a project which involves delving into the culture of an organization is not without challenges. Some of these challenges have already been pointed out by culture scholars. In the normal flow of things, Edgar Schein writes, "cultural data are unintentionally concealed; the 'natives' are not conscious of what it is they take for granted. The researcher then has the problem of how to observe phenomena that occur at that level without, at the same time, upsetting the natives by delving into areas that may be defined by them as private, or even unwittingly intervening in those cultures by raising questions that the natives may never have thought about."[10] Accordingly, Schein outlines three routes into an organization's culture: the insider's role, the consultant's role and the formal researcher's role. The first one, the insider's role, requires that the observer remain in the system long enough to figure out what things mean and to seek informants and develop a relationship with them. However, unless there is a tangible reward for the informants, the latter are usually unwilling to cooperate. At the other end of the insider's role, one finds the consultant's role, whereby the researcher is called upon by the client — i.e., the organization — to deal with a well-defined problem or issue. Here the researcher is licensed to ask questions and dig deep into the nitty-gritty of the organization. The third and most relevant role to the kind of research conducted here is that of the formal researcher who is allowed limited entry but is not really helped until a relationship of trust develops between him or her and the members of the organization and the latter feel that what will come of the research will be helpful rather than harmful to them.[11] Short of the trust and involvement of the organization, it is doubtful that the inquirer will be able to dig deep into the culture of the organization.

Getting organizational insights and getting media organizations to trust the researcher in a culture that is information averse is not always easy. More generally, doing research on media in the Arab world poses notable difficulties. Researching the culture of an organization can be greatly facilitated by access to information and a high degree of cooperation. But these are not always forthcoming. The scarcity of research on Arab media and the unavailability of relevant data and statistics, official and otherwise, pose yet another problem. As one observer put it, "Arab society is opaque and statistics and demography are not part of ordinary life."[12] This is true to a certain extent even for a network like Al Jazeera, which set out to change this very culture from a media standpoint and which encourages open-minded journalistic investigation. An independent researcher is usually received cautiously unless introduced and recommended by inner circles or members of the network. Even so, it is hard for researchers to scratch beyond the surface if they rely on the organization itself for providing them with sources of information. What this means is that serious and engaging research on Arab satellite TV is scarce and disproportionate to both the rate at which satellite TV has been developing and the growing impact Arab media have been acquiring. Even more alarming is the dearth of debate on the need to develop methodologies and envisage new or alternative ways for thinking through and approaching Arab media — in fact, methodological insights that can rise to the challenges researchers of Arab media encounter in a new area of investigation and research. Short of the cooperation of the organization, short of access to company data and research, and short of developing adapted methodologies, research on Arab media is left walking a thin line.

When it comes to an indigenous Arab organization, the challenges outlined above are enormous. The difficulties we encountered while conducting the research for this book are telling. One of the elements which draws attention to itself is the lack of openness of Al Jazeera. When we sought some help and assistance in facilitating our visits and talking to some staff in the network, we felt that Al Jazeera was not prepared to deal with us. It was acceptable and expected to visit or call, but when it came to a long and focused visit which involved interviews, data collection and observations, the reaction was not the same. One media researcher and journalist told us that when she contacted Al Jazeera to request a ten-day visit to collect data for her book project, she was dissuaded from spending all that time on the grounds that what there was to uncover did not need more than one or two days. Nonetheless, she ended up staying a week. Although seemingly insignificant, this incident suggests that Al Jazeera is somewhat insecure. Commenting on the newly launched Al Jazeera's English language news channel, Corey Pein concurs. "Faced as they are with a number of significant unknowns," the author of the article notes, "the leaders of Al Jazeera International have been advised not to talk to reporters."[13] One also can surmise that because of the perception that their setup or headquarters is not particularly impressive — from the inside "a match box," as President Hosni Moubarak once described it, and from the outside a nondescript "dusty compound of squat buildings and satellite transporters" as a *New York Times* journalist put it[14] — they don't feel outgoing. More importantly, one gets a sense that the attention one receives is of a public relations nature aimed at influencing the image about them. According to the assistant to the general manager, Al Jazeera receives daily requests to visit its Doha head-quarters or to talk to someone in the network. Naturally, the management has to deal with these requests; otherwise they convey a bad image about Al Jazeera. Hence, it is in Al Jazeera's interest to be courteous and accommodating to those who have an interest in the network so as to convey a good image about it. Presumably because Al Jazeera is also keen on getting legitimacy in the West, Western researchers tend to get more attention and cooperation. For Westerners with an interest in Al Jazeera, having access is less of an issue. For example, in his book on Al Jazeera, Hugh Miles recounts, "Fortunately for me, Al Jazeera's management happily acquiesced to my request for help in researching this book. Since Al Jazeera had nothing to hide, they said, it was in their interest to let an independent observer have a snoop around, especially since the network was planning the launch of its English-language channel."[15]

But that was not at all our experience. It is true that we were tolerated, but we were hardly given any significant data on or insights about Al Jazeera. Although we went through the public relations and media department and although we provided the head of international relations with a full-fledged research proposal about the nature and scope of our project with a list of pointed questions and adapted scales requesting access to the network and appointments with certain administrative and journalistic figures, we did not receive much interest in or assistance with our research. In fact, what we got instead was a tour of the newsroom, which we had already visited on more than one occasion on previous research trips. Even benign questions such as how many staff members Al Jazeera has or straightforward requests such as an organization chart which shows the different departments and the hierarchy within the network were hardly satisfactorily or precisely answered. Compared to the BBC, which provides detailed information on its website about its organization, including the way it is run, the policies and guidelines it has in place for various circumstances and the reports it produces yearly, Al Jazeera is distinctly discreet.[16] Overall, it was extremely hard to meet with people and when we did manage to talk to members of the network staff, we were often met with some suspicion which naturally affected the level of cooperation. The input we got from some of the decision makers and spokespeople we met with was an official story in line with the public narrative about Al Jazeera. Many of the network staff we talked to were not forthcoming and some of them were reluctant to speak; even when they talked to us frankly and openly, we could feel that they were taking some unnecessary risks. Understandably, some people had stakes with the network and were either not comfortable talking critically about Al Jazeera or were not willing to meet with us at all. Not surprisingly, perhaps, most of the revealing data we were able to gather was collected outside a formal fact-finding framework.

Seen from one perspective, the difficulties that were encountered while collecting data for this research are a hindrance to the research. Seen from another perspective, they are telling insofar as they are part of the culture itself and help provide valuable insights about that very culture. It was certainly instructive to find a dearth of information in a media organization which made a name for itself by prying open Arab states' affairs and by championing the freedom of speech in a part of the world where censorship is a widespread practice. The corporate communications department was willing to talk to us but unwilling to provide us with any documentation or internal publication about Al Jazeera. Even in its relationship with the press, Al Jazeera hardly commits itself to anything of substance beyond asserting its commitment to "the view and the opposite view," partly because Al Jazeera is a relatively small organization (with developed interpersonal relationships among the staff) that is operating in a predominantly oral culture, and partly because it wants to leave room for itself to tweak its positions if need be as it is changing, especially being at the forefront of Arab news broadcasting in a fast-changing post–September 11 world where all eyes are on the Middle East.

In spite of the difficulties we have encountered, we believe we have been able to get to the bottom of this organization — if not, at least to develop a deep understanding of this organization — thanks in part to our steadfastness in gathering information and to getting insights. Over time, we were able to build a small but valuable network of connections with people, which proved to be critical. Once we broke the ice, we were able to sustain the momentum — albeit with some setbacks. A few of our interviewees valued what we do. Some of the people we talked to gave us the benefit of the doubt when they came to realize we were not journalists after a story or in search of a scoop. Others trusted us because we were recommended to them by an insider or because a good word was put in for us. Still, others were spontaneously cooperative because they did not feel the need to hide whatever discontentment they have with Al Jazeera. One light-hearted senior staff member who trusted us found in the interaction with us an opportunity to voice his disenchantment with existing practices within the organization. Particularly useful were people who, at one point in time, were associated with Al Jazeera but are no longer with the network. Having acquired a distance from their former employer for some time, these former staff members tend to speak their minds more freely. Their perspective is often informed by a comparative perspective, as many of them moved on to work with competing regional media outlets but kept in touch with many of their former colleagues in Al Jazeera. Ultimately, our determination to knock on every door, our keenness to pursue every possible source we could have access to, and our tendency not to discard any source of information proved to be rewarding. Even people who were not critical of the network provided us with information that turned out to be useful. At the end, the disparate experiences with and impressions about the network we gathered from the various people we interviewed fell together like pieces of a jigsaw puzzle; even with some of the pieces missing, the picture was clearly discernable. Naturally, we never relied on a single source and as much as possible checked or validated the information we obtained for key findings and assertions. Last, throughout this project, we tried to keep an openminded attitude such that we were willing to revisit issues and question foregone conclusions when relevant information or evidence was provided. As researchers, we tried to be accurate and objective, professional and impartial. Although being subjective at times may have been unavoidable, we tried not to take sides. We hope our attempt at neutrality in the ensuing pages will not be lost on the reader.

The book consists of 13 chapters. The introduction, which sets the background for this study, places Al Jazeera in the context of Arab media. The opening chapter focuses on the rise and eminence of Al Jazeera while paying special attention to its contribution and its controversial nature. Chapter II outlines Al Jazeera's success factors. Chapter III is an attempt to determine the core capability which distinguishes Al Jazeera and sets it apart from its competitors. Chapter IV tries to understand the characteristics of the organizational model which best describes Al Jazeera. The ensuing four chapters deal with the various facets of Al Jazeera's organizational culture: what its core beliefs and values are, who pulls the strings, what drives the staff members, how employees experience the culture of the organization and respond to it, and to what extent Al Jazeera fosters and values talent. Chapter IX looks at the extent to which

Al Jazeera harnesses the knowledge it has acquired over the years. While probing the different facets of Al Jazeera's culture, this study also takes heed of the internal tensions and contradictions and how these affect the organization. Chapter X draws together the case study findings in order to reach substantive conclusions regarding the current state of affairs in Al Jazeera. The next two chapters examine the ways the organization is changing, evolving and expanding. The concluding chapter looks at the cultural constraints of Al Jazeera and outlines the limits of its experience.

Introduction

No other media outlet has drawn so much attention, hypnotized so many Arab viewers, ruffled so many feathers in official Arab circles or risen to international eminence so unexpectedly in recent history as Al Jazeera — a satellite channel beamed out of the obscure Gulf capital Doha. In its few years of existence, Al Jazeera has managed to establish itself as a media player to contend with during times when all eyes are on the conflict-ridden Middle East. Although it may be difficult to quantify with any certainty the changes wrought by the emergence of Al Jazeera on the Arab media scene, such changes are real.[1] In many ways, the emergence of Al Jazeera has changed the face of Arab broadcasting, putting an end to decades of state media monopoly marked by self-serving propaganda, inculcation and mind-numbing programs. By breaking ingrained taboos and treading uncharted paths, Al Jazeera has not only made a name for itself but also opened up a field of possibilities which, until not long ago, were unthinkable in the Arab world. Clearly, Al Jazeera has also proven to be a trend setter in news broadcasting — albeit a controversial one. In doing so, it has positioned itself as an influential media player in a region that has been increasingly under the spotlight.

At the same time, the peculiarity and unconventionality of Al Jazeera have made it a source of controversy and a subject of heated debate. In fact, Al Jazeera has caused so much stir both within the Arab world and in the West that speculation about its intentions and agenda have become rife. It has been taken to task for its populist appeal, its political agenda, its "biased" reporting, its footage of dead and captured American soldiers, its graphic images of war scenes and its "anti-American" rhetoric, among other things.[2] Although Al Jazeera is becoming increasingly conscious of what it broadcasts and is in fact trying to revamp itself and change its image, it continues to be a controversial network with published opinions about it stretching from the overwhelmingly positive to the vehemently negative. One thing its critics and defenders agree on, though, is that with Al Jazeera, Arab media is not business as usual.

The new kind of media tradition Al Jazeera epitomizes stands in marked contrast to a long tradition of state-run television. Broadly speaking, state-owned media tend to be dull, shallow and parochial. They lack good content and quality broadcasting. The standard fare of Arab television is over-wrought programs designed, as David Hirst put it, "to keep the Arab mind off politics."[3] A typical newscast and public affairs program advertises the achievements of the government and extols the virtues of high-ranking officials. News consists to a large extent of footage showing heads of state and prominent political figures receiving or sending off dignitaries or diplomats, stepping off an airplane, waving on airport runways and waiting on the tarmac, dubbed with music playing in the background. The cult of personality is imposing in Arab broadcasting, giving the impression that media exist to broadcast the activities of the local potentate and to glorify the leadership.

But this is hardly surprising. Media in the Arab world have always been perceived as an extension of the government. In this framework, the function of the media is to speak for the government and preserve the regime in power. Since their inception, TV channels have been a state establishment. Historically, state monopoly of mass media, whether it be television, radio or newspapers, was designed to promote nation-building in Arab states. In this sense, state media were designed to meet the needs of the government. Aside from entertainment and to a lesser extent education, the mission of state TV is to serve the state. Being state-owned, state-sponsored and state-run, TV naturally imposes the authority's official point of view. Overall, the function of media is to exhort the public, rally support for the ruler or government in power and dissipate official viewpoints. Media maintain the political legitimacy of the government, enhance regime support, and promote political values, if any. Even after the early stage of nation-building which called for national unity, state TV continued be mobilized as an ideological state apparatus and as heavy-handed political propaganda with tailored pro-government programming.

Because the free flow of information can hinder the government's control and destabilize the regimes in power, media have always been feared. For one thing, Arab governments have sought to control people by tightly controlling the means of communication, making media a closed sphere, so to speak, and the dissemination of information subject to control. In *Mass Media, Modernity and Development*, Fayad E. Kazan summarizes the communication policy in the Middle East:

> The communication policies of the Gulf countries tend to be authoritarian, prohibiting the press from criticizing the rulers, the Gulf governments, members of the ruling families.... Gulf media are discouraged from propagating any ideas or principles that might be conceived as destabilizing to the Gulf states' established orders.... The political systems of the Gulf countries are concerned about the threats to their legitimacy bases, the existence of internal and external threats to their stability and security, the political activities of opposition groups, and about uncontrollable currents of social change.[4]

In an environment where the free flow of information represents a threat to the existence of some governments and a potential destabilizing force in society, limiting access to information is an exercise of power. Accordingly, public dissent is usually not tolerated and opposition media are hampered by either bans or violations. Media are usually controlled by information bureaucracies which restrict information flow and dictate press content, subjecting it to the regime's security concerns and thus turning it into a propaganda instrument which inculcates sanctioned values. Information ministries are the official apparatuses that oversee media policy, determine red lines and decide what is aired or published and what is not. Such a systematic censorship not only makes it impossible for media to provide objective information to the public, to engage in professional journalism or to provide quality and innovative programs, but also shuts off all possibilities for entertaining a dialogue with those who have opposing views or hold different convictions, thus reducing media to a near-monolithic discourse.[5]

Although "a variety of legal control mechanisms still exist on Arab media,"[6] censorship is starting to wither. Arab governments seem to be fighting a losing battle in attempting to censor the media. Not only are people getting more suspicious of state media and distrustful of government-sanctioned news, but the role of the government as such is gradually declining and its monopoly on information is becoming less and less realistic. To be fair, even in the most controlled environments, there have always been sources of information at the disposal of the Arab public such as Radio Monte Carlo and the BBC. Likewise, there has always been a margin of free expression in what may be described as pockets of free press. For example, critics of the state have often expressed themselves in the pages of Lebanese newspapers, and they are still doing so to a certain extent without official reprisal, although Lebanon is an exception. Likewise, the influential pan–Arab London-based newspaper *Al Hayat* publishes daring dissent opinions, although such a window of freedom has been possible only to the extent that it is based outside the Arab world. The latter is an important precedent, though, insofar as it has provided a working model and style for media to develop and thrive along lines other than those afforded by the narrow margin of freedom available in the Arab world. In fact, in the nineties, this model and style were extended to satellite TV as a number of predominantly Saudi channels were launched in European capitals, epitomizing a new trend which can be loosely described as "offshore democracy."[7] Spurring these changes is a digitally based communication revolution, namely the growing sophistication and rapid diffusion of powerful new information and communication technologies. These new technologies prompted a diversification of delivery systems such as cable and satellite TV; they led to the multiplication of satellites and the explosion of satellite channels in a regional media environment. Contributing to this change is a host of other new media in the 1990s, including electronically distributed Arabist and Islamist newspapers, listservs, and email.

Naturally, these changes did not occur in a vacuum. Contributing to these developments is a global media revolution which manifests itself in the free flow of information, the increasing consumption of mass media in an age of globalization, the emergence of a global media society and the pervasiveness of global communication. The current phase in the history of Arab media thrived within a post–Cold War open climate marked by a global interconnectedness which can be pointed out not only in the explosion of digitally based information but also in the encroachment of free-market economies and the advent of privatization as a defining concept in (inter)national economies. With the breakdown of communism and the changes brought about by economic and political globalization trends, the Arab governments' tight control over media operations began to loosen.[8]

The plunging prices of satellite dishes in the 1990s have also made access to satellite TV affordable. Because of the growing number of satellite dishes sprouting up on the rooftops and the multiplication of satellites orbiting the earth, people started to have an increased ability to access information. The proliferation of satellite dishes enhances and is enhanced by the proliferation of satellite channels and the teeming of broadcasters in the Middle East and the Gulf region. The diversity of television stations and range of programs that are becoming available to audiences are indeed phenomenal. The widespread use of information is becoming unlimited, making it increasingly hard for governments to control images, screen information, black out satellite-beamed programs or enforce a ban on satellite dishes. Although in some countries satellite dish ownership is taxed or nominally banned, such control mechanisms are either not fully enforced or simply not enforceable.

Not only has control over media been somewhat relaxed, but also the extent to which censorship can be tolerated has changed. Ordinary Arabs who have long been put off by the pandering waffle transmitted by state channels and who are keen on breaking free from the pattern of news that just talks about official journeys and proclamations have come to value independent media. Increasingly, people in the Arab world have become eager for unexpurgated news — a need which has been consolidated by the emergence of a new regional media market.

The various satellite channels that erupted have changed the media practices in the region, most notably through hard-hitting news, live debates on political issues and current affairs, and blunt interviews with decision makers and political figures. The new media scene has become diverse, ranging from government to semi-private to private channels. Still, even the most *avant garde* of these channels are not without limitations. Overall, the new media support official government policy and adopt the official discourse. There are few independent media outlets, and many of these were initially beamed out of Europe to escape the clutches of governments who are keen on keeping control on information. Even on private channels, treatment of sensitive issues and criticism of friendly regimes is carefully avoided. Kai Hafez aptly characterized the media scene: "Most private TV networks ... are 'loyalist' in the sense that, despite their professional, often Westernized news policies, their programs include critical reports and commentary only insofar as they do not concern the national government or the governments of befriended states."[9] Many promising alternative media channels are closely tied to the government that hosts them, and too loyal to the governments that sponsor them. In one way or another, many of these channels have somewhat fallen under government control. David Hirst paints a sober picture of the new Arab media landscape: "Along with the vast, overwhelming vacuous superfluity of domestic media which it already controls or manipulates, every government must now have a pan–Arab outlet of its own."[10]

Broadly speaking, the Arab media scene, going all the way back to the Arab press, has been dominated by three prominent traditions, associated with three counties: Egypt, Saudi Arabia and Lebanon.[11] Given its size, population, and political weight, Egypt was an influential regional player and media was part of the equation. Gamal Abdel Nasser's radio *Voice of the Arabs*, which was launched to strengthen Arab nationalism and reflect Egyptian politics, had a tremendous impact on Arab audiences in the 1950s and 1960s. Even before the satellite era, Arab countries relied heavily on Egypt as a source of Arabic material for TV. With the influx of satellite TV, Egypt was keen on continuing to be a major program provider, initially through Arabsat and then through investing in its own satellites, Nilesat 101 and 102, launched by the government-owned Egyptian and Television Union and providing a variety of channels. More recently, Egypt has been attempting to consolidate its investment in program production by establishing a Media Production City and a Media Free Zone.

Seen from a regional perspective, these media investments, as Naomi Sakr explains, are geared toward enhancing Egypt's ability to provide a counterweight to Saudi Arabia.[12] Certainly, the latter is a media force in the full sense of the term, given the size of its media investments and the size of its population (or viewers), at least relative to other Gulf countries. Through semi-private, technology-conscious, Western-oriented, foreign-based media ventures, Saudi Arabia has come to build a media empire which extends from the printed press to satellite TV. Either directly or indirectly, Saudi Arabia owns well-established media conglomerates such as Orbit Communications, Arab Radio and Television (ART), and Middle East Broadcasting Center (MBC), which is part of ARA Group International, a media conglomerate that includes a number of radio and television companies beamed throughout the Arab world — not to mention print media, as Saudi Arabia puts out a number of publications, the most prominent being the pan–Arab London-based newspapers *Al Sharq Al Awsat* and *Al Hayat*.

The concentration of satellite media in Saudi hands is motivated not only by economic considerations but also political interests — namely the ability to exert control in the region. Historically, as Douglas Boyd explains, Saudi Arabia belongs to a long tradition of Arab states that seek to influence what is written about them in the Arab press in general and the Lebanese press in particular through financing.[13] Not surprisingly, perhaps, the rise of Saudi media came at a time when the influence of the media in Lebanon — another regional player — has been receding, particularly because of the civil war that has torn the country for over a decade. Lebanon is a rich media country with an open and tolerant press which reflected the country's make-up and specificity. The Lebanese press reflected many of the political and power struggles in the region by addressing the concerns of a wider Arab audience. At the same time, the Lebanese media also obey ethnic, religious and political lines. Each prominent religious or political group in Lebanon has had a foothold in satellite broadcasting. For example, the Lebanese Broadcasting Corporation (LBC) is a Christian Maronite channel, Future TV is a Sunni channel owned by the Al Hariri family, and Al Manar is a Shiite channel and a mouthpiece for the controversial South Lebanon-based group Hizballah. Although fragmented, the Lebanese media scene has a strong presence in the Arab world which is often complicated by regional influences.

The proliferation of private Arab satellite channels is an unprecedented and in many ways unique development. With the emergence of a pan–Arab market in the media sector, it has become increasingly hard to keep up with the new channels that are cropping up in every corner of the Arab world.[14] What is even more interesting about these developments, though, is the emergence of new centers of media influence which operate outside the aforementioned three historical poles of media power. That Qatar and the United Arab Emirates rather than Egypt and Lebanon would become media hubs was just unthinkable in the not so distant past. Dubai in particular is attracting many new media projects as it is positioning itself to become a regional media and advertising center with a super-modern communication infrastructure, flexible laws, and a hands-off policy. Likewise, Doha, the capital of Qatar, is positioning itself as a media player to contend with, thanks to Al Jazeera. The latter is noteworthy not only because of its rise to international eminence, but also because of the political thrust of the kind of broadcasting it engages in. Al Jazeera has a lot of clout in the Arab world and is also attracting the attention of many policy makers in the West, if nothing else for its potential to influence Arab public opinion, which many believe it reflects as much as it fuels. Not surprisingly, the market of Arabic news channels has been thriving in the wake of Al Jazeera's popularity.

Clearly, there has been an increasing interest in news channels, some of which are more politicized than others. The Al Hayat-LBCI news venture, Al Ikhbariya, and ANN are a few examples. Al Jazeera's most immediate competitor, though, is Al Arabiya, which was launched a month or so before the outbreak of the war in Iraq in 2003 to position itself in the midst of an increasingly information-rich environment in the Arab world. Al Arabiya's all-news format includes hourly bulletins with an emphasis on news of interest to Arab viewers, commentaries, business, sports, and documentaries, among other programs. This Dubai-based all-news Arabic channel, which is operated by Middle East News (MEN), is another addition to the Saudi media empire which has come to eminence over the past two decades or so. Although the new channel is a venture that is backed in part by Kuwaiti and Lebanese money, it is primarily a Saudi investment and can in many ways be considered the news division of Saudi Arabia's eminent channel MBC — it is in fact located in the same building in Dubai's media city.

The rise of Al Jazeera has invited not only regional but also international competition. In the wake of the September 11 events, the U.S. government became more convinced than ever before of the need to have a media foothold in the Arab world. In order to influence a region that is vital to its interests, the U.S. launched a radio station, Sawa, and a news channel, Al Hurra (literally "the free one") — both of which are subsidized by U.S. money, delivered through the Broadcasting Board of Governors. Like Radio Sawa, which established itself on the ruins of VOA Arabic Service, Al Hurra is part of an attempt on the part of the U.S. administration to reach the people of the Middle East, to counter anti–Americanism in the region and to challenge Al Jazeera.[15] But the Bush administration is not the only party interested in countering the influence of Al Jazeera. In the UK, the BBC has also decided to flirt again with Arabic-language broadcasting after its short-lived partnership with a Saudi media company came to an end in the mid–1990s because of editorial disagreement. In 2005, the BBC World Service, which has a well-established and trusted Arabic radio channel, announced plans to shift its resources from Eastern Europe in order to launch a new government-funded Arabic-language news channel (BBC Arabic Television Service) which is also expected to rival Al Jazeera.[16] Clearly, the success of Al

Jazeera has spawned a host of noteworthy competitors. What effect such competition is likely to have on Al Jazeera and on the regional mediascape as a whole remains to be seen. What is certain, though, is that Al Jazeera has given both Arab broadcasting and regional politics a new dimension.

I.

An Unconventional
Media Player

Even a cursory look at the proliferation of Arab satellite channels and the phenomenal rise of Arab broadcasting suggests that the Arab world, in general, and the Middle East, in particular, are in the midst of an information revolution. The vigorous growth and spread of satellite TV in the Arab world is not only an irreversible trend but also a momentous one. Some of these media outlets have more scope than others to tackle serious political, social or economic issues, but nowhere do they compare with the "success" of Al Jazeera Satellite Channel — a pioneer and still a leader in Arab broadcasting. Since its inception in 1996, this pan–Arab satellite broadcaster has revolutionized Arab-language television news, winning over scores of Arab viewers with its hard-hitting programming and its daring, though often controversial coverage of news and events, and forcing a change in the way official and semi-official media handle the news. The contribution of this media experiment to the development of Arab broadcasting is hard to ignore. According to a 2002 report on Middle East communication published by Spotbeam Communications, "Al Jazeera is center-stage in the modernization of Arab-language broadcasting."[1] Undoubtedly, Al Jazeera has been a significant media player, an influential broadcaster and a stirring force in Arab politics. There is a growing realization that, its problems and biases aside, Al Jazeera is becoming increasingly influential — arguably the most important non-state actor in the Middle East today.[2]

By Arab standards, the very existence of Al Jazeera is revolutionary. Al Jazeera has brought noteworthy innovations to Arab broadcasting and reporting, airing hard-hitting programs, bold and uncensored news coverage, passionate political debates, and on-the-ground reporting. The network introduced new programs and institutionalized certain program formats, broadcasting many of its shows live on the air, soliciting viewer participation and taking heed of the voices of ordinary people. Al Jazeera is particularly noteworthy for breaking boundaries and building a reputation for being outspoken on issues traditionally deemed as sensitive or taboo in the Arab world. It has been hailed as a beacon of free press, a bold initiative in journalism, and a revolutionary force among Arab media long constrained by state control. It has an approach to the news that was unthinkable in the Arab world not long ago. With its heated debates, daring commentary, bold coverage, public affairs interviews and viewer participation, Al Jazeera appears to be breaking new media ground and venturing into a realm of open discussion rarely attempted by other broadcasters in a region where public political debate is considered subversive — so much so that it has been perceived as a *de facto* forum for pan–Arab political debates. What partly distinguishes Al Jazeera is its attempt to reach out to a large Arab audience, discussing political issues of the day in the Arab and Muslim world, in general, and the conflict-ridden Middle East, in particular. In the words of Jon Alterman, "Al Jazeera has pushed the boundaries of knowledge, built a massive audience and helped unite Arabs in a community of concern."[3]

Naturally, the rise of Al Jazeera was far from being smooth. Both inside and outside the Arab world, Al Jazeera's coverage has been regarded with skepticism. Some viewers question its agenda while others doubt its objectivity and question its independence given its financial dependence on state funding. Still others are suspicious of the motives of its host country. During its formative years, Al Jazeera has garnered official loathing as much it has generated viewer enthusiasm. Over the years, some of Al Jazeera's programs ruffled nerves in several Arab capitals and rankled many an Arab government, prompting some governments to take retaliatory action against Al Jazeera and even close down its offices. Alarmed that the Qatar-based network granted time to opposition figures and critical voices, several Arab governments clamped restrictions on its reporters, closed its bureaus or discouraged advertisers from spending on the channel. In Arab official circles, there was a perception that Al Jazeera was a nuisance, a potentially destabilizing force and a catalyst for change, providing alternative voices and opposing views with a high-profile platform that resonates around the region. Not surprisingly perhaps, Al Jazeera is seen as developing the potential to influence Arab policies and, in some cases, has succeeded in applying pressure on Arab governments, pushing them to be more than a limp witness to what is happening both regionally and internationally. As such, Al Jazeera has become a force which neither governments nor decision makers can afford to ignore. For Al Jazeera, such a growing influence is a source of pride. As one staff member put it, any Arab official who is paying an official visit to the USA has to think of three things: the agenda of the president or monarch, the reaction of the USA and the coverage of Al Jazeera.

Such an influence is an achievement of sorts. In the words of Jihad Ballout, Al Jazeera's former spokesman, the network perceives itself as "a credible alternative source of news pertaining to the Middle East which is now at the very core of Western thinking."[4] The succession of events in the Middle East and the monolithic discourse of mainstream media have heightened the need for alternative outlets and perspectives. This has helped Al Jazeera position itself as the "the anti-news" or the channel with the "corrective view." For better or for worse, Al Jazeera has come to represent the pioneer, the dissident, the maverick, the oppositional, the anti-establishment, and the eccentric. It takes risks, does things differently, and ignores the culture of political restraint and media practices in the region. Al Jazeera has a desire to break molds and do things differently. Some of Al Jazeera's practices have become standard and in fact have been adopted by other media organizations. Even state broadcasters who have long enjoyed broadcasting monopolies have felt the need to keep up with the wave of change; they have come to offer flashier graphics, more field reporting and slightly less propaganda.

The rise to eminence of Al Jazeera is intriguing. It is hard to determine whether Al Jazeera's success — and in fact its claim to being the right channel in the right place at the right time — is a matter of ingenious planning on the part of its founder or a stroke of luck, or maybe a bit of both. Seen from a business perspective, Al Jazeera is in many ways something akin to a start-up company based on an innovative idea which eventually was turned into a resounding success. It seemingly came out of nowhere, and in fact its immediate success and its subsequent rise and claim to international fame took the network itself by surprise. Still, even though the network benefited from some fortunate circumstances, its rise is not all that circumstantial.

Technology is arguably one of the foremost driving forces behind changes in media. The changes in technology have expanded the possibilities for satellite TV to develop, whereas in the past the need for both being heavily financed and having high skills made satellite TV in the Arab world a government monopoly. Changes in audio-visual technology and advances in global communication have created new media industries, new ways of producing messages, new ways of distributing information, and new ways of marketing and selling media products. Some technologies are reducing the media organizations' capital investment substantially, making it possible for satellite channels to mushroom. With the changes in technology, the cost of news gathering has also fallen significantly. The internet in particular has become a cost-effective means of transmission, whereas in the past satellite feeds were the norm. The falling cost of news gathering and the proliferation of news and views have made satellite TV particularly appealing — although, as Greg Dyke points out, few of the emerging channels are profitable. For many of the new media ventures, the purpose is either not to die or to have an influence worldwide. In this respect, Al Jazeera is no exception.[5]

That technological changes have facilitated the rise of alternative media should not obscure the fact that Al Jazeera's roots are partly political. According to Oliver Da Lage, Al Jazeera cannot be adequately understood independently of the politics of Doha — even though the consequences of such an anomalous media project in a part of the world that has succumbed for decades to state media monopoly, inculcation and propaganda could hardly be assessed or predicted.[6] Qatar wanted to have an improved media for various reasons. Internally, Al Jazeera fits within the vision of the Emir, Sheikh Hamad bin Khalifa Al Thani, to liberalize the country and introduce social and political reform before it is mandated. At the regional level, Al Jazeera has to be understood in the context of Qatar's geopolitical constraints and its rivalry with the Kingdom of Saudi Arabia. Al Jazeera would enable Qatar to get out of the shadow of its big Gulf brother — neighboring Saudi Arabia, which has a political weight as well as a media clout to contend with. These factors determined the very conception and identity of Al Jazeera — being an independent channel which can attack its neighbors without Qatar suffering the consequences or being accountable for what its network broadcasts. Internationally, Al Jazeera has been serving Qatar well by enhancing its international reputation. It would hardly be an exaggeration to say that Al Jazeera has put Qatar on the map.

Although Qatar's Emir contemplated the idea of launching a news channel back in 1994, while still crown prince, the actual preparation for such a media venture did not start until a year later.[7] A three-member committee — made up of Sheikh Hamad bin Thamir Al Thani, who later on became the director of the Al Jazeera board; Adnan Al Sharif, a journalist who came later to serve as the network's interim director in the wake of the resignation of Mohammed Jassim Al Ali; and Muhammad Suhlawi, a financial adviser to the Emir — flew to London to do the groundwork for the new channel. Al Jazeera came effectively into being in November 1996, airing its first broadcast from a modest one-story building inside the nondescript Qatar television compound. Broadcasting exclusively in literary Arabic, it started with six hours of broadcasting per day, to be increased gradually. After three years, it went to 24-hour transmission with news programming and a format comparable to that of major news networks — although operating with a smaller budget and with fewer resources. When it came to the world's attention in 2001, it had an international network of reporters which comprised 50 correspondents and 35 bureaus in 31 countries. The station had in fact already expanded from a starting staff of 250 with no foreign bureaus to employ 380 people, the majority of which were not locals. Currently, the network's staff comes close to 1400. Out of these, 750 are based in Doha and 450 are journalists.[8]

Al Jazeera is certainly not the first or only satellite channel in the Arab world, nor is Qatar a pioneer in the field of media. The Saudi-backed channel MBC in particular was an achievement of sorts. Launched in 1991, the then London-based channel was a promising and successful channel during its early years, breaking decades of state monopoly over the broadcasting sector[9] and projecting what some described as "an offshore democracy" during a time when "Arab satellite broadcasters were clearly scared of operating from within the core region."[10] But MBC was more entertainment oriented and, for that matter, shallow and with limited impact. With the influx of satellite channels in what may be described as a media-congested environment, MBC lost much of its thunder before making a comeback through its Dubai-based division Al Arabiya, a 24-hour news and information channel. The chosen location of what many media analysts perceive as Al Jazeera's immediate competitor is probably a minor but significant detail. Unlike Al Arabiya's parent company, MBC, which initially opted to operate out of London in order to avoid censorship and control, the Qatari network was set half a decade later in a Gulf country, thus defying the assumption that a free and professional Arab media cannot thrive in a part of the world which is the least inclined toward democracy and freedom of speech.

Interestingly enough, Al Jazeera was born out of the ashes of yet another London-based Saudi media venture. The core team of Al Jazeera was recruited from the ex–BBC Arabic television service staff. In the mid–1990s, the BBC Arabic Services, widely known in the Arab world for the broadcast of its World Service Radio network, expanded into television in a joint venture with Orbit Communications, a Saudi company with links to the royal family. A year and a half into the partnership, the deal foundered and broadcasting was discontinued when the BBC's insistence on editorial independence collided with Saudi sensitivity over certain aired programs and figures. For Qatar — which at the time was seriously contemplating the idea of launching an "elite satellite news channel"[11] in line with the new image of the country the Emir wished to project to the outside world[12] and provide it with a way "to strengthen [its] fragile sovereignty and identity," and particularly "to give this small Gulf nation an image distinct from Saudi Arabia"[13] — this was a fortuitous turn of events. Al Jazeera founders seized this opportunity and recruited a handful of journalists, broadcasters, technicians and administrators, all of whom had an Arabic background, to form a nucleus of the staff that would make Al Jazeera. These BBC-trained recruits brought with them the long tradition of the BBC, with its professional standards and free spirit, to a new media environment marked by an exceptional freedom of expression — at least when considering what is generally expected from a Gulf setting.

Al Jazeera capitalized on this unprecedented margin of freedom by pursing an uncompromising editorial independence from the outset, which in turn earned it the reputation of an independent voice in the region. During the first years of its existence (the phase between 1996 and 2001), Al Jazeera tried to engage in a kind of professional journalism which defied the reigning mentality. Many viewers embraced Al Jazeera as the herald of a new media tradition. Both Al Jazeera's uncensored news and its daring talk shows stand in sharp contrast to government-controlled news in most Arab countries. To the extent that Al Jazeera has gone a long way toward breaking the sacred aura of authority in Arab countries, it has been a real and refreshing change from decades of censored news and superficial programs on state-controlled TV. Marc Lynch put it well when noting that "Arab news media resembled the desert: barren, boring, oppressive, repetitive, and (if not controlled by a national government) owned by the Saudis."[14] Covering news which Arab governments would rather cover up in a part of the world where media has long served the ruling elite rather than question them and where the only viewpoint the viewer is exposed to is that of the government, Al Jazeera has become a media powerhouse. Its uninhibited reporting and free expression stand in marked contrast to practices in a part of the world where strict state control over and occasional censorship of the media are the norm. By allowing its guests and commentators more latitude in expressing their views about issues which are controversial and traditionally shoved underneath the carpet,[15] Al Jazeera gained a reputation as an independent voice in a region where news media have traditionally been controlled by the government.

Overall, Al Jazeera breathed fresh air into the stifling climate within which political debates often take place in the Arab world. For the first time, Arabs are able to watch live debates on controversial or sensitive political, social, religious, cultural and economic issues they never thought could be discussed publicly. The network has made a name for itself by challenging old taboos and unabashedly tackling controversial topics. In testing the limits of what is acceptable in the Arab world, the Al Jazeera staff came to realize that there are very few red lines that needed to be observed. Its programs dealt with unmentionable topics such as government corruption, the human rights records of some Arab regimes, the persecution of political dissidents, the prevalence of police torture in Arab jails, the anachronistic state of dominant interpretations of Islamic law, the dialectic of Islam and democracy, and Islamic fundamentalism or revivalism. Various intellectual figures were invited to comment on issues that had long been considered forbidden topics in the Arab world. Likewise, a number of opposition figures inside the Arab world and dissidents living in sanctuaries outside their own countries were able to express their views freely on Al Jazeera and to challenge the official discourse, which earned it the reputation of "parliament on the air." What Al Jazeera did was provide a platform for opposing groups and views regardless of whether these were legitimate or illegitimate in the eyes of governments. Operating in what may be described as the disintegration of intermediate institutions able to connect the Arab individual, the state and society,[16] Al Jazeera came to be known as a channel that dared to probe matters of concern to the Arab world and defied the policies and practices of

Arab governments. In this regard, in much the same way opening offices in a number of Arab capitals during the first few years of its existence was an achievement of sorts, the change of attitude of certain Arab regimes towards the network, particularly since 2003, goes to the credit of Al Jazeera.[17]

More than anything else, it is probably the sustained and extensive coverage of the Palestinian-Israeli conflict which branded the Qatari network as a pan–Arab channel. As James Drummond put it, "the station's role in propelling the Palestinian uprising in the Arab public consciousness — and keeping it there — is considerable."[18] The network's instant coverage of the Al Aqsa intifada, which erupted in September 2000, has helped put the Palestinian question on the front burner. Airing raw footage and images which shed a gruesome light on the practices of Israel in the West Bank and the Gaza Strip and capture the brutality of the Israeli war machine in ways which have never been seen before is not without impact on viewers who have started to follow news with renewed vigor. Paradoxically enough, no other media or even political player had done more to break the taboo of "talking to the other" and promote negotiations with the Israelis than the network which is often criticized for glorifying the intifada. Even as it rivets its audiences with its coverage of the bloodshed and prompting a region-wide groundswell of sympathy for the Palestinian cause, Al Jazeera is actively pursuing an undeclared policy of normalizing media and information ties with the Hebrew state.

Although it broadcasts in standard Arabic from the obscure capital of Qatar, one of the smallest, most traditional and most conservative Persian Gulf countries,[19] Al Jazeera's influence extends beyond the Arab world. The so-called war on terrorism that has been waged in the post–September 11 era thrust Al Jazeera to the world media scene. The network caught the world's attention during the war in Afghanistan in 2001 when its correspondent Tayseer Allouni was the only correspondent permitted in Taliban-controlled Afghanistan. For a while, it became itself a valuable source of news. Footage of the war was shown throughout the world with the logo of Al Jazeera. The exclusive video and audio recording Al Jazeera received from bin Laden and his Al Qaeda associates has made it part of the news it covered — although such proximity to Al Qaeda also brought it a high degree of scrutiny from some Western governments.

But the war in Afghanistan was one of a series of events which ensued from September 11, 2001, and which gave Al Jazeera an international relevance. September 11 was indeed a turning point particularly in the interests and concerns of Arab viewers and in their priorities. It marked an important development in the thinking of the intellectual elite and the concerns of Arab media. Naturally, subjects of interest to the Arab and Muslim world which were prominent during the first few years of the network's existence were put on the back burner in favor of issues that are both more pressing and more international in scope. While keeping a distinctly Arab perspective, Al Jazeera's focus and attention underwent a slight change in scope which brought it to a new phase in its history.

The succession of events, crises and wars in the Middle East region and the prominence of such issues as international conflict, American dominance, weapons of mass destruction and oil have made Al Jazeera even more relevant. Nowhere is the clout the network acquired more evident and more controversial than in the case of Iraq, which continues to be at the forefront of world politics. Even before its ground-breaking coverage of the war in Afghanistan, Al Jazeera came to regional eminence during Operation Desert Fox in Iraq in 1998, providing live coverage of the Anglo-American bombing of Baghdad. Having an office in the Iraqi capital enabled Al Jazeera to compete with international networks such as CNN and the BBC. The various documentaries, reports, and programs Al Jazeera aired on the plight of the Iraqi people suffering long years of tight UN sanctions in the period between the second and third Gulf Wars[20] further enhanced the network's in-depth treatment of the question of Iraq and enabled it to position itself during times when wars are increasingly fought on the airwaves. The network's intensive coverage of the invasion of Iraq in 2003 and its continuous ability to scoop the world with exclusive material has provided a different, often corrective view of what is happening in Iraq during its invasion and throughout the tumultuous events and violent months of occupation that followed the fall of Baghdad.

By being at the heart of the events and crises that have shaken the Middle East and the Arab and Islamic world, Al Jazeera has enhanced its image as an international broadcaster to contend with, and occasionally made it a primary source of information worldwide if not "the most sought-after news resource in the world."[21] During the post–September 11 American-led military interventions, Al Jazeera has gained access to areas considered dangerous, enabling it to report stories ahead of other networks. Not surprisingly, the BBC signed a news gathering exchange agreement with Al Jazeera[22] and CNN courted Al Jazeera into an agreement to use its exclusive material — although the partnership between the two came to an end after the former released an interview which Al Jazeera's correspondent Tayseer Allouni conducted with bin Laden during the bombing of Afghanistan. Al Jazeera chose not to air the interview, allegedly because of its poor technical quality, and because bin Laden's tendency to ignore some of the questions addressed to him slanted the interview. Irrespective of this incident, Al Jazeera proved itself capable of emulating established international networks and in fact has on occasion served as a source of information for Western media networks, making "Al Jazeera" one of the most common search terms on such web browsers as Lycos. Its website, Al Jazeera.net, is one of the most popular sources of news for Arab-speaking audiences throughout the world, ranked at some point in time among the top five most visited sites,[23] with over 500,000 visitors and 40 million hits a day.[24] Outside the Arab world, Al Jazeera's popularity can be attested to by the soaring satellite subscriptions. For sure, these viewers are too important to ignore, particularly at a time when recent world events have again highlighted the geopolitical importance of the Middle East region and thrust Arab media to the center of world attention. In spite of its relatively short history, this Qatar-based news network seems to have left an indelible mark.

The foregoing analysis should not suggest, however, that Al Jazeera had a smooth ride. While Al Jazeera's coverage earned it a worldwide reputation, it has also made it the subject of a much-publicized controversy. Being at the forefront of Arab media, Al Jazeera attracted considerable critical attention. Since it catapulted into international prominence, it has been taken to task for what has been perceived as slanted coverage and criticized for its tendency toward sensationalism and demagoguery. In the words of Olfa Lamloum, Al Jazeera has come to be perceived as "the channel which advocates all the 'isms' which supposedly plague the Arab world: 'Islamism,' 'terrorism,' 'populism,' 'anti–Semitism,' and so on."[25] For the U.S. in particular, Al Jazeera has proven to be both a source of nuisance and a *bête noire*. Perceiving the Qatar-based network as hostile to U.S. interests in the Middle East region, the Bush administration has adopted a distinctly critical eye toward it. Former U.S. Secretary Colin Powell went as far as asking the Emir of Qatar to use his influence to rein in and to tone down Al Jazeera's coverage.[26] During the war on Iraq, Al Jazeera was accused of "false reporting," "biased coverage" and "inciting violence" against American troops — although the network denies that it has an agenda beyond living up to its motto of "presenting the view and the opposite view." Such an official reaction reflects a common perception in the United States that Al Jazeera is a biased outlet and a propaganda machine producing inaccurate reporting and providing slanted news which feed anti–Western sentiments. For its part, the American media has railed against Al Jazeera's anti–American tilt and its anti–Western tone. For some critics, Al Jazeera creates inflammatory lead-in segments to news reports which often feature violent scenes, foregrounds images of casualties and airs scenes of suffering. Such provocative footage tends to create a dramatic effect and appeals emotionally to the viewers. Al Jazeera also has a tendency to explain or analyze U.S. policies in the region unfavorably. Although the negative perceptions of U.S. policy in the Middle East are not all that uncommon in the region, Al Jazeera's treatment of the U.S. in its programs is not without impact. With the U.S. heavily involved in the Arab and Muslim world, Al Jazeera can be expected to play a significant role in reporting and interpreting U.S. foreign policy and its implications on the Middle East — a region which has been the scene of the war on terrorism, the conflict in Iraq, and the Palestinian-Israeli conflict.

More than anything else, Al Jazeera is often criticized for galvanizing Arab radicalism. For Jeffery Tayler, "the spirit of Al Jazeera's reportage often accords with anti–Western sentiments pervading both the Arab street and the more educated milieu of the Islamic world, especially when it comes to Osama bin Laden and the U.S.-led invasion on Iraq."[27] Amir Taheri concurs. In his view, the reason for Al Jazeera's success is simple: "it rubs the Arab fur in the right direction, confirming Arab prejudices and misconceptions. It tells them that they are innocent victims of a plot hatched by Jews and Christians, and that their poverty, lack of freedom and weakness are not their own fault in any way."[28] In Iraq, Al Jazeera was criticized and even banned allegedly for taking a pro-resistance stance, manufacturing militancy, spreading hatred and violence, and fueling sectarianism. The latter accusation also resulted in the closure of its office in Tehran. More broadly, Al Jazeera has earned the status of a lightning rod throughout the Arab world. A common take on the network is that it sows dissent. Some of Al Jazeera's programs have discussions that are of doubtful quality. At least one of its flagship programs has fallen into a set pattern of furious debate and political invective directed at the United States and its loyal allies in the Middle East region.

For Al Jazeera's managing director Waddah Khanfar, "some of the criticism directed against [the network] by Western politicians is similar to what [it is] used to from Arab politicians — in that it is politically motivated."[29] At the same time, Khanfar acknowledges that Al Jazeera "has made mistakes."[30] Recently, and presumably under regional and U.S. pressure to close or reform, Al Jazeera has been shifting into a new phase that is more in tune with Middle Eastern changes. With its new look, its lighter substance, its internal restructuring and its large-scale expansion, Al Jazeera seems to be embracing change. As it positions itself to look more like an international network than a pan–Arab all-news channel, the image of the network has started to change. In fact, although it continues to occasionally air footage of insurgent strikes on U.S. troops in Iraq and recorded video messages from Al Qaeda leaders, and although it continues to broadcast its trademark combative programs, Al Jazeera is gradually being perceived in a more favorable light. According to a *Washington Post* article, "Al Jazeera has become a leading vehicle for the region's budding reform movements,"[31] reporting on reform initiatives and giving voice to reformers. Its airwaves are saturated with coverage of elections in Palestine, Iraq and Egypt, and political changes in Lebanon in the aftermath of the assassination of Prime Minister Rafiq Al Hariri. If for nothing else, its intensive coverage of Middle Eastern experiments in shared governance, much like its extended coverage of the U.S. presidential primaries, conventions and elections, contributes to educating the Arab public opinion on the democratic process.[32] Increasingly, though not uniformly, the network is looked at as a potentially dynamic force for political change in the Middle East. To what extent a media player like Al Jazeera can be credited for ushering in political change in the Middle East and North Africa region, particularly in the absence of both a sound tradition of political participation and sound political institutions, remains a controversial issue.

II.

Critical Success Factors

Asked publicly about the secret recipe for Al Jazeera's success, prowess and vibrancy during a 2005 media summit hosted by the Emirates Center for Strategic Studies and Research, Al Jazeera's general manager, Waddah Khanfar, admitted plainly and without hesitation that "there is no secret recipe behind Al Jazeera's success," adding that "it just happened."[1] Judging by the spontaneity of the answer, it did not appear as though Khanfar was dodging the question; if anything, his reply came off as genuine. A subsequent meeting with a senior staff member at Al Jazeera's London office echoed this same view. Our interviewee bluntly but sincerely noted that studying Al Jazeera leads nowhere as there is really nothing to unravel.

To some extent, the rise and eminence of Al Jazeera defy rational explanation. As one staff member put it, "it is not a success that can be rationalized based on an objective set of tenets or elements." While Al Jazeera staff do not miss the opportunity to boast about their professional standards, aggressive reporting and strong commitment, they also tend to think of Al Jazeera's success partly as a stroke of luck. Doubtless, luck has been on Al Jazeera's side, as it has been thriving on scoops, hoping for better days which — at least so far — have not failed to come. Whether it be an exclusive coverage in Afghanistan, an Al Qaeda video-tape featuring bin Laden and his associates, footage of captured soldiers during the invasion of Iraq or a live controversial statement by Suha Arafat amidst speculations about the real cause of the sudden deterioration of the health of Yassir Arafat as he lies on the brink of death, Al Jazeera has been on several occasions the right channel in the right place at the right time. However, Al Jazeera's success can hardly be reduced to a stroke of luck. In fact, if one can venture a set of key factors which contributed to the success of Al Jazeera, chief among these are the wealth of talent, the structure or system in place for handling the news, and most importantly the margin of freedom available to the network.

To start with talent, management literature tells us that one of the elements of a good management strategy is to identify competencies and reward excellence — and this principle is to a large extent operative within Al Jazeera. Clearly the network has managed to attract considerable talent. Although, as one senior Al Jazeera staff member was quick to admit, the network's journalists and staff "are not exceptionally talented or particularly gifted," there is something to be said about the competencies Al Jazeera had managed to attract. The initial pool that was hired consisted of well-trained staff. Many of these were former members of the BBC Arabic Television, had a BBC training and experience, and in the words of Ian Richardson, former managing editor of BBC Arabic Television, were "fervent believers in the BBC ethos of balance and fairness."[2] When the short-lived partnership between the BBC Arabic Service and Saudi Orbit Communications Corporation fell through, the pool of journalists (reporters, presenters and producers) and technical staff (picture editors and directors) who were to be laid off saw in Qatar's new media venture a venue that was worth considering. Tempted by the job opportunity and lured by the financial rewards of working in an energy-rich Gulf country, many of the ex–BBCers took up Qatar's offer and ended up being recruited by Al Jazeera. This pool of BBCers was enhanced by regional talent; in fact, besides the "founders" of Al Jazeera who came from the BBC, Al Jazeera also hired staff members from various Arab nationalities. The outcome was not only the concentration of a wealth of talent but also a diverse make-up which eventually benefited the network considerably. It was important not to have a dominant nationality, a single political strain or a prevailing ideology. In fact, Al Jazeera was conceived from the beginning as a mini–Arab League comprising various nationalities from every corner of the Arab world[3] with different experiences which blend under a *modus operandi* which in turn is guided by a set of editorial guidelines and a follow-up system.

Surely, the BBC training some of the staff had was an important and significant element not only because it entailed new possibilities but also because it meant work ethics and standards. Many of Al Jazeera's journalists brought with them BBC journalistic values they had seen at work, if not practiced, such as objectivity, accuracy and speed in news reporting, checking the sources and showing different angles of the story. Naturally, these values thrived within a system or structure which was set in place in the news division and which addressed such varied issues as the format of the news, the handling of the news materials, the production of the news, the casting of the news, the distribution of foreign correspondents and the allocation of tasks. The nature of 24-hour news broadcasting is such that rigidity is a liability. In certain instances, there were instant decisions to be made, which required not only talent and professionalism but also flexibility, cooperation, freedom, motivation, delegation and empowerment. These were not missing in Al Jazeera as the staff members were empowered to act.

More critical than any other factor in the success of Al Jazeera is perhaps the margin of freedom available to its staff members. Reflecting on a visit to Al Jazeera headquarters in Doha, the spin doctor of Number 10 Downing Street during the invasion of Iraq, Alastair Campbell, wrote reflectively: "Raised on the BBC, we are so used to a modern, vibrant media that perhaps we underestimate the scale of change that Al Jazeera has brought in the region, given relative freedom by its main backer, the Emir of Qatar."[4] Sure enough, if Al Jazeera's predecessor, BBC Arabic Television, launched by the BBC in 1994 with Saudi funding, was short-lived, it is because "the guarantees of editorial independence," as Ian Richardson put it, "proved to be a sour joke, only barely obscured by a thin smokescreen about the BBC's alleged failure to observe 'cultural sensitivities'— Saudi code for anything not to the royal family liking.... The failure of the BBC Arabic Television is a sad story because of the death of a dream."[5] Out of the ashes of the defunct channel, Al Jazeera was born — or so the story goes.

However, the independent journalism legacy of the BBC could not have carried over were it not for the freedom of expression. In fact, if Al Jazeera has done well it is because from the outset it has been given a long leash. In an interview by *Foreign Policy*, Al Jazeera's managing director noted that "Al Jazeera has its reputation not because of some magnificent technology; it is only because of the freedom that our newsroom journalists and reporters have. We are going to maintain it, and I think Qatar understands that."[6] Nearly everybody we talked to insists on the importance of the freedom of speech and the margin of freedom Al Jazeera has enjoyed all along. One senior producer we interviewed pointed out that what gives Al Jazeera an edge is "the margin of freedom — and that's it." Several staff members who were interviewed independently said that they would not hesitate to resign their positions if they felt the pressure of censorship. This kind of freedom is amenable to producing daring and bold journalism. It is also key to Al Jazeera's credibility. In a published interview, Adnan Al Sharif, the interim managing director in 2003, explains how Al Jazeera's credibility is indeed contingent on the margin of freedom it enjoys: "We have undoubtedly had an effect on world opinion. Most of our close neighbors thought we would simply be another Arabic news station that would have very little impact globally. Public opinion in the Middle East had only seen the BBC model, and it was where I and many of my colleagues learned our craft. Nobody expected any Arabic channel to match or be a threat to the BBC, CNN, Fox News or Sky News. Viewers were more than surprised, they were shocked at the effect we had. The magic word is credibility, and from our first minute on the air, we have tried to provide that credibility. We have done well, helped by the 100 percent margin of freedom in the station. There are no restrictions on us, and none of our Arabic rivals enjoy these freedoms, despite what they might say."[7]

Al Sharif's view is shared by many of Al Jazeera's staff. In a media forum organized by the Beirut-based Center for Arab Unity Studies, the host of *Open Dialogue*, Gassan bin Jeddou, reiterated the same argument: "In Al Jazeera, we enjoy such a peculiar margin of freedom whereby 90 percent or so of what we do is broadcast." Bin Jeddou then went on to tell a personal anecdote which further elucidates the degree of freedom available to Al Jazeera staff:

> During the Millennium Summit, which also coincided with the eruption of the Palestinian intifada, it was brought to my attention that the Emir of Qatar may be meeting with Israeli Prime Minister Ehud Barak. As soon as the news editor in chief got word of the likelihood of such an event, and in order to be absolved from responsibility, he rushed to book a satellite link. It happened that I found myself approached by a Qatari, who intimated to me, presumably on behalf of Barak, that the latter was willing to make a statement to Al Jazeera. Although I pointed out that no such statement was solicited, I was made aware that there is a strong desire to do so. I met such an insistence with rebuke, this time in English, to the effect that I would not be honored to speak with Barak. To my surprise, I came to realize that Barak knew Arabic and that he understood what I had said. In response to my rebuke, the Israeli Prime Minister mumbled a few words dismissing the whole matter and then walked away. Because the exchange took place in the presence of the Emir of Qatar, I felt the urge to justify my decision to the

latter. When I told the Emir that he was at liberty to meet with Barak and that it was my professional duty to cover such an event, but I just couldn't get myself to do it, he simply pointed out that it was my call.[8]

In his book on Al Jazeera, Hugh Miles finds bin Jeddou's experience common among Al Jazeera journalists: "they rarely think of Al Jazeera even as a Qatari network — they shoot and edit packages in the field, uplink them and they are broadcast a few hours later. They do not stop to think for even a second about the nationality of their station or its financier."[9] This margin of freedom extends beyond the confines of Qatar to include tightly controlled media scenes such as Iran. However, this comes with clear signals as to which red lines are not to be crossed. Again, bin Jeddou's experience as a reporter and bureau chief in Iran is instructive:

> Once I asked a guest on the difference between the Shah and the grand religious leader of Iran Ayatollah Khamenei when it comes to the freedom of the press, pointing out that there seems to be little difference beyond the fact that the former wears a crown while the latter a turban. Naturally, this sent jitters to my interlocutors. Later, President Mohammad Khatami conveyed to me Ayatollah Khamenei's unease with what I said and his recommendation that I tone down my rhetoric. Naturally, he had all means at his disposal to do whatever he wished with me; however, he chose not to take action against me. Such is the case, it is important to capitalize on the margin of freedom available to us.[10]

The insistence that one of the critical elements that gives Al Jazeera an edge is the margin of freedom it enjoys is particularly noteworthy when it comes from a staff member who left Al Jazeera to work for the Dubai-based Al Arabiya. To the claim that the latter is roughly comparable to Al Jazeera in terms of what it can talk about and what it broadcasts, our interviewee shook his head, explaining that, in a place like Al Arabiya, things are "tightly controlled.... In fact, the editorial line of Al Arabiya is committed to two things — the supremacy of Saudi Arabia and loyalty to the United States." This perception is widely held, particularly since "Al Arabiya's owner," as the author of an *Economist* article points out, "put a new, staunchly pro–American editor in charge."[11] As such, the margin of freedom available to Al Jazeera remains higher than that at any other regional outlet and perhaps understandably so. Surely, the political agenda of Al Jazeera is more flexible than that of Al Arabiya, for instance. It is clear that Saudi Arabia has more at stake than Qatar when it comes to a free press. This enables Al Jazeera to be something like a chameleon — to wear different hats and to bear different colors. Not surprisingly, one of its promotional ads reads "with all colors of the spectrum." Al Jazeera can afford to give a platform to the Islamists, the secularists and the nationalists among other groups which want to claim a voice and have an influence. This gives the network an edge not only over its main competitor in the region, Al Arabiya, but also over such international media organizations as CNN and the BBC. These media organizations have a major complex of interest which does not so much weigh on Al Jazeera. The only restriction Al Jazeera has is presumably Qatar. Although Al Jazeera has drawn praise for its willingness to delve into political topics previously considered off limits in Arab media discourse, critics point out that Al Jazeera is rather discreet about the internal affairs of its own host country.[12] Even so, it is occasionally willing to cross the red line and report on the internal affairs of Qatar — a country barely the size of Connecticut, as per the *CIA World Fact Book*[13] — and, being such, its politics are relatively insignificant. Qatar is free of political strife and void of political parties altogether.[14] Being a country that does not have the conventional elements of power, as Mohammed El Oifi explains, Qatar has acquired "influence without power."[15] If this has been possible in spite of the disproportion of forces when considering Qatar in the geopolitical map of the Middle East it is through what Olivier Da Lage calls the imposition of the will of the weak on the strong.[16] If anything, the position and status of Qatar have made Al Jazeera a loose network, so to speak. It can afford to be a populist channel partly because it is not accountable and the stakes for its host country are arguably not high.

Seen from this standpoint, the question as to why Al Jazeera could not have sprung up elsewhere in the Arab world becomes particularly compelling. The launching of a channel like Al Jazeera in an obscure Arab country like Qatar may seem counterintuitive when, in fact, one would think that it is more likely to have been a Lebanese media project, for instance — for, according to William Rugh's classical typology of Arab media, Lebanon, along with Kuwait and Morocco, have a "diverse press" that is characterized by a relative margin of freedom and a certain degree of independence which are conducive to more information and opinion for people to choose from.[17] To a large extent, Lebanon remains a country that is marked by political and media openness, but such an openness is as much constraining as it is empowering; in fact, it is as much a liability as it is an asset. This is so because the Lebanese media, as Olivier Da Lage put it, is "too Lebanese"[18] insofar as it reflects and is caught in a type of sectarianism which gives prominence to "confessional pluralism" over "ideological pluralism."[19] The religious, political and ethnic make-up of Lebanese society has made the local media scene rigid and the differences the media outlets project often reducible to a black and white picture. It is a well-known fact that Future TV is Al Hariri's TV, LBC is a Christian Maronite channel and Al Manar is the mouthpiece for the Shiite Lebanese group Hizballah. Among these three channels, the latter is probably the most predictable, with an unmistakable discourse.[20] Not so with Al Jazeera. The network enjoys an ideological flexibility it has capitalized on to wear different hats and to speak freely and unabashedly on various timely and controversial political issues.

This is not to suggest that Al Jazeera has a *carte blanche* to speak about anything. It should not go unnoticed that Al Jazeera is silent on a number of pressing social, economical and cultural issues. According to one of the hosts of an Al Jazeera program, the fact that the network may have transgressed all red lines when it comes to politics does not make it a truly free medium. For the host of *The Book Is the Best Companion*, Khaled Al Hroub, "The ceiling of criticism on Arab regimes is high. My worry is about discussion on social and cultural issues. We have had critical discussions on political structures from Algeria to the Gulf States, Saudi Arabia, Jordan, and Palestine. However, approaching social issues is like walking through a minefield. We enjoy relatively a higher degree of freedom in talking politics than in cultural and social matters, particularly where religion is concerned. We can't touch these things. This is the true red line."[21]

Even if we concede that Al Jazeera has an independent editorial line with very few limits, the margin of freedom available to it makes it vulnerable as this competitive edge may not be enough to sustain competition in the future. The network has a reputation for being extremely outspoken on issues traditionally deemed sensitive in the Arab world. But if the margin of freedom in the Arab world becomes bigger, Al Jazeera will find itself faced with a real challenge — namely competition from Arab networks which may come about better equipped, better financed and with a clearer vision and a stronger sense of mission. The margin of freedom aside, the extent to which Al Jazeera has been able to develop a distinguishing source of strength which sets it apart from other news media organizations in the region and beyond acquires an added significance as it gives a clue about Al Jazeera's ability to fare well in the future.[22]

III.

In Search of a Core Capability

A convenient starting point for understanding the prowess of Al Jazeera — over and above the fact that it enjoys a margin of political freedom that is so far hard to find elsewhere — is the set of distinctive attributes that have contributed to its performance and can be considered as a source of the organization's strength or as a core competency. Broadly speaking, core competencies (or core capabilities) refer to the organizational processes and abilities that distinguish a company from its competitors and make it unique or successful. Companies and organizations usually develop their strategic vision, actively and consciously defining themselves in relation to a unique core capability or a single core competency which gives them a continuous competitive advantage because it cannot be easily or readily copied.[1]

Media organizations are no exception. A case in point is the BBC. According to Lucy Küng-Shankleman,[2] the core competency of Britain's preeminent broadcaster is broadcasting creativity — that is, the organization's commitment to, and record in, the consistent production of innovative high-quality intelligent programming: "The BBC's outstanding competence is its ability consistently to produce excellent and original programmes over a wide range of genres and subject areas that appeal to a broad cross-section of taste and interest groups."[3] The BBC's dedication to program excellence, innovation and originality ensures the best practice in, and highest quality of broadcasting in the world — so much so that the BBC has come to be associated with high national prestige and is often seen as setting the standards in world broadcasting. However, the organization's core competency does not exist in a vacuum. Going hand in hand with the BBC's professional standards is its public service ethos. Likewise contributing to the BBC's core competency is a number of organizational attributes. To start with, being a large bi-media organization (involving both radio and television), the BBC benefits from the cross-fertilization of staff and ideas between its various units. This creative mass can deliver partly because of the organization's protected status, which translates into guaranteed income and relatively little competition. Enhancing the organization's performance is its tendency to foster an environment that is conducive to teamwork, its inclination to have elitist recruiting practices, its ability to attract leading creative talent, and its belief in the value of elite professional skills and high-quality technical and support services. These organizational attributes go a long way toward enhancing the BBC's outstanding competence, namely its ability to produce excellent, original, intelligent and high-quality programs with great editorial depth and with a British flavor primarily for UK license-fee payers.[4]

The foregoing analysis of Britain's premier broadcaster leaves us with a set of questions when considering Al Jazeera. What unique capability or special character does Al Jazeera have which differentiates it from other networks in the region and leads it to make a difference in the market? Which characteristic of and variable in the experience of Al Jazeera cannot be easily imitated or readily replicated? Or is Al Jazeera's success simply due to the fact that it happened to be the first in a market niche where almost any media organization with some degree of freedom of expression and minimum programming would still be seen as a high performer?

In a 2004 public opinion poll conducted jointly by the University of Maryland and Zogby International in six Arab countries, Al Jazeera was found by far the most-watched satellite channel for international news.[5] Likewise, according to a 2002 Gallup poll on the Arab and Islamic world conducted in nine countries, Al Jazeera is widely watched and is in fact perceived positively in the Arab world.[6] The poll, which probes the viewers' perceptions of and attitudes toward Al Jazeera in Saudi Arabia, Morocco, Kuwait, Jordan and Lebanon, reveals a number of attributes which make the network stand out. A high percentage of those who participated in the poll credit Al Jazeera with providing comprehensive news coverage, having unique access to news, presenting daring and unedited news, offering good analysis, being constantly on the site of events, and to a lesser extent aiming at objectivity.[7] These Gallup poll findings are hardly surprising. In fact, a series of separate focus groups conducted in three Arab countries confirm these findings.[8] By and large, Al Jazeera can be said to be a phenomenon in the Arab world for a number of reasons.

Chief among these are the ability to provide a credible alternative to Western media, consistency in quality, appeal to Arab masses, instinct for airing breaking news, immediacy, comprehensiveness of news coverage, daring unedited news, unique access to information, good analysis, timely debates, vivid commentaries, Arab orientation, multiple perspectives, international standards, live and unedited news, interactive programs, taboo-free shows, tendency to shock, and keenness on presenting balanced views. A Spotbeam Communications report on Middle Eastern satellite communication concurs with the spirit of these findings: "Al Jazeera ... offers what no terrestrial broadcaster in the region does — a world class, free, uncensored, professional source of news and opinion provided by Arabs and targeted at Arabs."[9]

Content-wise, Al Jazeera offers a combination of news and scheduled programming. Its regularly scheduled programs fall into two categories: political programs which deal with the issue of the hour, and lighter programs that are directed toward relaxing the viewers and giving them a break from the high-paced programming that characterizes much of what Al Jazeera airs. These would include dubbed documentaries as well as recorded programs like *The Book Is the Best Companion, Correspondents, In Depth, An Encounter with an Arab Expatriate*, and to a lesser extent "the lighter side" segment of the news. Al Jazeera's style is somewhat a mixture of the BBC style with its emphasis on analysis and the CNN style with its inclination for hard-hitting news, focus on real time and eye on action. It tries to strike a balance between the desire to have strong program schedules and the commitment to the continuous flow of news, between the tendency for regularly scheduled programming and the rush with attention-grabbing news drama. The former is based on high-profile individuals whose personalities draw audiences, while the latter is based on the instinct for breaking the news and the ability to provide sustained and continuous live coverage. Al Jazeera is dedicated to round-the-clock coverage of big breaking stories while at the same time providing its viewers with fixed immovable scheduled programs (appointment-based scheduled programming) which do not dilute the organization's focus on news, as a great majority of the fixed programs deal with current affairs and political issues that are of interest to the Arab world. Naturally, some of the fixed programs, namely those which are considered flagship programs, are presented by high-profile hosts. These hosts may have branded the program and given it a specificity which makes it readily associable in the minds of the viewers with the presenter of the program, but overall it is the content of the program more than stardom that is the driving force. During times of crisis, priority is given to breaking news. This is the case for instance during the war against Iraq, when Al Jazeera discontinued its regular programs and devoted itself to live coverage. At times, the two strategies converge so that its regular programs focus on hot issues while its star reporters or high-profile program hosts become on-the-ground reporters. Such was the case with Maher Abdullah, who covered the fall of Baghdad in 2003, and Ahmad Mansour, who covered the siege of the Iraqi city of Fallujah early in 2004. Al Jazeera does not hesitate to interrupt a scheduled program which is aired live in order to air a White House briefing or a press conference. During times of less tension, Al Jazeera includes a blurb or banner on the bottom of the screen to announce breaking news.

Although some of these attributes give Al Jazeera an edge over its competitors in a congested media scene in the Arab world, they hardly ascend to being core capabilities. When it comes to Al Jazeera, identifying a set of core capabilities is no easy matter. The foregoing analysis of widely held perceptions about Al Jazeera's experience reveals a set of attributes which may distinguish it from other competing media organizations in the region, but does not crystallize fundamental characteristics and basic features which define the organization's essence. In other words, it is hard to single out one or two make-or-break characteristics which are idiosyncratic of Al Jazeera and which can rise to the level of a core component. For example, it is true that Al Jazeera has pioneered some program formats such as aggressive on-the-scene reporting, interactive political talk shows with viewer participation and exclusive interviews, but these are more "core products" than "core capabilities." The former are visible end products while the latter are invisible assets, so to speak, which is tantamount to saying that a core capability is not a service or product that can be sold: "as bodies of knowledge, core capabilities cannot be managed in the same way as are the tangible assets of the firm."[10]

In "How to Link Strategic Vision to Core Capabilities," Paul J.H. Schoemaker outlines a number of characteristics which help define and identify a core capability: (1) it evolves slowly through collective learning and information sharing, (2) its development cannot be greatly speeded up by doubling investment, (3) it cannot be easily imitated by or transferred to other firms, (4) it confers competitive advantage in the eyes of customers, (5) it complements other capabilities in a 2 + 2 = 5 fashion, and (6) investment in it is largely irreversible, which means that the firm cannot cash it out.[11] By definition, then, a core capability is not something that can be easily or quickly acquired. Rather, it is something that is developed slowly: "these assets and skills cannot be bought off the shelf but must be developed over time through investment and information exchange in the firm's human capital. By their nature, they involve time and evolution."[12] More importantly, a core capability protects the organization in the sense that it makes it immune to competition. A core capability is such that it is hard to easily duplicate or swiftly imitate. In the words of Dorothy Leonard-Barton, core capabilities "are created over time and can be sustained over time. They are not easily imitated, transferred, or redirected on short notice."[13] Several examples of core capabilities for well-established companies and international corporations come to mind here: for Sony, it is miniaturization; for Toyota, it is reliability; for Apple, it is innovation or creative product design; while for Wal-Mart, it is the company's distinctive approach to multi-service stores. To take a more relevant example from the world of media *strictu sensu*, the BBC's core capability, as Küng-Shankleman put it, is its genuine commitment to excellence in program making — that is, its instinct for broadcasting creativity.[14] Küng-Shankleman's analysis of what the BBC does best and what core competency sets it apart from other media organizations is worth quoting at length:

> The BBC's core competence, its broadcasting creativity, rests on an amalgam of creative, professional, technical, technological and behavioral components. While some of these are "structural," arising from the organization's unique history and position — its protected environment, the creative mass provided by the scope and range of its activities, its tradition of recruiting the best and the brightest, and the length of time in which it has been able to experiment and learn — the majority of such elements could, albeit at great expense, and with varying degrees of difficulty, be replicated by a competitor. What is not reproducible is the spirit that mobilizes them, that catalyzes them into a world bearing capability, and that is the emotional investment underlying the capability.[15]

When it comes to Al Jazeera, a core capabilities–centered approach which takes into consideration Schoemaker's criteria for defining core capabilities — namely that they are unique, scarce, important, controllable and hard to imitate — is tricky. It is hard to identify a distinct core capability which forms the basis for sustainable competitive advantage, sets the network apart from other organizations and makes it difficult for a competitor to emulate. Al Jazeera has come to eminence partly because of a vacuity that has long characterized the media scene in the Arab world. The network seized a market niche and carved a place for itself within what is otherwise a mediocre Arab mediascape. To put this in a different way, Al Jazeera was able to deliver to a market that lacked credible information in an environment that is information-averse (to say the least) during a crucial juncture in the history of the Arab and Muslim world. What this means in part is that Al Jazeera's success — at least from an organizational perspective — does not rest on a distinctive core component nor does it emanate out of a strategic vision. This is all the more true when considering that Al Jazeera did not have enough time to create and develop a core competency. In fact, Al Jazeera falls short of a distinctive and significant core capability that brands it. The elements which, according to the aforementioned Gallup poll, give Al Jazeera a competitive advantage and edge over its competitors in the Arab media scene can hardly be said to be core capabilities because, by definition, a core capability is not easy to duplicate and imitate. There is a sense among the network's critics that if censorship in the Arab world recedes, Al Jazeera may no longer be able to shine. For others, like Barbara Demick, there is a sense that "imitators are likely to come along, perhaps better financed and equipped, that might eventually drive Al Jazeera out of business."[16]

At the same time, the difficulty one faces in identifying a set of core capabilities which distinguish Al Jazeera is itself telling. It suggests, among other things, that perhaps Al Jazeera's success does not lie with a set of identifiable competencies, nor is it the sum of such competencies. In other words, Al Jazeera's success cannot be adequately analyzed from the standpoint of core capabilities. Al Jazeera may have certain attributes or capabilities which give it a competitive advantage, but these can arguably thrive only within a certain configuration of these concepts. These capabilities cannot be discussed in isolation and are not sufficient by themselves or potent if they are considered independent of the management model which nurtures them. Of course, core competency and organizational model are not necessarily discrete variables, which is tantamount to saying that while a core competency analysis may not yield answers to the questions that motivate this research, it cannot be ignored altogether because in fact it can provide valuable insights into what the organization does best and how it does it. Seen from this perspective, a more inclusive, general evaluation of the organizational model of Al Jazeera may provide a better understanding of its deep-seated practices and the philosophy that underwrites them. In other words, what should be the center of attention and the subject of inquiry is the organizational model that characterizes Al Jazeera.

IV.

Unraveling the Business Model

According to John M. Lavine and Daniel B. Wackman, media organizations tend to have one of two structures: a vertical structure or a horizontal one. Broadly speaking, what distinguish the two structures are the layers of management. Whereas vertically structured organizations have numerous layers of management, horizontally structured organizations have only a few.[1] Which of these two structures is better or more likely to be successful is a tricky question, the answer to which depends on a number of variables and a variety of factors, such as the amount of supervision required, the degree of routinization of tasks, and the interdependence of jobs in the workflow. Nonetheless, Lavine and Wackman ascertain the increasing tendency of media organizations to be organized horizontally partly because "many of them are comparatively small, tasks are complex and non-routine, and staff members must interact with different managers about different projects."[2]

More recent organizational studies literature provides a more nuanced typology of organizations. For the authors of *Information Technology for Management*,[3] there are at least three common formal models of organization: the hierarchical model, the flat model and the network model. In the hierarchical or classical model, the default management model is the hierarchical control-based model. In the so-called tall organization, the hierarchy has many layers, and managers have a narrow span of control. In the flat(tened) model, there is more autonomy for the operational levels. In the flat organization, the hierarchy has fewer layers, and managers have a wider span of control than the hierarchical organization, and in that sense can be considered to be an improvement over the latter. The system is based on delegation of power, with fewer hierarchical levels and fewer reporting relationships. What distinguishes the network model from the former two models is mainly its minimal hierarchical levels. This model, which is more congenial to an information-based economy in general and an information-intense environment in particular, is characterized by the full empowerment of line people. It rests on having more empowered and knowledgeable employees work with minimal supervision and with better information management.[4] Although insightful, this classification is tricky when considering the case of Al Jazeera. In fact, determining which of the three organizational models describes Al Jazeera's structure best requires a small detour.

Until recently, the dominant structure of media organizations, at least in the United States, was dictated by the need to have a high level of stability and a high degree of predictability. In an information company which is expected to deliver in a timely and persistent fashion, a formal hierarchical structure was believed key to success. For modern management theories, however, such a formal and highly structured approach may be a liability more than an asset, given the fast-paced, constantly changing nature of media and media organizations that are expected to deliver media products which feed existing structures, cater to set timetables and meet pressing deadlines while at the same time produce quality programs that are creative and innovative. As Lavine and Wackman point out, "in organizations as time driven as the media, tasks need to be performed on time, and at a high level of quality and effectiveness and at a reasonable cost."[5] The demands for efficiency and effectiveness point to different pulls, the attention to which calls for a less rigid structure than the traditional vertical hierarchical approach operative in many media organizations can afford. In order to be able to deliver and in fact to survive in an increasingly competitive environment, media organizations have increasingly opted for a more flexible horizontal structure.[6]

It would probably be unfitting to examine media organizations in the Arab world in light of the development of its Western counterpart, given the specificity of the historical, cultural, political and economic paradigm within which they operate. Still, in the literature on Arab media, one can point out a fairly old but relevant classification of various media experiences in the Arab world which — although far from being an exemplification of the three normative organizational models highlighted above — can nonetheless, with some degree of adaptation, help elucidate the likely implications of such organizational models. The work that readily comes to mind here is William Rugh's threefold classical typology of Arab press: the mobilizing press, the loyalist press, and the diverse press.[7]

The first type is characterized by the quasi-total subordination of the media system to the political system. The second type is less aggressive or revolutionary in the sense that it supports, albeit passively, the regime in power. The third type is characterized by a relative margin of freedom and a certain degree of independence which are conducive to more information and opinion for the people to choose from. More recently, Muhammad Ayish has extended the threefold typology Rugh outlined in the press to analyze Arab broadcasting. According to Ayish, Arab satellite TV can be categorized into three patterns of political communication: the traditional government-controlled TV pattern, the reformist government-controlled TV pattern, and the liberal commercial television pattern.[8]

It is tempting and convenient to align the three organizational models outlined above with the three patterns Rugh has outlined and Ayish has elucidated. At least theoretically speaking, these three patterns can be cautiously said to coincide with the three organizational models outlined above. Thus, state media, which is part of a more entrenched state bureaucracy, can be said to epitomize the hierarchical model of organization;[9] semi-private TV can be said to work along the lines of a flat organizational model; and, finally, private TV networks are likely to be aligned with the network model of an organization which empowers its employees by giving them more autonomy in decision-making processes, among other things.

Still, although the aforementioned types of organization are most useful as a conceptual tool for conceiving of and theorizing about various Arab media organizations, they should not be treated as normative. Clearly, there is a theoretical danger in imposing a preconceived formal model in a strait-jacket manner, as such an approach risks obfuscating the very specificity of the media organization under consideration. One may cautiously venture that the dominant features of a traditional government-controlled TV like Qatar TV are close to the hierarchical model, the dominant features of the reformist government-controlled television like Abu Dhabi TV are reminiscent of the flattened model, and the dominant feature of a liberal television pattern such as Al Jazeera are in line with the network model. At the same time, it is important to recognize and emphasize two points. First, organizational models are abstractions, which is tantamount to saying that organizations do not fit them completely and perfectly. Second, the organizational models outlined above are theoretical extremes, the rigidity of which may not reflect how organizations flow in between. To that extent, a particular organizational model should be treated as an unfolding empirical concept that is attentive to the specificity of the cultural environment (organization-wise and otherwise) within which the organization thrives, rather than a normative model imposed on the subject at hand. For example, in much the same way the organizational model of Abu Dhabi TV can be said to oscillate between the hierarchical model and the flat model, the organizational model of Al Jazeera can be conceived as closer to the network organization than the other two types.

But even a fluid formulation which posits that Al Jazeera may not be a network organization but an organization which has some of the characteristics of such a model poses theoretical difficulties which cannot be overlooked. In any organizational model, the organization has two main concerns: control and coordination, or, more accurately, coordination through control. In other words, its management strategy aims at bringing the different elements of the organization to operate in a coordinated way. Because the flatter the organization is the more difficult it is to control, more sophisticated control structures and mechanisms are needed for network organizations than for flat or hierarchical ones. In the latter case, the hierarchy itself ensures an appropriate level of control. Investing in an integrated information technology system and effectively managing the knowledge of the organization can harbor a strong and normative culture amenable to ensuring the control and coordination of organizational activities. At least so far, Al Jazeera does not seem to fit this model for, as will become clear, it has neither predictable features nor a sophisticated control system. If anything, Al Jazeera's control system is loose and its integrated systems are not up to the level of sophistication required in a network model. With the departure of the founding director, Mohammed Jassim Al Ali, the strong culture of the organization which could have ensured an appropriate level of control, hence coordination of the network's activities, is slowly eroding and the organization has no strong alternative control system to fall back on as the culture that was settled in starts to weaken. The simmering conflicts between the major poles in the network and the latest changes to the channel's program offerings may signal the organization's inability to coordinate its offerings for a changing market.

While anchored in a classical business model, the study of Al Jazeera's organizational model cannot overlook the latter's indigenous nature. Particularly important in conceiving of Al Jazeera's organizational culture is the specificity of the society and culture, in the broad sense of the term, within which Al Jazeera operates. Taking heed of the socio-cultural environment in which Al Jazeera has been thriving compels us to look at Al Jazeera not only from a corporate model perspective but also from a family business perspective which, although not specific to Qatar, is particularly intrinsic to the culture of a small Arab country where kinship, tribalism and nepotism are still prominent concepts.

Even in the Arab world, the family business is not a uniform concept. In fact, there is a wide range of organizations which can be grouped under this label. At one end of the spectrum is the family business that is run like a modern organization; at the other end of the spectrum, there is the entrepreneurial type of family business, which is of particular interest here. In the latter case, and in its most extreme manifestation, either the founder or someone from the family is usually in the position of leadership. Power tends to be centralized and the management of the organization is usually informal in the sense that it is far from being systematic. Strategy is often nonexistent, structures are loose, meetings are rare and participation in decision making is weak. Important issues are often dealt with on an individual basis, which is amenable to making decisions and taking actions. In this setting, change is almost nonexistent and it is unlikely to play a significant role or to be a priority. Likewise, trust and loyalty are as much important as competence and skills. In terms of recruitment, the emphasis is usually not on "leaders" or "decision makers" but on "doers." In this setting, initiatives are rare as the staff have to refer back to their boss, who controls their work and its results. By and large, the success of the family business is usually associated with a charismatic and energetic leader who is usually from the field, who has organizational skills and who knows how to be pro-active and how to seize an opportunity when it presents itself. Interestingly enough, the role the founder/leader plays in a family business is as much a liability as it is an asset. Partly because things are centralized and partly because the founder/leader is often left to act on his own and is often called upon to be omnipresent, decisions tend to be monopolized. Because the family business is an extension of the founder, and in this sense lacking in transparency, when the latter retires or passes away, the inheritor is often not able to grasp the complexity of the structure put in place. In other words, once the founder is gone, the organization is likely to be at great risk to lose its edge or even fall apart. Increasingly, however, family businesses are run like modern organizations, emphasizing vision, competency, delegation, management by objective, strategic planning, and use of an integrated infrastructure. There is also an awareness of the need to educate and prepare the younger generation which is bound to inherit the family business and involve it in the management of the organization to ensure its survival and continuity beyond its founder.

Clearly, the family business paradigm can be said to permeate Al Jazeera, particularly when we contemplate the way it was founded and the way it was managed during its formative years. Though it was created as a state-sponsored organization, the autonomy and access to resources that the founding director Al Ali had while running the network allowed him to mold the network on a family business model. As is the case with family businesses, the omnipresence of the founder in running the affairs of the network gave it impetus. When Al Ali was eventually replaced after some five years of service, the new director walked into "family turf," so to speak, to replace the family chief without having the legitimacy or the capacity to run a family-like business. Attempts at formalizing, structuring and institutionalizing activities in Al Jazeera were also attempts to move away from a family-like business to a more professional model based on explicit structures and modern management practices. The risk in doing so is that one can unsettle an existing working model without replacing it with an alternative working model. This seems to be the case in Al-Jazeera. However, if we concede that the replacement of Al Ali was inevitable, Al Jazeera would still be faced with the issue of appointing somebody who could fill his shoes and who could then ready the organization for takeover by a "non-family" member. As things currently stand, there seems to be a missing link between the old management and the new management.

Still, Al Jazeera is not a family business any more than it is a network organization. If anything, the foregoing analysis suggests that Al Jazeera could be operating under different models during different time periods, such as being a "family business" like model under Al Ali and a network model afterward. To impose a prescriptive model on what is otherwise a complex model is to reduce its complexity. In the final analysis, it seems that Al Jazeera's organizational model is more of a hybrid model than a normative model — one which has traditional Western management practices, but which is also imbued with idiosyncrasies which make it all the more interesting and worthy of study. Seen from this perspective, what should be the focus of the analysis and what is of interest here is not pinning down Al Jazeera to a particular model, but tracing the changes that occurred in its organizational model over time. Such an endeavor will make it possible to assess and foresee the likelihood of success of the network at different times.

V.

Values and Beliefs

Each organization defines an objective or a set of objectives for itself. These objectives derive from the mission of the organization, which usually focuses the attention of the members of the organization and its external constituents on the organization's core purpose (broadly perceived as the creation of goods and services for customers).[1] In "The Future of Work," Robert Reich explains the centrality of a mission: "Talented people want to be part of something that they can believe in, something that confers meaning on their work, on their lives — something that involves a mission."[2] Without a mission and a goal, an organization stagnates; instead of being proactive, it merely reacts to situations.[3] The mission of an organization is generally formalized in a clearly articulated mission statement which describes the organization's overall direction and general goals: "mission statements are written to communicate a clear vision in respect to long-term goals and future aspirations."[4] The actions that follow from a company's adopted strategy reflect and influence its direction, its choices, its management, its product development, its recruiting practices, its make-up and its financial management, among other things. In order to implement their vision, accomplish their mission and fulfill their objectives, organizations pursue a strategy — i.e., a means to transform the desirable to the doable. While mission is abstract, strategy is more concrete and refers to the means through which an organization achieves its strategic objectives. Choosing a strategy helps focus attention and provide a sense of direction (although it tends to eliminate options to a certain extent).

When it comes to their role and mission, many Arab broadcasters have been grappling with an identity crisis. Although these broadcasters have a mission, it is for the most part rhetorical. Not so with Al Jazeera, which comes off as uncommonly conscious of its mission. In a 2003 interview, the then Al Jazeera chief, Adnan Al Sharif, took special note of Al Jazeera's mission, particularly as an element that distinguishes it from its competitors in the region: "Our competitors in the area do not have the same aim as we do.... They want to compete with us, but the mission is not the same."[5] For Al Sharif's successor, Waddah Khanfar, the questions as to who Al Jazeera is and what its mission is are of utter importance. Since the coming to the scene of Khanfar as Al Jazeera's managing director, the network has been, more than ever before, conscious of and articulate about its vision and mission, which one finds posted on bulletin boards inside the network as well as on its website: "Al Jazeera is an Arab media service that has a global orientation. With its motto 'the view and the other view,' it acts as a forum for plurality, seeking the truth while observing the principles of professionalism within an institutional framework. While endeavoring to promote public awareness of issues of local and global concern, Al Jazeera aspires to be a bridge between people and cultures to support the right of the individual to acquire information and strengthen the values of tolerance, democracy and respect of liberties and human rights."[6] Al Jazeera considers itself a "unique" Arab media project. Its objective is to be an "alternative media organization" that escapes the mediocrity of the media scene in the Arab world: "Al Jazeera ... is a quantum leap in the development of Arab media which has long been shackled by censorship and government propaganda."[7] By freeing itself from censorship and government control, Al Jazeera is aiming at reinstituting the Arab citizens' right "to be informed."[8] As such, Al Jazeera is consciously "attuned to the aspirations of the Arab viewers."[9] It aspires to be an authentically Arab news source and strives to offer "an Arab perspective" in news and information which can "bridge the gap between Arab viewers"[10] and ensure a certain affinity between Arab viewers throughout the world. Overall, Al Jazeera is committed to fostering a culture which encourages dialogue, promotes tolerance and pursues objectivity.

To implement its mission, Al Jazeera has been pursuing what seems to be a clear strategy. The network is committed to offering "lively quality programs" which can rise to the expectations of the Arab viewer.[11] As a "responsible" media organization, Al Jazeera strives "to live up to its motto 'the view and the other view' by providing the viewer with various perspectives and viewpoints while upholding the highest professional standards of objectivity."[12] To keep its viewers abreast of what is happening around the world, Al Jazeera has pursued an aggressive strategy of "providing live news and on the ground reporting through a wide network of reporters, correspondents and bureaus world-wide."[13] As a news network, Al Jazeera strives to be "independent" and "professional" in its approach to the news as well as its production of purposeful talk show programs.[14] The network does not recognize red lines and in fact does not shy away from discussing controversial issues or addressing taboo subjects. This has branded Al Jazeera as a daring network. Through the pursuit of an objective approach, quality programming and serious journalism, Al Jazeera aspires to be the best in the Arab media scene.

It is only judicious to say that, although Al Jazeera comes off as having a distinctly strong mission and a clear strategy, the awareness of the mission — at least in the formal sense — within the network is not as pointed as one might expect. It is interesting to note that, in the aforementioned interview, the interim general manager of the network distinguishes Al Jazeera from other competitors in the region on the basis of its goal and mission, but falls short of articulating such a mission: "Our competitors in the area do not have the same aim we do. When we launched Al Jazeera, our goal was not only to supply a high quality news channel, but for it to be free of any restrictions. There were simply no boundary lines we would not cross, either political or regional. Our rivals have a different agenda. Yes, they want to compete with us, but the mission is not the same. Some seem to favor certain political or religious points of view. But from our audience's point of view ... we remain firmly in the lead."[15] Although we are told that what makes Al Jazeera stand out are its aim, goal and mission, we do not get a glimpse of that mission. Instead what is pointed out is a competitive edge — namely the margin of freedom the network has been enjoying all along.

Although Al Jazeera claims to have a strong mission, such a mission is not always evident even for its network staff. In fact, many of the staff that were interviewed could not articulate a clear mission. Although the network does have an explicit and written mission statement and although its top management is very conscious of it and articulate about it, the staff we interviewed do not seem to have a well-defined mental map of such a statement. When prompted to articulate the mission of the organization, one of the pioneer anchors who has been with Al Jazeera since its inception attempted to do so, but unable to articulate it in a concise and clear way, referred us to Al Jazeera's website. Although hardly significant in and of itself insofar as many of the staff have developed an instinct for the organization's beliefs and values, this particular encounter suggests that the mission and vision of Al Jazeera have not been fully internalized by many of those who work in it, including its BBCers. Not surprisingly perhaps, BBC's Peter Feuilherade took pains to note that Al Jazeera's staff readily admitted "they have been at loggerheads over the channel's objectives"[16]— something Al Jazeera's general manager admitted to the authors during an interview, pointing out that "Al Jazeera's mission has been the source of heated debate within the network."[17]

A few of the Al Jazeera staff that were interviewed do not feel there is a clear vision or purpose that is holding everybody together or a common goal that is drawing the commitment of everybody. For these people, the very identity of the channel is elusive even for those who work in it: Is it a channel with ideological orientations? Is it an Arabic channel or is it a channel for Arabism? Is it a channel that has Islamist inclinations and affinities? There is a perception that, in spite of the channel's proclaimed commitment to multiple views, its editorial line is not all that neutral. Even within Al Jazeera, there is a feeling that Al Jazeera has a "channeling dimension." Furthermore, there are certain orientations at the level of news broadcasting which are indicative in and of themselves. Rather than a clear-cut editorial policy that is well thought out, what prevails in Al Jazeera are poles of power which often translate in the work environment into bonding and grouping based on a common school of thought, an ideological affinity or a religious rapprochement.

More challenging and more difficult to pin down than Al Jazeera's mission and strategy are its beliefs and values, as these are not always evident either to the network staff themselves or to the viewer, being deeply ingrained and therefore hard to uncover. Still, the organization's website, publications, official literature, and public statements provide a valuable first-hand account of Al Jazeera's core beliefs and values. As such, Al Jazeera stands out for its instinct for breaking news, its alternative journalism, its tolerance for difference, and its Arab orientation.

1. Instinct for Breaking News

Al Jazeera is the first Arabic satellite channel dedicated solely to news, information, and current affairs. It perceives itself as a leader in news broadcasting in the Arab world. This leadership position entails certain priorities. As a news provider, so to speak, it prides itself on its immediacy and its ability to be constantly on the site of events, providing first-hand accounts of events as they occur. As such, Al Jazeera news smacks of a combination of the precision of the BBC and the speed of CNN. In organizational terms, Al Jazeera's immediacy — its ability to react immediately to breaking news and events — puts an emphasis on rapid production turnaround while still paying attention to high production values. In terms of infrastructure, this entails a high investment in technology, while in terms of programming paradigm, it means the freedom to interrupt any program in order to move to a news scene or to broadcast a press conference live on the air. In terms of programming, this also means that the image Al Jazeera projects is that of the right channel in the right place at the right time: "Al Jazeera has truly become a media channel for media practitioners, so much so that news agencies and international networks are finding themselves rushing to strike deals with it in order to benefit from having its reporters in the right place at the right time."[18]

Al Jazeera positions itself everywhere. It has a network of on-the-ground journalists and correspondents which enables it to provide first-hand accounts of events: "Al Jazeera supports its news bulletins by closely following events through a comprehensive network of correspondents who are strategically located and who are well trained to conduct live interviews on site in record times."[19] Not surprisingly, Al Jazeera has a unique access to news sources which enables it to secure exclusive news, interviews and tapes: "Al Jazeera has managed on numerous occasions to secure exclusive interviews with figures who usually prefer to stay away from media or to be anti-camera."[20] In its search for truth, Al Jazeera is determined "to seize every opportunity for exclusive reporting, to take hold of unforgettable moments in history."[21] Consequently, Al Jazeera has "managed on several occasions to scoop the world with its stories."[22] The organization's news-gathering coups have made it a preferred channel for various controversial parties to broadcast videotaped messages (whether it be from Osama bin Laden in the remote mountains of Afghanistan, a Hamas militant in the Gaza Strip, an Islamic resistance group in the Iraqi city of Fallujah, or footage of insurgent strikes on U.S. troops in Baghdad), which in turn consolidate even further its ability to scoop the world. However, while striving to be the first on the site of the news and to secure exclusive reporting, Al Jazeera is not oblivious to the dangers with which such an undertaking is fraught. As such, article 4 in the Al Jazeera code of ethics stipulates that it "welcome[s] fair and honest media competition without allowing it to affect adversely [its] standards of performance so that getting a 'scoop' will not become an end in itself."[23]

2. Alternative Journalism

Al Jazeera is an independent news channel established by an Emiri decree, on 8 February 1996, which stipulates that "it is an independent Qatari public organization."[24] Initially, the government of Qatar contributed $140 million to finance the network's operations for five years, after which the network was expected to finance itself—although so far that has not happened, as the Emir continues to generously bankroll Al Jazeera. Such arrangement has left Al Jazeera's status ambiguous, and perhaps purposefully so. The network's continued dependence on Qatari financial backing has, as Jeremy M. Sharp put it, "blurred in the line between its status as a private or public organization. Al Jazeera has demonstrated characteristics of both a privatized and a state-run news network."[25] As such, Al Jazeera is owned by the government, but has an independent editorial policy; it is publicly-funded, but independent-minded. Nearly everyone in the network boasts that Al Jazeera enjoys an unprecedented margin of freedom, giving it the courage to break taboos. In the words of the host of one of Al Jazeera's flagship programs, the network "left no stone unturned."[26] As such, Al Jazeera "has succeeded in breaking away censorship walls."[27] According to a 2002 report on Middle East communication published by Spotbeam Communications, Al Jazeera "offers what no terrestrial broadcaster in the region does — a world-class, free, uncensored, professional source of news and opinion provided by Arabs and targeted at Arabs."[28] In its few years of existence, it has proved able to remain steadfast in the face of pressure: "Al Jazeera is committed to objectivity in [the programs] it produces, as evidenced in its strong resistance to the kinds of pressures which have plagued Arab media."[29] The kind of freedom available to Al Jazeera's journalists has enabled the network to take Arab media into a new era: "Free from the shackles of censorship and government control, Al Jazeera has offered its audiences in the Arab world a much needed freedom of thought, independence, and room for debate.... It offers a different and new perspective."[30] Al Jazeera claims to offer alternative journalism based on daring reporting, a rich network of correspondents and high professional standards. In its code of honor, it pledges to "adhere to the journalistic values of honesty, courage, fairness, balance, independence, credibility and diversity, giving no priority to commercial or political considerations over professional ones."[31] Part of the success of Al Jazeera lies in its ability to breed a common set of journalistic values among its staff which helps it live up to its mission: "Our team of dedicated journalists with their multi-national education and diverse backgrounds share a common set of attributes: objectivity, accuracy and passion for the truth."[32] Al Jazeera is also very conscious about the need to "distinguish between news material, opinion, and analysis to avoid the pitfalls of speculation and propaganda."[33] The amount of freedom available to Al Jazeera journalists and reporters, along with the kind of professional journalism it promotes, makes it possible for Al Jazeera to emulate internationally renowned broadcasters: "Al Jazeera is one of the most credible news sources and media outlets in the world. This is evident when comparing it not only with Arab news channels but also with reputable international media organizations like the BBC and CNN which often quote Al Jazeera as their news source."[34]

3. Tolerance for Difference

Al Jazeera does not shy away from taking up "hot topics and heated debates,"[35] and does not hesitate "to deal with controversial issues"[36] or "raise thorny issues."[37] However, what distinguishes Al Jazeera is not simply the range of issues and nature of topics it engages in, but also the multiplicity of viewpoints it is willing to entertain during times when reflecting every shade of Arab and Islamic opinion has never been more important. Al Jazeera's motto tells much about the network. Al Jazeera sells itself as the channel of "the view and the opposite view"—a slogan it does not miss the opportunity to reiterate both on screen and off screen. Passengers bound to Doha find it hard to miss a panel fixed on the wall in Qatar's international airport which defiantly reads:

- View of Point Different A

  If Arabs write from right to left, they probably also look at and see things in another way. We can help you understand that way by offering the other side of the story; it is important after all that you get the whole story.

Unlike Arab state TV which presents only the official point of view uncontested, as it were, Al Jazeera strives "to cover all viewpoints with

objectivity, integrity and balance."[38] According to the aforementioned
Spotbeam Communications report on Middle Eastern communication,
Al Jazeera's strength "is that it is not cowered into self-censorship and it
allows dramatically opposing views to be aired."[39] The network takes
pains to forcefully articulate the centrality and extent of its tolerance of
difference. Article 5 of Al Jazeera's code of ethics stipulates that the network "present[s] diverse points of view and opinions without bias or par-
tiality."[40] Article 6 of the same document goes a step further, making the
diversity and multiplicity of perspectives not just an approach to the
news but a whole philosophy: "Recognize diversity in human societies
with all their races, cultures and beliefs and their values and intrinsic
individualities in order to present unbiased and faithful reflection of
them."[41] Committed to "the view and other view," as the motto of the
network has it, Al Jazeera has come to project itself as a pluralistic forum
and "a platform for various views."[42]

4. Arab Orientation

The conceivers of Al Jazeera had in mind an Arab channel broadcasting
from the Arab and Muslim world in Arabic to Arabs. Naturally, this
defined its choices and orientation. If Al Jazeera found itself in a privileged position in Afghanistan, it is because of its interest in Afghanistan
before it came to the attention of the whole world in the post–September 11 era. Al Jazeera had an inherent interest in Afghanistan, which at
the time was controlled by the Taliban, partly because it is a Muslim state
in a strategic yet tumultuous region and partly because it continues to
be the host of many "Arab freedom fighters," as they were called then.
As Al Jazeera's former managing director Mohammed Jassim Al Ali
explains,

> When we started the channel, we first concentrated on opening offices
> in Arab countries and Islamic countries. We started with Palestine and
> Iraq, because these were hot areas and there was news happening. So we
> opened an office in Jerusalem, with sub-offices in Gaza and Ramallah,
> and at the same time opened in Baghdad, then moved to other Arab
> countries. When these were in place, we moved to the other Islamic
> countries, first Iran and Pakistan, then we tried to get into Afghanistan.
> We got permission from the Taliban — and at the same time permission
> was granted to us, it was granted to CNN, Reuters, and APTN.... We

opened two offices, in Kabul and Kandahar. The others didn't move in because they didn't consider it very important and didn't see much news coming out of there. But for us, it was important because it's an Islamic country.... They are looking through international angles. The difference between CNN and Al Jazeera is that they look first to international news, then maybe to Asian, Middle Eastern specific issues. We look first to Arab and Islamic issues in detail, and after that to international questions.[43]

Even when Al Jazeera became an international broadcaster with a world-wide audience, it did not lose sight of its "Arabness." When asked if Al Jazeera has a reformist agenda or is simply an eyewitness to what is happening, Al Jazeera's manager Waddah Khanfar replied: "Naturally, being professional and objective is more important than 'having an agenda.' At the same time, [Al Jazeera] should not lose its edge. It should not dissociate itself from dealing with important issues in the region such as reform in the Arab world. Seen from this perspective, the changes Al Jazeera has in mind will try to focus on having a vision without dissociating itself from its environment."[44]

What Al Jazeera shows and says is a stark contrast to a long tradition of state-run programming and official government-sanctioned news. State-controlled and state-sponsored media are parochial to say the least. They provide news reports which reflect the official viewpoint and glorify the leadership. The function of media is to exhort the public, rally support for the rulers or the government in power, and dissipate official viewpoints. A channel like Al Jazeera makes it possible "to bypass the spoon-fed government propaganda that passes for news coverage in much of the Arab world and watch programs that their own state-run stations would never dream of broadcasting."[45] Underlying the change in style and substance from the state-sponsored news services that went before is arguably a *mise en valeur* of the audience itself. Al Jazeera is successful partly because it takes the viewers seriously with its content and programming. One of Al Jazeera's objectives is "to meet the expectations of the Arab viewer."[46] Article 3 of its code of ethics explicitly states that Al Jazeera takes it upon itself to "treat [its] audience with due respect."[47] In the words of Mohammed Jassim Al Ali, Al Jazeera aims "to bring the Arab audience back to trusting the Arab media, especially the news.... We treat them as an intelligent audience, rather than the conventional idea that they will take whatever you give them."[48] Al Jazeera provides food for an audience that is hungry for serious political analysis and eager for unex-purgated news. For Al Jazeera's former communications and media rela-tions chief, Jihad Ballout, "Al Jazeera has sharpened the sense of intuition that already exists in Arab viewers."[49] It caters to an audience that is politically conscious, that cherishes reliable political news and that craves intelligent political debates.

Al Jazeera has arguably changed news-watching habits. It aims not only at providing Arab viewers with reliable news from a distinctly Arab perspective, but also at conveying their views: "Al Jazeera is keen on pro-viding Arab viewers with an outlet to their opinions and to give them a chance to get their voice heard on the Arab and international media scene live and uncensored through fax, phone or email."[50] Al Jazeera listens to the people as much as it speaks to them. Whether it is through the call-in segments of its talk shows or through the polling and open fora avail-able on its website, Al Jazeera strives to be interactive and to involve its audience in a two-way communication stream: "Our ultimate goal is to set up a more proactive relationship with our audience, where the audi-ence is not simply a visitor at the other end of the line. They are and they will always be an integral part of the news reporting and news mak-ing process."[51]

In many ways, Al Jazeera draws much of its energy from the affinity it has with the Arab viewer. The network, as one critic points out, "knows that it will always be controversial to cover the Middle East. It is count-ing on its popularity among its viewers to stay on the air."[52] Viewer involvement and viewer feedback are an integral part of Al Jazeera's strat-egy and the structure of its programs, many of which are interactive. More than merely developing an affinity with the Arab viewer, this ten-dency has given Al Jazeera an overtly populist orientation. As such, Al Jazeera affects and is affected by Arab public opinion; it listens to the beat of the street and capitalizes on an existing public discourse, giving people what they want while at the same time shaping that which they want. People relate to Al Jazeera because it both shares and stages the malaise and sorrow of Arabs. Al Jazeera emerged in an environment marked by a succession of wars and crises and during a time marked by the spirit of defeat and disappointment. As such, Al Jazeera is the chan-nel of Arab disenchantment, articulating what people want to say but cannot say with a rare sense of audacity. Over the years, it has come to give an outlet to people's fears and anxieties and to allay much of the anger and frustration many Arabs feel. This side of Al Jazeera transpires not only in its many interactive or call-in programs, but also in its reports and documentaries. Part of Al Jazeera's mission is "to shed light on important eras and crucial stages in the history of the Arab nation which can provide a better understanding of history, which is necessary to acquire a more profound understanding of the present and a better conception of the future."[53]

As envisaged by its founders, Al Jazeera had a wide reach from the very beginning. Although set in and funded by Qatar, Al Jazeera smacks of an undeniably strong pan–Arab identity. The network has gone a long way toward strengthening the sense of pan–Arab identity — although in the view of some commentators this identity remains a distant prospect, as the ties that bind Arab viewers are based largely on sentiment, emotion and memory, making the virtual pan–Arabism that is fostered by a satellite channel like Al Jazeera more of a rhetorical effect. In the decline of the Arab nationalistic cause, pan–Arab satellite TV in general and Al Jazeera in particular have allowed Arabs to feel imaginatively bound in a common cause. Still, pan–Arabism is not only paramount to Al Jazeera but is also a driving force. This is inherent in the very image the network projects: opting to air its programs from within the Arab world (during times when its most prominent competitors — mostly Saudi media outlets — were based in European capitals), broadcasting in modern standard Arabic, and favoring a diverse and inclusive workforce from almost every corner of the Arab-speaking world. In terms of subject matter, Al Jazeera's programs deal with a range of timely issues that bear either directly or indirectly on the Arab world. The network widens its appeal by providing, among other things, a distinctly Arab perspective on issues that embroil the Arab and Muslim world: "Al Jazeera addresses itself, in a pointed way, to an Arab public, covering key and decisive topics that are of interest to Arabs."[54]

Through some of its journalists, guests and programs, Al Jazeera has come to play an eminent role in bringing sections of the Arab world together and in fact in broadening the scope and extent of pan–Arab interaction. Forging a common perspective on important issues and speaking directly to a group of people who already believe they constitute a community on some level, Al Jazeera, as Jon Alterman put it, has made that community real.[55] By appealing to Arab viewers both inside and outside the Arab world and by regularly inviting passionate and articulate guests, speakers and commentators who provide an Arab nationalist perspective on current affairs and timely issues, Al Jazeera often gives prominence to the theme of pan–Arabism, so much so that the very issue of "Arabness" has become paramount on its waves. Al Jazeera is branded, so to speak, by the Arab nationalist discourse it promulgates. In the words of Suleiman Al Shammari, "the channel promotes an Arab nationalist discourse wrapped in a democratic style which makes it easy for viewers to palate."[56] The fact that some of Al Jazeera's regular Arab guests who toe a pan–Arab line live in Europe, as is the case with the editor in chief of *Al Quds Al Arabi* Abdul Barri Atwan, who is frequently invited to comment on a variety of political issues, is not without significance. In his reflections about his own program *The Opposite Direction*, Faisal Al Kasim further explains the additional value the Arab diaspora bring to Al Jazeera: "Arab expatriates are particularly valuable for a channel like Al Jazeera. They are the ones who can appear on television, dare speak their minds and return home safe and sound. It is true that Al Jazeera has done them a great favor by giving them a platform to express their views, but they have been of paramount importance to us as well. A program like *The Opposite Direction* thrives on dissenting Arab voices. Not surprisingly, most of the episodes which hosted expatriate Arab dissidents have raised a big row in the Arab world."[57]

Part of Al Jazeera's strategy is not only to tap into Arab figures outside the Arab world and to capitalize on political figures in exile, but also to appeal to Arabs outside the Arab world: "Al Jazeera ... strives to reach the largest number of Arab viewers, particularly Arab expatriates in Europe, who long for the truth."[58] In fact, Al Jazeera has helped nurture a sense of community between Arabs in the Arab world and the Arab diaspora; it has also helped enhance the cultural connection between Arab viewers overseas and the Arab culture, thus bringing Arab countries and their diaspora in an ongoing public dialogue about a variety of timely issues.

VI.

The Power Game

For organization culture theorists, culture and leadership are two sides of the same coin.[1] The role a leader plays in building and shaping a strong culture is paramount. More than mere management, leadership entails having an impact and making a difference. In the words of Lavine and Wackman, "leadership provides direction for the organization by capturing people's attention and mobilizing their energy and support for a particular purpose, goal or strategy. Leadership provides stability and strength for the organization."[2] As such, leadership calls for a number of abilities — such as developing effective strategies to achieve the organization's objectives, harnessing participation at all levels, mobilizing commitment to the organization's vision, critically assessing the practices taking place within the organization against the stated vision, and using the artifacts of the organization to embed values and endorse the taken-for-granted assumptions — as well as traits — such as those of a facilitator, promoter, agitator, innovator and communicator.[3] Empowering employees and providing good leadership can help the organization harness the collective intelligence, knowledge and skills of people in the organization. In the absence of such a culture, demotivation is likely to seep in.

The founder of an organization often plays a significant role in laying the foundations of its culture, and, in fact, the beliefs and the cultural values laid by Al Jazeera's founder(s) are important and strategically enabling to the organization in an increasingly competitive environment, particularly as the network considers adaptability to environmental developments. Al Jazeera can be said to be the outcome of a visionary and transformational leadership at the highest political level — the Emir of Qatar. Governing Al Jazeera is a board of directors which sets the general policies of the network, leaving its mission and goals to be implemented by the upper management. These layers of leadership deserve more than a cursory attention.

To start with, Al Jazeera's cultural paradigm cannot be discussed independently of its political leadership. In fact, the political identity of Al Jazeera is hard to ignore as viewers are constantly reminded that Al Jazeera's news bulletins and many of its programs are aired from Qatar. As such, Al Jazeera is a showpiece of the Emir of Qatar and a symbol of his resolve to modernize his country under his "institutional monarchy." Since assuming power, Sheikh Hamad bin Khalifa Al Thani embarked on what has been described as "a limited course of political liberalization"[4] which, according to some commentators, is "geared toward satisfying U.S. policy goals of promoting democracy in the region,"[5] while for others it is a voluntary reform aimed at keeping up with the demands of the people and preempting dissatisfaction and disenchantment.

As part of the modernization plan, Sheikh Hamad launched Al Jazeera, which has since proven to be a valuable means for carving a role for an otherwise obscure tiny country in the Arabian Peninsula. Claiming a strong voice in the Arab mediascape gives Qatar prominence and enables it to extend its regional influence and to get out of the shadow of neighboring Saudi Arabia — "Gulf Big Brother," as David Hirst calls it.[6] Al Jazeera has not only enabled Qatar to heighten its diplomatic presence but also served its host country well as an instrument of foreign policy. As a leading regional news provider, Al Jazeera certainly promotes, albeit subtly, Qatar's political outlook. For sure, the network is a source of pride for Qatar and has even become a brand name, so to speak. Increasingly, there is an awareness of the strong international image Al Jazeera is building and the implications of that on the tiny Gulf country which, until not long ago, was hardly heard of. In the minds of many people, Qatar has become synonymous with Al Jazeera, which in turn has become one of the country's attractions. An advertisement in Doha's international airport based on a Brandchannel.com rating of brand names which puts Al Jazeera ahead of Coca Cola and behind such brand names as Apple, Google, Ikea, and Starbucks reads: "The fifth most powerful brand globally. Al Jazeera channel is currently among the five most recognized brands globally and the one brand named amongst media networks."

Not surprisingly, "the reform minded ruler of Qatar," as a Congressional Research Service Report described him,[7] has given Al Jazeera free rein, protecting it from pressure by creating a favorable, censorship-free environment for the emergence of such a channel — a noteworthy initiative in one of the regions that are less inclined toward freedom of expression. What is known about Sheikh Hamad is his contemplation of political reform in a part of the world that is more prone to keeping the *status quo*. Long before international pressure, particularly in the post–September 11 era, compelled the Arab world to pursue a course of political reform, Qatar was willingly flirting with "democracy" and voluntarily initiating some changes to liberalize life in Qatar — an achievement of sorts when compared to other Gulf countries with little or no appetite for reform. Particularly noteworthy is the Emir's initiative to liberalize the press. Shortly after taking power, the Emir did away with the Ministry of Information — a move which set a precedent, for since then Qatar has abolished the Ministry of Transportation and that of Heath Care in a move aimed at "building institutions which have enough financial independence, administrative autonomy and more flexibility in fulfilling their objectives.... The move is part of Qatar's strategy to improve performance levels."[8] Abolishing the Ministry of Information has even more profound implications than the subsequent dissolution of the two other ministries, as loosening the grip on information is anathema to the Gulf region in particular and the Arab world in general. The Ministry of Information is, in fact, the government body whose name in Arab countries is traditionally associated with censorship and with it a whole system that kept tight control over the country's newspapers and broadcasting. The Ministry of Information, as Sheikh Hamad bin Thamer Al Thani, chairman of the board of Al Jazeera, explains, "is the Ministry that controls the news media, be it television, radio or newspaper.... We don't see that a Ministry of Information has any positive role to play in future media projects."[9]

Although not revolutionary by any means, Qatar's initiative to do away with the Ministry of Information is more than a token decision. According to the 2001 Country Report on Human Rights Practices, released by the U.S. Department of State's Bureau of Democracy, Human Rights and Labor, the censorship office, which has been moved to Qatar Radio and Television Corporation, is more concerned with material that is culturally insensitive than politically incorrect: "The Office reviews materials for pornography, sexually explicit material, and material deemed hostile to Islam. There were no reports of political censorship of foreign news media or foreign programs."[10] A subsequent Country Report on Human Rights Practices is more cautious but equally favorable, pointing out that although in 1995 the Qatari government lifted formal censor-ship of the media, some restrictions still remain in practice and journal-ists continue to engage in self-censorship, particularly when reporting on government policies, the ruling family and relations with neighboring states. Still, the report takes pains to mention that the government did not prosecute anyone for the expression of views considered offensive.[11] The importance of the government's decision to do away with the Min-istry of Information lies not only in lifting censorship but also in giving Al Jazeera a free hand to operate at various levels. If Al Jazeera has made it so far, it is also in part due to Qatar's decision not to exercise direct control over the channel's policies and its tactful pursuit of a hands-off policy when it comes to official complaints about Al Jazeera's programs and requests to rein in the network. Qatar has indeed resisted pressure from Arab and Western leaders to bring back Al Jazeera to the straight and narrow of the region's conformist tradition. It is in this context also that one should understand Olfa Lamloum's contention that although Qatar benefits from Al Jazeera, the latter is far from being a tool in the hands of its host country. More than that, "the channel can fulfill its function for the Qatari regime only if its editorial independence is respected."[12] Naturally, this has made Al Jazeera "uncontrollable" even for Qatar.[13]

Another official figure whose name is often associated with Al Jazeera is Sheikh Hamad bin Jassim bin Jabr Al Thani — the Foreign Minister and the ruler's influential and outspoken cousin. In his book on Al Jazeera, Hugh Miles claims that "Besides being Qatar's Foreign Minister, Sheikh Hamad is also a major shareholder in Al Jazeera."[14] A regional newspa-per article even called Al Jazeera Sheikh Hamad's channel. Not surpris-ingly, when Sheikh Hamad is occasionally hosted on Ahmad Mansour's show *Without Borders*, Al Jazeera itself is often the subject of discussion and debate. Likewise, when there are official complaints about Al Jazeera, these are usually lodged at the Foreign Ministry, which is headed by Sheikh Hamad — although he publicly distances himself from the net-work. When traveling, Sheikh Hamad also receives frequent complaints about the network. During a trip to Washington and in response to the concerns of high-placed officials in the Bush administration, Sheikh Hamad told the press that he is "not responsible for Al Jazeera," nor was the Qatari government responsible for its output: "We will take this con-cern back to Al Jazeera and they have to review it because we need Al

Jazeera to be professional and we don't want anybody to send lies or to send wrong information."[15]

Al Jazeera is also tied to the Qatari government financially. It was launched in 1996 with a loan from Qatar's government. The latter contributed $140 million to finance Al Jazeera's operations for five years, after which the network was expected to finance itself. But a decade or so after its launching, the station has fallen short of securing independence from the government by supporting itself financially. Al Jazeera is far from breaking even by relying on production sales or on commercial advertising. The latter remains notably low as its controversial reporting is still scaring off advertisers, many of whom have succumbed to a politically motivated advertising ban imposed on Al Jazeera. As Mohammed Jassim Al Ali put it, "advertising in the Arab world is driven by politics and not by viewership figures.... In general, the trend for advertising in the Middle East is more towards buying around entertainment shows than around political, controversial and news programs."[16] Having failed to prevent Al Jazeera from invading their subjects' homes, some Middle Eastern governments have resorted to economic pressure. As a consequence, many companies steer clear from Al Jazeera partly for fear of a backlash from powerful and more economically viable countries which represent large markets in the region, the most obvious being Saudi Arabia, which, according to one report, controls about 40 percent of the Gulf advertising market.[17] Either because of the *de facto* Saudi embargo or Al Jazeera's own controversial programs and editorial stance which deter some advertisers from buying airtime, the network has not turned a profit despite its proclaimed huge viewership.

Seen from this perspective, it is only natural to ask how long Al Jazeera's financial backer is willing to sustain its losses; but that may not be a pressing question when put in context. Al Jazeera may not be the only channel which is not making headways financially. Overall, the political economy of Arab satellite TV and the size of the Arab advertising market is such that turning a profit is difficult for most channels. In fact, the Gulf advertising pie may not be big enough for an ever-expanding satellite TV market.[18] Some observers believe that "not one Arab satellite channel, including Al Jazeera, could survive without political and financial support either from an Arab government or from a wealthy member of the Arab elite who has close ties to its government."[19] So far, Al Jazeera, whose need for cash has become all the more insistent with its envisaged expansion, is still heavily dependent on the Emir, who continues to bankroll and subsidize it.

That Al Jazeera maintains its operations in spite of failure to sustain its operations on the basis of its self-generated financial resources is indicative of Qatar's own political priorities. One may even suspect that the plan from the outset was to furnish a channel for reasons other than profit — what is often termed "vanity broadcasting."[20] After all, the motivation for launching a private TV channel that is financially losing may not have been a random choice.[21] Interestingly enough, although financed for the most part by the Qatari government, Al Jazeera is perceived as being more independent than, say, Al Hurra, the U.S. government-sponsored Arabic language television station which was launched to bolster public diplomacy efforts in the Middle East.[22]

The Qatari government's conduit to the network is its board of directors — although the relationship between the latter and upper political leadership is neither direct not straightforward. According to the 2004 Country Report on Human Rights Practices, released by the Bureau of Democracy, Human Rights and Labor, "newspapers are not state owned; however, the owners or board members generally are either high-level government officials or have ties to government officials."[23] Al Jazeera operates in a similar manner. One of the key figures in Al Jazeera is Sheikh Hamad bin Thamer Al Thani, who served as the deputy Minister of Information before chairing Al Jazeera's board of directors since its inception. Although the seven-member board is appointed for a renewable one-year term, it has been marked by a sense of continuity for the first few years of the network's existence. In November 2003, some seven years after its launching, Al Jazeera underwent a noteworthy reshuffle of its board. A royal decree by Qatar's Emir, Sheikh Hamad bin Khalifa Al Thani, appointed three new directors, including Al Jazeera's former general manager Mohammed Jassim Al Ali, to replace three members.[24] Sheikh Hamad bin Thamer Al Thani's chairmanship of the board was extended and so was the assignment of his deputy, the head of finance, and the head of administrative affairs. It is noteworthy that the newly appointed board members include, and for the first time in the history of the network, a non–Qatari and a woman. The changes were such that Al Jazeera was quick to assert that the new appointments do not indicate a shift in editorial policy.

One staff member we interviewed recounted an interesting incident where a Qatari news reader in Al Jazeera stood up during an open meeting the network staff had with the chairman of the board, Sheikh Hamad, and publicly criticized the board. The complaint pertained to the often obscure nature of the board and its secretive deliberation. The staff member complained that the only thing he knew about the board is Sheikh Hamad himself. As such, he is the interface of the government with the board. For most of the network staff, as one interviewee put it, "the board comes down to Sheikh Hamad." Many of the staff we talked to agree that although Sheikh Hamad hardly interferes in the day to day activities of the network or is concerned with details, he is heavily involved with it. Granted that Sheikh Hamad's direct involvement is minimal, the fact that he is a member of Qatar's ruling family is never far from the mind of the network staff.

In a traditional society, such kinship, particularly to the ruling family as is the case here, is not without significance. In social and cultural anthropology, as Thomas Hylland Eriksen explains, "kinship can give a practical advantage. One can usually trust one's relatives, since they are tied to oneself through webs of strong normative obligations. In many societies, and especially stateless ones, the kin group usually forms the basis for political stability and for the promotion of political interests. The group is tied through mutual bonds of loyalty."[25] In spite of the pan–Arab current that runs through it, Al Jazeera is after all a Qatari channel — one that is sponsored by and beamed from Qatar, and entrusting its direction to someone with ties to its creators makes it easy for the piper to call the tune even with the proclaimed sacrosanctity of the principle of editorial independence. There is even a perception that he is the one who calls the shots and pulls the strings. He frequently visits the network, often every other day or so, but is rarely seen in the newsroom. When he comes, it is usually to meet with the general manager, a position which until the sacking of Al Ali entailed being part of the board of directors. For years, Al Jazeera's board included the managing director of the network, and even when Al Ali was relieved of his duties as general manager of Al Jazeera, he maintained his membership on its board of directors. With the restructuring of Al Jazeera and the coming to the scene of Waddah Khanfar, the managing director of Al Jazeera channel is no longer part of the board; rather he is part of an administrative structure which reports to the board. Naturally, such an administrative hierarchy gives the chairman of the board more leverage and more of a say in Al Jazeera's affairs.

At the level of management, the relationship between Al Jazeera's board of directors and Qatar's political leadership has at times served Al Jazeera well. Being a member of the ruling family and having served as a high-ranking official in the Qatari government before assuming the directorship of Al Jazeera's board, Sheikh Hamad enjoys the benefits of leading an independent organization and the privilege of being well connected to Qatar's political leadership. For instance, if Al Jazeera's bureau in South Africa runs short of cash and alternative arrangements have to be made, a network staff member told us, a phone call to the Qatari embassy in Pretoria will suffice for it to immediately disburse the necessary funds to Al Jazeera with the understanding that arrangements for reimbursing the money and clearing the books will be made in Doha at high government levels. In this sense, Al Jazeera's links to the government — which the latter takes pains to publicly downplay — can be an asset which benefits the network and facilitates its operations.

However, there is a less bright side to Al Jazeera's leadership. Some members of the staff perceive leadership at Al Jazeera as problematic, to say the least. Partly because of its covert political dimension, Al Jazeera is fragile, which is tantamount to saying that the politics of Qatar is not without potential effects on Al Jazeera. For one thing, the awareness that Al Jazeera has a political weight takes away from the myth of its independence. Furthermore, Al Jazeera depends on the good will and support of its sponsor, being unable to wean itself off Qatari state funding. The problem, however, is that if the priorities and goals of its patron change, the network will definitely be affected. There is also the specter of effacement, as is the case with Abu Dhabi TV, a channel which found itself succumbing to internal management problems and allegedly yielding to outside pressure to "tame" it because of its coverage of the war on Iraq. It is a fact that Al Jazeera depends on the Emir of Qatar politically. Such a political leadership is a double-edged sword, giving Al Jazeera a free hand to operate — for if Arab leaders have to a certain degree tolerated Al Jazeera it is because they know full well that any attack on Al Jazeera is also an implicit take on its host country. Qatar, in spite of its keenness on publicly dissociating itself from the network, has been vital to the success of Al Jazeera, particularly when it comes to probing the politics of Arab states publicly — while at the same time making it unable, at least so far, to operate outside the parameters envisaged by its political patron and to transform itself into an institution in the full import of the term.

At least initially, Al Jazeera has been conceived as the Emir's pet project more than a full-fledged institution, which in the words of Louay Bahry means that "any serious domestic change in Qatar, such as instability in the ruling family or even change of government — though currently unexpected, always a possibility [considering the history of palace intrigue that marked Qatar since it gained independence from Britain in 1971] — would impact Al Jazeera. Without strong support from the Emir and political will to continue this media experiment, Al Jazeera could fall prey to external pressure to curtail its daring style. Over time, such pressure could leave it weakened, resulting in a loss of appeals to Arabs outside Qatar."[26] Not surprisingly perhaps, such a concern is also on the minds of some of the network staff. As Hafez Al-Mirazi, Al Jazeera's Washington bureau chief adamantly states, "Al Jazeera has got to be self sufficient in order to guarantee its independence in the long run.... Until now, the whole of Al Jazeera has been dependent on Emir Hamad of Qatar, who has views on modernization. There is no guarantee whatsoever that if there is any change in his approach or in the government or in anything whatsoever that Al Jazeera will continue to be there."[27] Hugh Miles concurs; in his view, Al Jazeera, being a sign of liberalism and not of democracy, "could be unmade as quickly as it was made if one day the Emir changes his mind."[28]

Although the above scenario is not imminent, considering the slow pace of change in the Middle East and the survival instinct of Arab regimes, the very way power changed hands in Qatar during the country's recent history and, probably more significantly, the political incidents that have befallen Doha, particularly after the fall of Baghdad, leave a lot of room for speculation. The assassination in a car bombing outside a mosque in 2004 of Zelimkhan Yandarbiyev, the former Chechen President who fled Chechnya to settle in Doha in 1999 after the start of Russia's second military campaign, and the car bomb attack on a theater near a British school in Doha in 2005,[29] came as a shock to Qatar — a tiny Gulf emirate with tight though not always obtrusive security which serves as the home of one of the largest U.S. bases.

Upon visiting Al Jazeera's headquarters not long after the latter incident, we got a sense that security had been stepped up in Al Jazeera's compound. As we had an appointment with the manager of Al Jazeera, the network arranged for us to have permission at the gate to enter Al Jazeera. However, when prior to leaving the newsroom we requested permission to come back to the network the following day to observe the staff's interactions inside the newsroom and informally talk to some of the staff who did not mind sitting with us but were busy then, we were denied permission on the grounds that such a visit would have to be arranged, that we had to have a *vis-à-vis* visitor we were bound to meet and that someone would have to accompany us at all times while inside the network. Compared to our experience with the security-conscious but professionally handled procedures for accessing the MBC-Al Arabiya building in Dubai's media city, which we visited on several occasions to interview former Al Jazeera staff who had relocated to Al Arabiya, there were noteworthy restrictions which suggest that there was not as much openness as one would expect from a network which made a name for itself by unraveling the otherwise obscured truth about what is happening in the Arab world and for leaving no stone unturned. When in the course of a conversation with a female news anchor who has been with the network since its inception we mentioned the hassle of getting to Al Jazeera during our short trip and the notable lack of ready access to the network even though it was clear that we were doing academic research about Al Jazeera, she admitted that the bomb attack on a Doha theater had created a sense of fear, even among the network staff, that Al Jazeera may be a target. "You have to understand," she added in a slightly cautious tone, "everybody around here is nervous."

Naturally, Qatar has its own politics which are hard to ignore when considering Al Jazeera, which some observers perceive as a foreign policy tool. It is obvious that there are geopolitical factors which cannot be overlooked when considering Al Jazeera's host country, particularly in light of the debate about Al Jazeera's ability to deliver the facts without a domestic agenda.

Qatar is an institutional monarchy governed by Sheikh Hamad bin Khalifa Al Thani. It gained independence from Britain in 1971. In a 1995 bloodless coup, Sheikh Hamad, then crown prince, replaced his father, who had ruled the country for nearly a quarter of a century — although later, the two reconciled to some extent. With its small territory (11,437 sq km) and narrow population base (the country's population is around 800,000, with foreigners outnumbering native Qataris nearly four to one),[30] Qatar has been increasingly relying on external support for its security. In the aftermath of the second Gulf War (the war between the American-led allied forces and Iraq following the Iraqi invasion of Kuwait in 1991), bilateral defense and security cooperation between Qatar and the U.S. in particular have expanded considerably and rapidly. In the wake of the September 11 attacks, Qatar has emerged as the most important base of operations for U.S. forces in the Gulf, when in the not so distant past, the U.S. had a stronger military presence in Saudi Arabia and Bahrain. "Few countries in the Persian Gulf region," Mark Bixler writes, "have welcomed U.S. forces as eagerly as Qatar."[31] Thus, the U.S. combat air operations center was transferred from Saudi Arabia to Qatar. Both Al Udeid airbase and Al Sayliyah army base, which was also host for U.S. CENTCOM during the 2003 invasion of Iraq, were instrumental in America's so-called war on terrorism. To recognize Qatar's steadfast support for the war, George Bush hosted the Emir of Qatar in 2004.[32]

When considering that in much the same way the U.S. imports virtually no oil from Qatar, the latter does not purchase U.S. weapons[33] or planes,[34] the close and growing military alliance between the two countries is telling. Such an alliance arguably enables Qatar to position itself in a fast-changing region. For sure, it enables it to make headways, political and otherwise, over Bahrain, whose royal family, the Al Khalifa, has kinship ties with the ruling family in Qatar, the Al Thani. More significantly, perhaps, it enables Qatar to get out of the shadow of neighboring Saudi Arabia (as Qatar adheres to the Wahhabi brand of Sunni Islam, though the Wahhabi tenets are not as strictly enforced as is the case with ultra-conservative Saudi Arabia). At the heart of such rivalries are not only historical reasons, but also geopolitical considerations — Bahrain because of its maritime proximity, the relevance of which will become clear, and Saudi Arabia because of its weight, not the least being a heavy OPEC member.

There is something to be said about Qatar's relationship with its neighbors Saudi Arabia and Bahrain — two countries with which Qatar had strains but also with which it had recently resolved its long-standing border disputes. Qatar's relation with Bahrain has been marred with territorial disputes which have been settled to the satisfaction of both parties at the International Court of Justice. Equally significant is its relation with neighboring Saudi Arabia. The relationship between the two counties has never been that warm, and was often marked by strains — the Saudis being suspicious that Doha is supporting opposition figures, while the latter resentful about Riyadh's alleged involvement in an attempted coup in 1996, a year after the Emir, Sheikh Hamad, seized power from his father.[35] A 2003 incident which put Qatar under the spotlight whereby some 6,000 members of the Al Ghofran clan, a subset of one of Qatar's largest tribes "seen in ruling circles as a vehicle of Saudi interests," were stripped of their citizenship is indicative of the ebb and flow in the relations between Qatar and Saudi Arabia.[36] Although in 2006 Qatar reinstated the citizenship of those who settled their dual citizenship problem which Qatar claims is the real bone of contention, the political aspect of the incident is hard to ignore.[37] A Congressional Research Service Report sums up the nature of the dispute between Qatar and Saudi Arabia: "Relations between the new Emir of Qatar and Saudi rulers were strained in the first few years of his rule. Some Qatari officials accused Saudi Arabia of plotting to restore the former ruler of Qatar in 1996. Since then, Al Jazeera's treatment of Saudi Arabia in its programming has been the largest point of contention between the two regimes.... A combination of factors — strains with Saudi Arabia and Bahrain and aspirations to a more influential role in regional affairs — has contributed to Qatar's increasingly independent foreign policy since 1992."[38]

Qatar has come out of the shadows not only politically, but also economically, capitalizing on its significant oil and natural gas revenues. During the late 1980s and early 1990s, as one report has it, Qatar "was crippled by a continuous siphoning off of petroleum revenues by the Emir, who had ruled the country since 1972."[39] Under Sheikh Hamad, who seized power from his father while the latter was out of the country to become the sitting Emir in 1995, Qatar embarked on a reformist course which includes several liberal reforms. Currently, oil is the mainstay of the economy of Qatar, which is strategically located in the central region of the Persian Gulf near major petroleum deposits. According to the *CIA World Fact Book*, "proved oil reserves of 16 billion barrels should ensure continuous output at current levels for 23 years." Even with oil reserves likely to be exhausted and oil production declining in the foreseeable future, presumably within a few decades, Qatar is still well positioned for economic prosperity, and is in fact becoming one of the world's fastest-growing and highest per capita income countries. It is no news that Qatar sits on the third (second according to a recent *Middle East* economic report)[40] largest gas reserves in the world and has ambitions to become a world energy giant. With the long-term goal of developing offshore natural gas reserves, it has expanded its liquefied natural gas production (which incidentally is not subject to OPEC production quotas), has signed many agreements with international energy companies, is in the midst of building the largest gas-to-liquids plant in the world, and is envisaging building underwater pipelines to export natural gas.[41] Gas revenue is expected to outstrip oil income by 2007.[42] Understandably, Qatar counts itself among Washington's closest allies in the Middle East and is in fact "building an increasingly close defense relationship with the United States, possibly to ensure that its neighbors do not try to encroach on its huge gas reserves," as a Congressional Research Service Report put it.[43] There is a perception, common among many analysts, that Qatari authorities who "are acutely aware of neighbors with larger and more powerful militaries ... want the American military in their country"[44] in much the same way their forefathers put themselves under British protection in the eighteenth century for fear of being absorbed by the Turks. From the American perspective, this tiny Gulf peninsula "which allows its resources to be exploited and its desert to be colonized"[45] is an ideal partner in a conflict-ridden but oil-rich Middle East where anti–American sentiments are running increasingly deep.

If Qatar has served the Americans well by hosting U.S. bases on its soil in return for its own protection, it has also been aligning itself with Arab public opinion by playing a populist tune on the airwaves of Al Jazeera and often riding the mood of the Arab street. As Alastair Campbell put it, the complexity of Al Jazeera's situation is such that "they report anti–Americanism, but deny anti–Americanism is part of their ethos."[46] In addition to its populist tendency, Al Jazeera is also often criticized for its Islamist affinity. Critics of Al Jazeera often complain that Al Jazeera's broadcasts are biased in favor of Islamist causes; others perceive the network as having close ties with Islamic extremists and accuse it of having a religious agenda. In Sam Cherribi's view, "the image Al Jazeera inculcates in the public mind of offering 'the opinion and the other opinion' is really *trompe l'oeil* or as cover-up for a larger religious message.... Al Jazeera is not a 'liberal' or 'neutral' channel; it is a religious channel that allows other programs that are liberal or neutral to be shown occasionally."[47] For Molley McKew, Al Jazeera has "close ties to an extremist religious agenda"[48]—which may go some way into explaining its perceived jihadist propaganda. A Congressional Research Service Report goes as far as claiming that Qatar "harbored Al Qaeda terrorists"[49] while another one speculates that "Al Qaeda activists were present in or transited Qatar" prior to September 11.[50] Even among some of the people we talked to inside Al Jazeera, there is a perception that if Qatar has been spared the kind of unrest that befell neighboring Saudi Arabia or the sporadic incidents that took place in Kuwait, it is to some extent because it has been particularly keen on not alienating the Islamists.

But to avoid being on the wrong side of the Islamists is not to buy into their agenda. Although Al Jazeera has given generous airtime to so-called radical Islamists, as John Bradley put it, "there is no evidence that [the Emir] personally sympathizes with the often extreme opinions broadcast. Indeed, his close cooperation with Washington during the war on Iraq would suggest the opposite."[51] Seen from this perspective, Al Jazeera's perceived relationship with the Islamists has to be understood within the constraints and considerations of the country that hosts it and sponsors it. For Amir Taheri, "having allowed the U.S. to build its biggest military base in the Middle East in Qatar — a move bound to provoke Islamic rage — the Emir needed a gesture in the opposite direction. Creating a television channel that specialized in vilifying the United States was a balancing act.... There is little doubt that Al Jazeera ... has bought Qatar protection from Islamist terrorists."[52] Not surprisingly, many viewers who find Al Jazeera's journalism laudable are willing to look the other way when it comes to Qatar's decision to invite the U.S. to use its Al Udeid airbase, which seems like a *de facto* support for an attack on Iraq. So far, Al Jazeera's host country has managed to walk the thin edge of the wedge; how long it can keep in check these irreconcilable strains in its foreign policy remains to be seen.[53]

Within the network, the issue of the Islamist influence is not absent from the minds of some staff we talked to. One presenter we interviewed pointed out that Al Jazeera has always had a strong Islamist inclination which has grown stronger with the new management. Another network staffer we interviewed was particularly vocal about Al Jazeera's ideological affinity with the Islamists: "When the general manager is in a position to be influenced by a staff member who has been with the channel for only a few months just because he is an 'Islamist,' there is something fundamentally wrong." In another instance, and upon hearing that we got to interview Al Jazeera's general manager, one prominent Al Jazeera program host we met with sarcastically inquired if we managed to get anything out of the interview after shedding off all the "Islamist rhetoric." Likewise, in "The War Inside the Arab News Room," Samantha M. Shapiro reports that "some former Al Jazeera employees defected because, they said, Al Jazeera's management these days is too Islamist for them. Women were discouraged from wearing tight pants, they said, and some men refused to shake your hand if they knew you did not follow Islamic law."[54] This perception of the network as having Islamist affinities is not an uncommon one. Accounts on Al Jazeera in the Western press often point to an ambivalence stemming from the coexistence of the BBC ethos among some of the network staff, on the one hand, and allegiances to a brand of political Islam, on the other hand: "The TV station's reporting staff is a mixed bag. The core are former British Broadcasting reporters, steeped in Western news values. But other reporters are said to have links with the Muslim Brotherhood, a radical Islamic organization with ties to a member of Al Jazeera board."[55] Likewise, following the leaked information in the *Daily Mirror* regarding a confidential Downing Street memo in which George Bush allegedly discusses bombing Al Jazeera headquarters in Doha in April 2004, a newspaper article took heed of the presence the Islamists have in the network: "Many believe that behind the new momentum Al Jazeera is gathering stand the political allegiances of many network staff members, and more specifically an allegiance to the Islamic Brotherhood."[56]

However, not everybody we talked to in the network shares the view that Al Jazeera is increasingly becoming the channel of the Islamists. Incidentally, three interviewed female journalists with what could be termed a liberal outlook do not buy into the Islamist takeover theory. For sure, this take on Al Jazeera is not shared by a prominent female network staffer we interviewed, and was brushed aside by yet another female anchor who resigned her position with Al Jazeera to join Al Arabiya. A third female interviewee, who could tell with certainty that such an allegation was coming from a woman who left Al Jazeera for Al Arabiya but was still holding a grudge against her former employer, took the whole criticism with a grain of salt. If anything, we were told, there has been a spirit of tolerance in Al Jazeera. This same former female producer confided to us that she was an Arab Christian and yet her two best friends during the years she spent with the network had very strong Islamist inclinations, and that in fact one of them was the host of the prominent talk show *Islamic Law and Life*. It may be, the same person continued, that Al Jazeera has a visible Islamic front or veneer, but it is far from being Islamist; it just happened that some of the prominent figures or senior staff have such Islamist ideological inclinations.

Interestingly enough, a senior Al Jazeera staff member observed, the more aware Al Jazeera became of the Islamist image it has been projecting, given the prominence of key staff members and journalists, the more conscious it grew of the outside image it needs to project. Al Jazeera's management realized that, being an international broadcaster, it had to develop itself institutionally and to improve its image. For one senior staff member, however, such an endeavor often amounted to trading myopia for hyperopia. He complained that the coverage of the passing away of the pope, for instance, was "a bit exaggerated." When seen in the context of Al Jazeera's audience, a couple of hours of live coverage was more than the event warranted, particularly when considering that the death of the pope was not breaking news in the full sense of the term. If anything, such an extensive coverage is believed to serve in some ways as a cover-up for the network's Islamic front. According to the same senior Al Jazeera staff member quoted above, the incident hides "a desire to show that Al Jazeera is not an Islamist channel."

One former Al Jazeera staff member we interviewed pointed out that while it is true that Al Jazeera has figures who have Islamist affinities, that a member of the board of directors and at least two hosts of prominent programs, along with the regular guest of *Islamic Law and Life* who came to be one of the icons of the network, Sheikh Youssef Al Qaradawi, are perceived as being ideologically in tune with the Islamic Brotherhood, such an affinity does not necessarily make Al Jazeera an Islamist channel. This particular interviewee explained that Al Jazeera cannot be an Islamist channel if it is promoting radical sedition and contributing to sowing sectarianism in Iraq. There is indeed a perception that some of Al Jazeera's staff in Iraq have managed to impose their views and even foment ethnic strife. For example, the reports that are fed from Al Jazeera's bureau in Baghdad, we were told, give the impression that the Sunnis in Iraq are the majority when, in fact, this is not necessarily the case. Another example is Al Jazeera's coverage of the ethnic tensions in the oil-rich southwestern Iranian province of Khuzestan, located on the border with Iraq. The violence was spurred by the circulation of a letter allegedly attributed to former Vice President Mohammad Ali Abtahi outlining a plan to bring down the number of Arabs in the region by promoting the migration of Arabs to the northern provinces of the country. According to the Associated Press, Al Jazeera "is believed to have been the first news outlet to broadcast news of the unrest. The clashes also provided fodder for the station's talk shows."[57] Tehran suspended the operations of Al Jazeera in Iran, accusing its coverage of "inflaming ethnic disputes" and "exasperating the violence by Iran's Arab minority." The element of "media deception" in Al Jazeera, our interviewee observed, points partly to deficiencies in the recruiting process and partly to shortcomings of management. The channel can have journalists with strong views and convictions, but has to implement control mechanisms so that the output is written in an objective way.

VII.

The People Organization

Particularly striking about Al Jazeera is the dedication, commitment and loyalty of its staff. Many of the network staff who were interviewed are very enthusiastic about Al Jazeera and in fact effusive in their praise of its virtues. This enthusiasm has been a source of vitality and a driving force for a young broadcaster with relatively minimal resources. Many of the network staff we talked to have considerable faith in what Al Jazeera does. For some, such a commitment emanates from a belief in Al Jazeera as an independent Arab media project with high professional standards and an unprecedented margin of freedom. For others, the experience of Al Jazeera defies rationalization; behind its success lies a somewhat transcendental element. In the words of one staff member, the network "makes the unthinkable possible." Working for Al Jazeera is a real change and even a revolution. This is so not simply because it gives some people the chance to talk about that which is often shoved under the rug, but because it affords them "the opportunity to dream about the future" as one interviewee put it — something which cannot be taken for granted in a part of the world where people do not grow up dreaming. Naturally, this makes Al Jazeera a source of immense pride. Among many of those who work for it and those who watch it, Al Jazeera "engages and enlarges the field of the possible in the Arab and Muslim world."[1]

Throughout its formative years, the network was motivated by a sense of purpose more than it was driven by a particular vision. For better or for worse, the staff had in mind the notion that they were changing the face of Arab history. Overall, there is a deeply held belief and an utterly motivating conviction that Al Jazeera matters and that the news and programs it airs make a difference. At the same time, these people do not have an articulated common cause; what they have instead is "a common denominator," as one staff member put it, and that was enough to bring them together. Coming from countries which have autocratic governments whose agendas are not in synch with the people's aspirations, these staff members — many of whom have experienced the bureaucracy of Arab state television stations — share a sense of frustration about the condition their countries are in.

Seen with hindsight, though, some of the excessive faith in the network was more of a hype which the staff strongly believed in and subscribed to, so much so that during times of crisis or even when there was breaking news, many of the staff who were not on duty would drive to Al Jazeera's headquarters to see if they can be of any assistance to their colleagues. One producer remembers how the spirit of dedication during the war in Afghanistan was phenomenal. When the bombing of Afghanistan first started, Al Jazeera's twelve producers — those who were on duty and those who where off duty — were present in the newsroom and were keen on helping out. Although most of them ended up sitting in the cafeteria and drinking coffee, they felt they had to be there simply because they could not resist the urge to be part of what Al Jazeera was doing. There is a strong sense of bonding and enthusiasm among the network staff. Most of the people we talked to believe in Al Jazeera and feel that the network is theirs, so to speak. One staff member recounted how they would go to meetings because they wanted to and not because they had to. Some staff members would finish at 1:00 P.M. but would hang around sometimes up until 4:00 P.M. In the words of one interviewee, "Al Jazeera was a family." For another staff member, "Al Jazeera is like a baby; it is everything.... When you work in Al Jazeera, you are engulfed in the whole experience.... It is as if you live in a bubble."

In a way, this sense of belonging Al Jazeera has fostered among its staff is reciprocated. There is a perception among some of the people we talked to that Al Jazeera is supportive of its staff. At least compared to a regional channel like Abu Dhabi TV, job security is not an issue at the network and the number of people who have been sacked or whose contracts have been terminated is not all that significant.[2] Some of the staff we interviewed value the kind of job security Al Jazeera offers. Others value Al Jazeera's commitment to its staff. One staff member remarked that Al Jazeera does not let down its employees, pointing out instances where the network was willing to pick up the tab when a staff member was hospitalized and had to undergo surgery. This is even more evident at the professional level, namely the way Al Jazeera stands by its staff when they are detained, injured or run into difficulties. Suffice it here to mention Al Jazeera's coverage of the death of one of its field reporters during the invasion of Iraq (and the network's decision to create a trust for the families of journalists killed or wounded while on duty), the detention of one of its cameramen in Guantanamo, Sami Al Haaj, and especially the prosecution of its star reporter during the war in Afghanistan, Tayseer Allouni, who was sentenced in Madrid to seven years in prison for "collaborating" with Al Qaeda — although Al Jazeera's standing by its journalists has proven at times to be a double-edged sword.

This is not to say that there are no rivalries, conflicts or competition between the staff members. One network staff member noted that the sense of bonding and the family business atmosphere are deceiving. It is true that everybody works for the good of Al Jazeera, everybody is proud of Al Jazeera, everybody wants to live the dream, and everybody longs to see Al Jazeera succeed; but that group mentality is often at the expense of self-denial or self-effacement, as one interviewee put it. Another staff member explained how there is a feeling of uniqueness which often overwhelms them, so much so that they are led to feel they are special — in fact they are led to feel they are better than anybody else. This complex is still there — call it refusing the other ... in spite of the fact that Al Jazeera is the channel of "the view and the other view." This partly makes Al Jazeera's work environment stressful. In the newsroom in particular there is considerable pressure. Initially, such pressure was due to the desire "to make it." With the rise of competition in 24-hour news, Al Jazeera finds itself suffering from the winner's complex. One female anchor who left Al Jazeera for a regional competitor compared Al Jazeera to a military camp where there is no room for mistakes. If Al Jazeera is afraid of something, it is nothing other than itself.

Still, these reservations do not undermine the sense of belonging among Al Jazeera's staff. Behind the spontaneous enthusiasm for Al Jazeera lies a culture of empowerment which, although it has become one of the distinguishing traits of organizations, particularly in the West, is still to a large extent an alien concept in the Arab world. Empowerment — which is to a large extent the result of a vision carried through the channel of a strong leader[3] — has become increasingly important as a way of harnessing the full capacity of employees in an organization. The concept refers to the vesting of decision-making in the employee, whereas traditionally such an authority is a prerogative of management.[4] Stated differently, empowerment means providing a framework whereby the organization's employees can explore their potential, develop their skills and use their knowledge to help the organization achieve its goals and to better themselves. As an organizational vision, empowerment means allowing self-managing or autonomous teams and individuals to be in charge of making decisions they deem necessary to help the organization achieve its planned objectives. As an organizational program, empowerment entails giving the employees the resources to unleash their potential, develop their knowledge, and utilize their skills to their fullest potential in order to address and resolve organizational contingencies.[5] As an organizational *modus operandi*, empowerment is arguably a form of management control rather than an erosion of such a control; by vesting decision-making in the employee, the organization creates the perception that the interests of the organization and those of the employee converge, thus influencing behavior unobtrusively and at the same time enhancing the legitimacy of organizational goals.[6]

Given the expectation of the job and the nature of the organization (being an information intensive organization), Al Jazeera's staff are compelled to maintain high performance standards. A culture of empowerment can go a long way toward fulfilling those objectives. In fact, the success of Al Jazeera can be attributed in great part to the fact that the network promotes a number of values which foster a culture of empowerment, chief among which are flexibility, independent thinking, willingness to take initiatives, involvement, self-development, and talent fostering. According to some of the interviewed network staff, these attributes make Al Jazeera a good environment to work in and in fact a place where the staff are well at ease.

In his book on Al Jazeera, Hugh Miles takes special notice of the amount of individual responsibility the staff members at Al Jazeera are given: "each reporter is an individual news cell, often writing, shooting and editing his own work, and staff can easily move laterally to different departments, trying their hand at new things and forming new connections."[7] Not only do Al Jazeera employees have considerable leeway in deciding how to get their jobs done, but also the various divisions within the network, including the administrative units, have a lot of flexibility, autonomy and control over their work. Since the early years of the network, Al Jazeera's staff have enjoyed a degree of autonomy and flexibility which is inconceivable in government institutions. In order to get things done, the restrictions of slow bureaucratic processes are simply bypassed, empowering the staff to make decisions and take actions when needed. In other words, people in the network are given a free hand. A staff member who served in the finance department in the early days of the network recounts a particular instance when he signed a major purchasing request for equipment without having to seek clearance from the board of directors first, thus enabling the network to acquire such equipment and use it in no time, which is very uncommon in a culture where red tape and state bureaucracy are deeply entrenched. What is even more telling is that the spending in question was eventually approved *ipso facto* by the board of directors as a matter of formality.

A comparative perspective can further elucidate the point. The difference between Al Jazeera's reaction to breaking news that needs to be reported and that of its immediate competitor — the Dubai-based Al Arabiya — is particularly instructive. Let us take a real-life scenario about an event that was widely publicized during the time the interviews for this research were conducted, and consider the likely course of action for each of these two channels. Pope John Paul II is suffering from worsening health problems including a heart condition and is showing signs of losing consciousness. Vatican officials have conceded that the 84-year-old revered pope is on the verge of dying. In St. Peter's Square, thousands of anxious Catholics have gathered to pray for and pay their last respect to the frail pontiff who led the Roman Catholic Church for more than a quarter of a century. On the eve of April 2, 2005, the gravely ill pope eventually dies. Naturally, this important event is to be covered promptly and prominently.

In the case of Al Jazeera, the senior producer on duty picks up the phone and talks to the news editor in chief in order to secure permission to get a staff member to the site of events to cover the unfolding of the drama in the Vatican — if no action has already been taken in this regard. Permission is more or less a formality and is usually granted immediately. The producer then contacts Al Jazeera's Paris office requesting that a correspondent and cameraman, along with a satellite news gathering device (SNG) be immediately dispatched to the Vatican. Within an hour or so, Al Jazeera's team is boarding a plane that is bound to Rome. The rest happens on screen.... In the event Al Jazeera's team does not secure an SNG to cover such a prominent event, it can always hire a feeding point from an international press agency like Reuters or resort to a local Italian TV station in Rome. Whether it uses its own SNG or hires a feed,

Al Jazeera's team is bound to cover the event in a timely fashion and live with picture and sound.

If the process is both smooth and efficient, it is in large part due to Al Jazeera's resourcefulness. In other words, Al Jazeera can be at the site of events faster than any of its competitors in the region partly because of its resourcefulness. A few weeks after the event, Al Jazeera's office in Paris sends the bill for relocating Al Jazeera's team from Paris to Rome to the main office in Doha, which picks up the tab. Clearly, money is not an issue: "they just sign," one staff member told us. A former Al Jazeera producer who later joined Al Arabiya concurs, adding that she has "never heard the word budget during her tenure with Al Jazeera." Al Jazeera is generously funded, which means that it has ample resources at its disposal. There is a perception that the network spends endlessly without consideration of financial returns. Compared to Al Arabiya which, being a profit-seeking organization, is compelled to spend effectively and with an eye on returns,[8] Al Jazeera does not have money constraints — at least so far. For example, when sending a large team on a mission, we were told, a producer will not get criticized, reprimanded or denied access to resources, but will simply hear a suggestion such as, "Was it necessary to send such a large team?" The lack of financial constraints and the abundance of (financial) means and resources have implications on the empowerment of the staff and consequently on the outcome. This resourcefulness translates, for instance, into a network of bureaus throughout the world. Naturally, such a network of correspondents gives the network not only prestige but also added value. For instance, because Al Jazeera has a bureau in Japan, Al Jazeera can provide live coverage of, say, an earthquake, and broadcast original perspectives from government and non-government sources in ways which cannot be provided by a report that is produced in the newsroom, thousands of miles away from the event.

Not so with Al Arabiya. Faced with the immediacy and significance of the event, Al Arabiya has also to react to the Vatican's announcement that the Pope has passed away. As in the case of Al Jazeera, a small team has to be dispatched to Rome to cover the ensuing events. The senior producer on duty contacts the head of assignments to request moving two staff members from London to Rome. Upon getting clearance for relocation, the producer calls the satellite desk to request an SNG device. The latter has to seek permission from MBC's clients (Bahrain's BTV and

Saudi Arabia's Al Ikhbariya) to move an SNG device from London to Rome. Upon getting a no-objection signal from all involved parties, the call desk comes back to the producer with a cost estimate of the operation for his or her perusal. If there are no objections, approval is then sought for the requested budget, which is more than a mere formality. When it comes to implementation, further complications may arise. For all practical purposes, the London office may not have the requested money, in which case approval for the budget of this operation may have to be requested from the Dubai head office, which means that the producer will have to contact the news editor in chief. Assuming that all goes well and that all involved parties are available and respond promptly, the process may take up to 5 hours, which in the age of live news coverage is considerable time. Even so, the outcome is not guaranteed. Should the attempt to secure an SNG device fail, the producer on duty will have to settle for a phone interview or simply air a report which, in this particular case, would still save the day as the passing away of the pope is more of a global event than an event that is specific to the Arab world — which is the niche Al Arabiya, among other regional broadcasters, has carved for itself. Even so, such constraints put Al Arabiya at a slight disadvantage. Eventually, it is a channel like Al Jazeera, with better financial resources and less cumbersome processes, which gets the scoop ... and the audience.

A comparison between the resources of Al Jazeera's bureau in the Russian capital of Moscow and that of its regional competitors illustrates the point further. As a former Al Jazeera reporter who served later as a correspondent in Moscow for Abu Dhabi TV before joining Al Arabiya as a producer explains, Al Jazeera is well provided for when compared to some of its competitors. To start with, its bureau is large, consisting of four rooms including a studio, and is well equipped for picture editing. The bureau chief has a backup reporter who handles the economic reports and acts as a substitute when needed, two cameramen, a producer, a car with a driver and subscriptions to wires from all the Russian information agencies and from AFP in Arabic. In contrast, Abu Dhabi TV had only a reporter during the period the Al Jazeera interviewee served as correspondent. If there is a story to be covered, the reporter has to call the assignment desk in Abu Dhabi, which will arrange for the booking of a cameraman from Reuters' London office, who in turn passes on the request to Reuters' Moscow office. Because the process may take up to two hours, the reporter does not always act on the spot or cover issues in a timely fashion. Al Arabiya is not better off. The reporter in Moscow has two desks, one cameraman and is compelled to use his own laptop to produce his reports. He has no access to editing equipment or to wire services. Recently, there has been talk in Al Arabiya to replace the Moscow correspondent with a freelancer, as Russia was not deemed a priority. Likewise, there has been a move to reduce the amount of time used on feeds, as in the case of Iran, since these tend to be expensive and to go for in-house reports rather than field reports or make use of phone interviews when the event being reported is not all that important. Clearly, the choices and decisions each of these three channels made is bound to affect the end product. Naturally, one would think that the absence of money constraints and profit considerations give Al Jazeera an edge over its competitors.

It remains to be said that the free hand Al Jazeera enjoys poses yet another question which eventually has to be addressed: What is Al Jazeera's philosophy of spending? If we consider CNN, the network has a pragmatic understanding of its role and a businesslike approach to its operations. Of course, CNN's financial realism may be part of a wider industry culture, but it is one which is more pointed in the organization. CNN is a cost-conscious organization which spends only on things which increase the value for its viewers. To what extent is this true for Al Jazeera, and further, is Al Jazeera able to provide good products to customers at a reasonable cost?

In the 2005 Arab Summit which took place in the Algerian capital, Al Jazeera dispatched a 25-member team while Al Arabiya had a small team of five. As many observers predicted, nothing much was achieved during this summit, which saw the absence of several Arab heads of state. For a political event which turned out to be as inconsequential as observers expected it would be, or as one observer put it "business as usual," clearly Al Jazeera may not be getting its money's worth and may prove expensive to run in spite of its being generously funded. In some instances, the resourcefulness of Al Jazeera may even prove counterproductive. One staff member recounts how the general manager, Waddah Khanfar, ordered an SNG device to be relocated to Amman to cover parliamentary elections in Jordan. This move was not met with enthusiasm in the newsroom. The then news editor in chief felt that the event did not deserve the attention it was about to get. Most importantly, live coverage of the event would help perpetuate the idea that Jordan in particular and the Arab world in general are taking serious steps toward political reform which bodes well for democracy in the region, when in fact this is far from being the truth. A phone call to the chairman of the board, Sheikh Hamad bin Thamer Al Thani, to discuss the issue further dissuaded the general manager from providing live coverage of the elections. Nonetheless the incident suggests that the resourcefulness of Al Jazeera, which many perceive as giving the network an edge over its competitors in the region, can sometimes be a double-edged sword.

These considerations notwithstanding, Al Jazeera's culture of empowerment is an achievement of some sort, particularly when seen in the context of Arab media. Unlike state media, Al Jazeera is open to the delegation of authority, which is necessary for routine operations. Because there is not so much of a formal or rigid system in place but a set of practices (many aspects of which were informal and unwritten before Al Jazeera adopted more formal measures), employees do not tend to communicate with managers frequently when it comes to routine matters. Al Jazeera journalists, reporters, anchors and editors have decision-making prerogatives which enable them to react to situations and deal with events without systematic and routine hierarchical referral, thus allowing self-managing teams to be in charge of themselves and qualified individuals to be at their best as they strive to achieve the company's goals and carry out its vision. Naturally, Al Jazeera's pursuit of minimal overseeing not only helps the staff act more rapidly, leaving time for the managers to deal with the unexpected or with newsworthy developments — which, as far as Al Jazeera goes, have never failed to come about — but also promotes independent thinking, encourages creativity and develops the instinct for taking personal initiatives. Therein lies an aspect of Al Jazeera's culture which far outweighs the edge its "lavish spending" gives it. Al Jazeera may be more generous with spending, but hardly spends significantly more than its competitors. For example, the very structures and procedures Al Arabiya has in place, as the foregoing analysis suggests, end up costing it more. In fact, with its behind-the-scenes procedures, the latter may end up spending more (if we consider cost, overhead, and corporate prices for transactions and services). What this means in part is that money may give Al Jazeera an edge, but it is by no means a decisive factor. More important than the lack of restrictions on spending is the freedom for people to work. The kind of flexibility Al Jazeera's staff enjoy cannot be emphasized enough.

A case in point is the experience of Jamal Demloj — a former BBC journalist who joined Al Jazeera as a correspondent when it was launched in 1996. He worked as a journalist and a correspondent before moving to Abu Dhabi TV when it was relaunched in 2000 to serve as its correspondent in Moscow, only to end up three years later as a producer with Al Arabiya. Almost five years after he left Qatar, Demloj still remembers well his major last assignment with Al Jazeera — reporting on the events in Kosovo. A few days before the start of the NATO bombing of former Yugoslavia in 1999, Demloj was to move to Kosovo. He submitted a plan to Mohammed Jassim Al Ali, the then general manager, delineating the mission — which consisted of covering the developments in Kosovo — and specifying the period of the assignment — in this case it was open. Al Ali usually acted on such requests promptly, either giving his approval on the spot or getting back to the concerned party as soon as he was through with the matter in his hands. The allocated budget for a particular assignment can be suggested by the correspondent, but is usually determined by the general manager, in some cases in consultation with the head of the assignment desk. In this instance, the approval was instantaneous, with a signature and a jotted comment authorizing the sum of $30,000 to be disbursed to Demloj. The latter then took the signed request to the administrative affairs division which acted on it immediately. In no time, the correspondent was in possession of the money and all set to go.

The next step was to secure the visa for entering Yugoslavia. Since the latter did not have diplomatic representation in Doha, Demloj boarded the first plane to Crete bound for the Yugoslavian consulate. Because he was affiliated with a media organization and was going on an assignment, he was told that he had to wait for clearance from Belgrade, and that getting such permission took four days or so. On the fifth day, Demloj headed back to the consulate only to come back empty-handed. For the next week, he would receive the same message from the diplomatic mission: "we have not received clearance yet." Time was not on his side as the NATO strikes were clearly becoming more imminent than ever. After 12 days in Crete, Demloj grew impatient and informed Al Ali that he had been held back in Crete longer than he could afford to wait because of paperwork and that he was bound for Athens. When he arrived in the Greek capital, it was 23 March 1999. That evening, in his hotel room, he watched the press conference held jointly in Brussels by Richard

Holbrooke and Javier Solana. It was evident from their rhetoric and tone that the air strikes were imminent. In the morning, Demloj took a cab and dashed to the Macedonian embassy. He figured that if he could not get a visa to enter Yugoslavia, he may have more success getting to Macedonia and from there he would have to find his way to Kosovo. Much to his dismay, he was informed that even here the process took a minimum of three working days. Knowing that tension was high and that he had no time to spare, he had no choice but to fill out a visa application and wait for his turn to submit his documents. When his number was up, he submitted the application to the diplomat at the visa desk and inquired about the application fees. Instead of the requested $30 or so, he withdrew $1,000 from his wallet, handed it to his interlocutor and asked if his application could get immediate attention. In a matter of minutes, he was in possession of a multiple entry visa and was on his way to Skopje, the capital city of Macedonia.

It was almost 9:00 A.M. and the next flight to Skopje was not until 6:00 P.M.or so. Knowing that time was of the essence and that waiting was not an option, he hired someone to take him with his car to the border between Greece and Macedonia, some 850 kilometers north of Athens. On the way, he called AP, with whom Al Jazeera has an agreement, to arrange for having a cameraman, picture editing service and a feed. Knowing that their client, Al Jazeera's correspondent, would be on the frontier soon, AP offered to send a car to pick him up. Demloj made it to Kosovo on 24 March 1999 — the same day the NATO strikes started. Although his first appearance on the channel was secured through phone correspondence as there was barely any time left before the evening news bulletin to make other arrangements, it nonetheless enabled Al Jazeera to be the only Arab TV channel to cover the American-NATO assault on Yugoslavia live.

A day or so later, Demloj acquired an SNG from AP, and hired a driver with the intention of exploring the frontier region. As he was cruising, he looked far ahead to see what looked like a flowing river — only to realize as he drew closer that this was a multitude of refugees fleeing the strikes in Kosovo in search of a safe heaven in neighboring Macedonia, forming an endless flow, the spectacle of which was unlike anything he had experienced before. The numbers were in the thousands and in fact subsequent estimates pointed to 20,000 refugees. The immediate instinct of Al Jazeera's reporter, who was equipped with an SNG and therefore had access to a feeding point, was to call Doha and request permission to appear live on the air. And so it was — capitalizing on a historical incident a few hours before French TV and nearly a day ahead of CNN.

When asked if he could have done the same thing if here were working with his current employer, Al Arabiya, our interviewee expressed doubts. A key difference between the two media outlets, as he put it, has to do with financial stakes. Al Jazeera, he explained, is not a commercial channel but more of a media venture which aims at communicating and connecting with the Arab viewer in the best possible way. This requires in part making every effort to get to the news through any possible means and to report events to the viewers as they occur. Not so with Al Arabiya, which is operated by Middle East News (MEN) and is first and foremost commercial in nature. Such a commercial mindset compels the heads of departments to be as cost-effective as possible. This is often achieved at the expense of the quality of the output. Imagine a scenario, our interviewee added, whereby a staff member has to be dispatched to Iraq to cover the elections. For this to take place, a reporter is designated, a plan is drafted for a one-week assignment, a budget is put together and a request is submitted for approval. The process may take up to two days. Even so, there are several restrictions which a reporter with Al Jazeera is not subjected to. For instance, even when the entire budget is approved, the reporter does not get a lump sum. He or she gets only part of the money in cash, the rest in services which are provided by the main office in Dubai. Al Arabiya would provide its reporter with some money based on a *per diem* rate, would acquire his or her tickets, and would arrange with AP for an SNG to be provided to him or her on site. In the latter case, Al Arabiya deals directly with the party that is providing the equipment. The reporter is then informed that he or she has a facility available at his or her assignment site whether it be a camera crew, editing services or feeds.

While in theory such a management approach is to ensure efficiency, in practice — at least compared with Al Jazeera practices — it is restrictive, rigid and often lacking common sense, particularly for media practitioners who work in a region that has been marked recently by a succession of wars and a proliferation of crises. In some cases, covering such crises has been more the norm than the exception. The budget restrictions, in terms of both the funds allocated for a particular assignment and the management of such money, is not conducive to producing a competitive output. For example, an Al Arabiya reporter is not in a position to make a decision to pay for vital and timely information he or she may not acquire otherwise or which may eventually fall in the hands of a competing network. There are even times when the reporter is confronted with a situation where he or she is approached by someone and offered exclusive pictures for sale but cannot take up the offer because if he or she takes the initiative to pay the requested $1,000 or $2,000, he or she will not be reimbursed, as a receipt will have to be provided for accounting purposes. There was an instance, we were told, where an Al Arabiya staff member acquired $100 worth of gasoline for the car he was using to move around in Iraq from one of the clandestine merchants who display fuel containers on the side of the road during the peak of armed clashes in the aftermath of the fall of Baghdad but was not eventually reimbursed for failing to provide a receipt — when in fact fuel was a commodity in Iraq, when security was an issue, when time was of the essence and, most importantly, when Al Arabiya was not officially welcome in Iraq. Not only is the *per diem* for going on an assignment to Iraq perceived as rather low to start with, but the whole approach to financial matters is constraining. Transferring money is made problematic partly because of unusual circumstances in the country of assignment and partly because of complications and red tape within the media organization itself. If a reporter needs additional funds, he has to get in touch with the assignment desk, which in turn refers the matter to the chief of news before ending with the accounting and finance departments who have to figure out which cost account should the requested funds come from, as current affairs programs and news have separate budgets. When the program overlaps, further delay is to be expected until the exact amount to be billed to each cost center is figured out.

The complications that arise from such a system are often beyond belief for the layman. One Al Arabiya staff member recounts an instance where Al Arabiya's office in Baghdad was left with no communication lines for a day or so because the telephone bill was not paid. Eventually, arrangements had to be made with the head office in Dubai before Al Arabiya's bureau was wired again. Likewise, a senior staff member who used to work with Al Jazeera and then moved to Al Arabiya pointed out that, by comparison to procedures at work with his former employer in Doha, the restrictions Al Arabiya puts in place often lack common sense and are not amenable to having an edge in an already media-congested environment. "Sometimes," this same staff member complained, "you find your hands tied up and you can't help it.... Finding yourself in charge of a bureau in Iraq during a time of siege with only $20,000 in cash at your disposal does not help. The only thing you can do is follow procedures, fill out paperwork and provide justification for the disbursement of more cash — all of which takes time." In comparison to procedures at work in Al Jazeera's Doha head office, this senior staff member, much like Demloj, finds the procedures, paperwork and layers of management in the MBC headquarters in Dubai unduly restrictive and often unfit to deal with contingencies which have been increasingly rife when reporting on the conflict-ridden Middle East.

At the end of the day, Demloj observes, the rigidity of the system drains the energy of the reporter, who finds himself or herself caught in a web of distractions that rearrange the sense of priority. Seen from this perspective, the effect of the kind of autonomy, delegation and empowerment Al Jazeera's staff are likely to be endowed with, as the foregoing analysis of the coverage of the Kosovo crisis suggests, is not to be underestimated. That Al Jazeera reporters get upfront the money that is approved for conducting their mission, that they have the autonomy and decision-making power to spend that money as they see fit to get the job done, that they are not bound with rigid red tape when it comes to accounting and finance purposes, that they know that they can get money wired to them any time when they run out of cash — all these are small details out of which transpires the culture of an organization which goes a long way toward accounting for the success of Al Jazeera and explaining how it managed to do what it did.

There is yet another minor facet of that culture which, although Demloj mentions only passingly, is nonetheless significant as it bears on drive, achievement and belonging, which Al Jazeera's management takes pains to foster. A few days after sending his report on the refugee crises in Kosovo, Demloj found an envelope under the door of his hotel room containing a fax from Mohammed Jassim Al Ali thanking him for his efforts and commending him on his performance. Needless to say, Al Ali's gesture meant a lot for Demloj. More importantly, it suggests that leadership has gone a long way toward building a culture of empowerment. At least in the news division, the management style is more employee-directed than management-directed; it involves high levels of supportive behavior and low levels of direction. The major feature of this leadership style includes encouragement of input, involvement of the staff and assurances that they can perform their job well. For example, the editor in chief of Al Jazeera news, Ahmad Sheikh, conceives of himself as a facilitator rather than someone who oversees the editorial policy of Al Jazeera. Even a cursory observation of how he conducts every operation confirms his claims. He has an open-door policy, making himself both accessible and approachable to the staff he works with, who frequently and informally pop in and out of his office. When he was not facilitating the work in the newsroom during the time we observed him, he was answering phone calls from the network's correspondents. In either case, he seems to positively channel the energy of his network staff and to provide input on and suggestions about staff initiatives as the need arises rather than dictating a particular agenda or rigidifying the work environment into set ways.

One gets the same impression from talking to the director of Al Jazeera Media Training and Development Center, Mahmoud Abdulhadi, who oversees the center and sets its goals and strategies but does not concern himself with the details of the activities of the center or interfere in the work of specific individuals or units unless there is a particular need to do so. Overall, he promotes a sense of responsibility by delegating and empowering while at the same time instilling the value of accountability. The nature of the products that come out of a media organization — whether it be a news bulletin, a talk show or a documentary — makes the staff accountable as they are expected to deliver a product that is up to the professional standards of the organization and meets the expectations of the audience. Notwithstanding this internal pressure to deliver that is inherent to the profession, Al Jazeera has created a unit to monitor its programs and set up an editorial board. Even those units or departments where the end product is not a media program are also accountable as they have to provide periodic reports and hold regular meetings to ensure follow-up.

For some of the interviewed staff members, what is interesting about Al Jazeera is how real the chance "to think and execute" is. This energy is evident even at the level of programs. Al Jazeera's programs consist not only of flagship programs which have been around since the inception of the network, such as *The Opposite Direction*, *More than One Opinion*, and *Islamic Law and Life*, but also a series of other programs, some of which are put together on the spur of the moment and in response to important events, such as *The Century's First Wars* or *The Iraqi Scene*. Some of the newly hired anchors were appreciative of the opportunity Al Jazeera affords not just to be part of the newsroom team but also to develop one's own program.

Al Jazeera encourages creativity among its staff. A member of the staff was particularly appreciative of the fact that the general manager, Waddah Khanfar, has a suggestion box which is open to everybody in the network. A newly hired member of the network staff was proudly recounting how staff in the Media Training and Development Center are required to come to their weekly meetings with two new ideas. Al Jazeera channels such energy and enhances creativity through talent fostering and self-development. As such, it believes and invests in its staff; it seeks people with talent and works on improving the skills of its existing staff. The latter are encouraged to take whatever training they need at the network's expense in order to improve themselves and perform better. The creation of Al Jazeera's own Media Training and Development Center further facilitates human resources development. During 2004, the center offered close to 60 training sessions with 800 participants; 55 percent of those who benefited from such training are Al Jazeera staff.[9] In 2005, the number of participants reached 1400.[10] Incidentally, Al Jazeera also uses its Training and Development Center to identify talent and possibly recruit good trainees.

However, not everybody is enthusiastic about what Al Jazeera has to offer to them. In fact, for some of the interviewees, the new initiatives are good as far as they go, but they do not go far enough. For example, some of the staff who took part in a few of the sessions Al Jazeera Media Training and Development Center held were disappointed in the quality of the training they were offered. One of the journalists from Aljazeera.net complained that the training session he was recommended to take was substandard, introducing staff who — given their experience with Aljazeera.net — are computer savvy to such basic concepts as search engines. This particular staff complained that the training he took part in did not take into consideration the knowledge and know-how of the group, nor was it tailored to the specific needs of the trainees, many of whom have become seasoned just by doing what they do. If anything, there is resentment that some of Aljazeera.net editors who distinguish themselves through on-the-job learning are often transferred to the newsroom of the channel. In spite of the opportunities Al Jazeera affords for professional development, some of the network staff do not feel they can fully realize their potential or implement some of the ideas they have.

Clearly, not everybody is thrilled with Al Jazeera. While some speak effusively about Al Jazeera, others are more critical of the network and of their colleagues' tendency to indulge in chauvinism, heaping more praise on the network than criticism — an attitude that may be understandable in a society which does not tolerate criticism but is unexpected from an organization which prides itself on breaking taboos in the Arab world.

To start with, the size of Al Jazeera presents a constraint for some of the hitherto less achieved journalists or less prominent staff. Compared to the BBC, which employs over 20,000 staff,[11] Al Jazeera is a relatively small organization with modest resources and few layers of management. The total number of staff is around 1,400. Being a relatively small organization, Al Jazeera requires few layers of management between the general manager and the staff members at the lower level of the organization. Such a setting offers limited opportunities for employees to increase their responsibilities, move up the ladder or advance their careers. Overall, Al Jazeera does not come off as particularly attentive to such issues as career development, advancement within the organization, employee motivation, continuous growth and job rotation which may go a long way toward retaining its best and most talented employees. In order to make headway, employees may be inclined to jump ship although, currently, this is not happening at any significant scale given the visibility and prowess of Al Jazeera itself and the absence of a vibrant news media scene in the Arab world which can absorb such talent. Although advancement is not precluded in Al Jazeera, at the moment it is not systematic. It is true that few network employees made it in the organization and that it was possible for some to move up from the position of news editor to program producer and presenter, but it is also a fact that in other cases there is a sense of restlessness even among Al Jazeera's prominent figures. Not surprisingly, perhaps, a recently hired achieved anchor we talked to admitted that he ended up in Al Jazeera for lack of a better alternative, and even so with the understanding that he would be able to develop his own program. Likewise, a veteran anchor and a former BBCer who has been with Al Jazeera since its inception has confided to us that he has been considering moving out of the network but none of the offers he received were appealing. What is revealing about these cases is that the loyalty is not to Al Jazeera in and of itself as much as it is for what Al Jazeera, as an Arab media organization, stands for and what it is all about — although the two can only be theoretically distinguished. Overall, such job mobility tends to favor orientation to the profession more than it fosters loyalty for the organization. With the increased competition and newcomers on the scene, this trend may be enhanced in the future, with potential effects on Al Jazeera.

There is also a perception that the network is not as independent as one is led to believe. At the level of news and programs, there is an increasing awareness that the network is not as free to air what it wants as one may think. An often-invoked example is the censoring of a documentary which exposes the inhuman practices of using very young camel jockeys in the Gulf. Likewise, in a recent *Herald Tribune* article, the host of one of Al Jazeera's programs bemoans the fact that Al Jazeera has yielded to pressure and refrained from airing a program on the truthfulness of elections in an Arab country.[12] Similarly, there is a perception that a few prominent talk show programs are orchestrated from above and that they have a political component that sets them apart from the other programs and puts them in a league of their own, making their hosts often unaccountable to the general manager, not to speak of the head of programs. In fact, there is a belief, both inside and outside the network, that some flagship program hosts have direct access to Qatar's political leadership and that their talk shows are often aligned with the host country's foreign policy. What this means in part is that Al Jazeera is only relatively independent. In the eyes of some of the interviewed staff, decision making in the network is often influenced by outside players and sometimes succumbs to the whims of parties that go beyond the general manager of the network. In fact, there is an awareness that some occasional decisions pertaining to certain programs or maybe topics come from an undeclared or anonymous source. Although such interference does not live up to the image of independence, openness and objectivity Al Jazeera wants to project, it does not seem to weigh much on the network staff we talked to. For better or for worse, they learned to live with it.

When it comes to human resource practices, the lack of transparency and objectivity becomes even more noticeable as these can have negative effects on the network. One of the casualties of a culture which allows for favoritism is meritocracy at the level of human resources. It is not hard to tell from the numerous network staff we talked to that Al Jazeera has a lot of real talent which is not fully utilized. Although many staff members started as journalists, then moved to assistant producers and later producers, internal promotion, job advancement and career enhancement are not all that easy, and when it occurs it is not always based on objective criteria. Naturally, certain practices, particularly with respect to appearance on screen, have invited resentment. Some of our interviewees lamented that the appearance of certain correspondences is sometimes related to personal relationships or a particular agenda, while on certain occasions the decision to entrust which anchor with which program either goes beyond the general manager or lacks rationality.

This of course affects the morale of the network staff. Not surprisingly, among some of the employees we interviewed, motivation was low. The kind of favoritism that is perceived to be practiced in Al Jazeera is also affecting the degree of the staff's commitment to the network. Increasingly, people within the network are starting to think more as individuals who have to look after themselves — acquiring the "what's-in-it-for-me attitude"—than as members of a team that is helping Al Jazeera move forward, which has always been a source of vigor for the network. While the notion of "belonging" and "being part of" Al Jazeera's project is quite prominent among Al Jazeera staff, it is being encroached upon, for lack of a better term, by the feeling of disappointment and the experience of setbacks which result from the organizational lacunae that permeate Al Jazeera. "If people in Al Jazeera continue to do their best and are driven to perform well," one member of the network staff explains, "it is not because the institution believes in them but because they believe in the institution." How long such a commitment can last with the same intensity when it is not reciprocated by the organization remains a pressing question.

Likewise, retaining well-trained and motivated employees presents a special challenge for Al Jazeera. So far, Al Jazeera relies on its staff's abilities (i.e., knowledge, experience and skills) as much as it benefits from their willingness to perform (i.e., their high level of commitment and motivation). In this regard, the excitement and challenge of the work, along with the spirit the staff share with each other, is one of the prime forces of motivation within Al Jazeera. The interviews that were conducted with some of the network staff reveal a fair degree of job satisfaction. By and large, Al Jazeera manages to maintain a reasonable level of work satisfaction among its employees. Chief among the "maintenance factors"[13] Al Jazeera has developed over the years are financial compensation, job security, working conditions, status and interpersonal relationships with employees within the network. What is less obvious is the pervasiveness of strong and enduring "motivational factors"[14] such as achievement, recognition, advancement, fulfillment, growth and development. To keep the network staff motivated and enthusiastic requires not only promoting a culture of transparency but also providing the opportunity and latitude within which the network staff can exercise their creative abilities to their fullest and perform at peak levels. Such job enrichment opportunities include increased responsibility, expanded decision-making authority and staff development opportunities.

Not only is Al Jazeera's claim to independence taken with a grain of salt by some of its own staff, but the very perception of the network as a beacon of free speech is starting to succumb to a reality check. Until recently, there has been a common perception that Al Jazeera is a safe heaven (or "Daar Abou Sofiane," to use an Arabic neologism that is current within the network) not simply for the guests (whether they be opposition figures, dissenting voices or independent thinkers) to speak their minds unabashedly about various issues, but also to the very people who chose to work with Al Jazeera. The latter are at liberty to entertain any discourse and express any views, provided these do not conflict with the ethics of the profession. Inside Al Jazeera, the talk-back system, which is an electronic bulletin board system, is open to all staff members and provides a context for the members of the organization to voice their opinions on a variety of issues from the programs to the administration to the health care system for the staff. In an interview with the authors, Khanfar proudly compared it to the Speaker's Corner in London's Hyde Park, where people can talk freely about anything. The official view is that the talk-back system is popular within the network and many people use it to communicate their views and voice their opinions.

However, not everybody is enthusiastic about the talk-back system. For one staff member, the talk-back system has gradually turned into a medium for sending congratulations and offering condolences. "People are reluctant to express their views on the system if it dissents from the opinion of the majority in the network," we were told. Overall, there is a feeling that the margin of freedom inside the network has been receding lately. For example, in the aftermath of the airing of an episode of

The Opposite Direction in which one of the guests made a statement that was believed to be unfitting of Grand Ayatollah Sayyed Ali Sistani, Al Jazeera — which stated publicly that it acted in accordance with the code of ethics — took the initiative to leave out the controversial statement of its guest when rerunning the program the following day.[15] Not surprisingly, some staff members believe that currently, there are a lot of restrictions on news. Because of previous mistakes, the network has a stricter editorial policy which may be intended to ward off the kind of criticism the network has been facing since September 11 but which nonetheless is gradually changing how Al Jazeera does what it does and potentially affecting that which previously gave Al Jazeera an edge. But internal dynamics are as much a source of anxiety for some of the people we talked to as are institutional demands or changes. One telling incident pertains to an editorial board made of senior staff members from within the network and established not long after Waddah Khanfar took over the management of Al Jazeera. The board is intended to act as an advisory body to the general manager. However, there is a feeling, even among some of the board members, that it is not all that effective and that it is more of "a rubber stamping committee." When some network staff publicly questioned the viability of a newly established editorial board on the talk-back system, they were taken to task. Several members of the editorial board reacted, some with resentment while others with vindictiveness, which is not typical of Al Jazeera's culture of tolerance. For one member, the criticism leveled at the editorial board was a clear case of misconduct which should not go unpunished. For another member, the critical staff members went overboard, while for a third one, they were a nuisance. The initial inclination of the general manager when this an incident was brought to his attention, as one member of the editorial board recounts, is to take action against the staff members who were critical of the editorial board and who incidentally happen to include some of the most seasoned and credible journalists in the network. Upon a more careful consideration of what has been written on the talk-back system, and with the realization that some board members overreacted to the views some of their peers hold in the network about the viability of the editorial board, the general manager dismissed the matter. Still, the incident is indicative of a changing culture whereby either censorship or self-censorship is tolerated.

Another incident whereby the contracts of seven members of staff were not extended led some people within the network to believe that the margin of freedom inside the network is not what it used to be. Among those who were sacked was a seasoned Qatari staff member from the production department and a director who was described by his peers as "very competent." There is a feeling among some of the people we interviewed that the decision to dismiss these staff members was not based on professional reasons as much as it was politically motivated, as these staff members were considered close to the former general manager, Al Ali. For some of the interviewees, incidents such as these mark a turning point, symbolic as it may be, in the history and mindset of the network. Although there have been no formal or official restrictions on what can be said and discussed, some people feel intimidated while others find themselves discouraged from wearing their hearts on their sleeves. In either case, there is a perception that the culture of openness inside Al Jazeera — namely saying anything one wants to say without the fear of reprisal — is no longer as sacred as it used to be.

VIII.

Beyond Money

The fundamental purpose or function of reward in an organization is to provide incentives to foster individual and organizational behavior that would enable the organization to create a competitive edge and to maximize its profitability.[1] In this sense, the role of reward systems in directing employees' energies and competencies is of utter importance. Broadly speaking, one can point out two types of reward: intrinsic and extrinsic. The former is part of the job and arises from the work itself; it refers to a culture of meritocracy whereby talent is recognized, competence rewarded and excellence encouraged. Examples of intrinsic reward include autonomy, variety, significance and enrichment. The latter reward falls outside the scope of one's job and includes financial reward (such as compensation, benefits and profit sharing) and non-financial reward (such as professional recognition, promotion and friendship). A quick review of some management literature suggests that intrinsic rewards are often assumed to provide enough incentives for the employees to engage in work activities.[2] For E.E. Lawler, though, intrinsic rewards have to be complemented with appropriate extrinsic rewards insofar as an extrinsic system of rewards prevents incompetent people from setting in and ensures that competent people are where they should be.[3] In Lawler's view, an organization can have and maintain a competitive edge only if it combines intrinsic rewards with a good pay package which meets the needs and expectations of the member the organization hopes to attract and retain.[4] A discrepancy between reward and performance may lead to a decreased level of job satisfaction and prompt the employees to withhold some of their critical knowledge and skills. Conversely, employees tend to utilize their knowledge and skills to their fullest if they perceive that the reward system emphasizes specific attributes that are conducive to rewards.

The question of reward is all the more important in the case of Al

Jazeera because competition within the Arab satellite TV industry has increased the demand for journalistic talent. Some well-funded Arab channels have aggressively gone after some of Al Jazeera's reporters, anchors and editors. Among Al Jazeera's senior staff who left are two BBC veterans who served at different times as the newsroom chief editors, overseeing the entire news division during key phases in the history of the network. Likewise, a few of Al Jazeera's news readers, reporters and other staff, including its communications and media relations manager, who as Samantha M. Shapiro points out "were poached for their expertise,"[5] have relocated to Saudi-financed all-news Arab channel Al Arabiya.

Although overall such a turnover does not seem to hide any particular trend, a few female staff we interviewed cite gender not so much as a reason for parting with Al Jazeera but as a contributing factor. For example, it is hard to find top ranking female producers, we were told. These do not have as much chance making it up the organizational ladder. Currently, for instance, there are fewer female producers at Al Jazeera than there used to be. Likewise, although recently a woman was appointed for the first time to the board of directors, the editorial board of Al Jazeera has no women figures on it. In spite of the tendency of Al Jazeera to promote eloquent females like Khadijah bin Ganna and Jumanna Nammour and to feature strong female reporters like Shereen Abu Aqla *à la Shahrazade*, as Fatema Mernissi put it,[6] women's image as articulate communicators is not without a ceiling. One former Al Jazeera female anchor who moved to Al Arabiya feels that the opportunity for women to be entrusted with political programs is slim compared to her new employer. Up to the summer of 2005, when Al Jazeera embarked on some changes, launching a number of additional shorter programs some of which are hosted by women, the only regular live program which had a woman as host was *For Women Only*. *Islamic Law and Life* was also temporarily hosted by Khadijah bin Ganna following the sudden demise of its original host, Maher Abdallah. Incidentally, the guest of the program, the Moslem cleric Youssef Al Qaradawi, is more regular and more imposing than the host, being in fact one of Al Jazeera's icons.[7] In the case of *For Women Only*, the program was assigned to a number of female presenters over its few years of existence for obvious reasons — being a program about women and for women and moderated by a woman. Even so, the program was axed during the same period of change and restructuring which brought *In Depth*, a daily talk show hosted by various figures from both genders. The topics of the program range from the Israeli withdrawal from occupied territories in the Gaza strip to video games and violence to safety on board airplanes to rising oil prices. Incidentally, the show does not have the same political intensity more prominent and longer shows do, which presumably makes it suitable for "benign" female figures. Somehow, there is a perception within Al Jazeera, the same female anchor who moved to Al Arabiya added, that men are better suited for political programs than women. Such conservatism, she concluded, is true even when considering Al Jazeera's stagnation at the level of programs, as there have been very few live current affairs or talk show programs — although recently this is starting to change.

These considerations notwithstanding, the turnover at Al Jazeera is far from being a liability. As some of the interviewed staff explain, the mobility of talent in the media industry is something that is not unusual or unexpected. The same interviewee pointed out that the turnover at Al Jazeera is relatively not high, adding that none of the people who left the network is a superstar or a big name — if anything, the opposite is happening as journalists from other channels and media outlets in the region are flocking to Al Jazeera. In fact, some of Al Jazeera's prominent figures and senior presenters have received tempting offers that are extremely hard to turn down but preferred to settle for a modest raise and carry on with Al Jazeera for the sake of "loyalty," as someone in the network put it. In one case, a senior correspondent in Palestine turned down a lucrative offer to move to a prominent Arab satellite channel on his own terms and conditions. In another case, an editor in the newsroom brushed aside the idea of moving to Al Hurra, the Washington-based new American channel aimed at Arabs, because he did not believe in its mission and goals or simply did not feel he could fit in a culture that is markedly different from that of Al Jazeera. One disenchanted interviewee confided to us that after having spent over half of his life in Qatar, he was considering leaving Al Jazeera but could not conceive of himself away from it. In a few instances, people left Al Jazeera because of differences with the general manager but came back with the change of management. In yet another case, a newly hired, low-ranking young Qatari administrator in the network passed up a better offer to work with Ras Gas, Qatar's preeminent gas company, in order to join Al Jazeera in pursuit of prestige and recognition.

It should not go unnoticed that while a few of the interviewed staff are tempted to leave if they find viable alternatives, there is clearly a sense of a loyalty to the network which emanates partly from the belief in what Al Jazeera is all about. The people who work at Al Jazeera tend to see themselves as more than just winning their bread. According to a senior producer at the network, people who work at Al Jazeera "don't just like their job — they love it." Al Jazeera staff, he added, "are willing to give a lot ... and when they know that their work is appreciated by their superiors and colleagues, they are motivated to give even more." For some of the people who work at Al Jazeera, the network has an existential meaning. The head of programs compares his love for Al Jazeera to his love for his daughter. "It is the most important thing for me in the universe," he told us wholeheartedly. This same staffer proudly recounted how he willingly puts in long hours in the newsroom, working at times from 10:00 am straight through till midnight, with only six days off the whole year. Although some people left Al Jazeera in search of other opportunities and a better financial reward, overall there is an attachment to and a pride in the channel. Merely being part of Al Jazeera is in and of itself a big source of motivation. The ensuing sense of satisfaction is particularly important for, as Lucy Küng-Shankleman reminds us, extrinsic motivators such as greater creative exposure, large budget and high pay cannot compensate for the lack of intrinsic motivators.[8] Still, some of the former Al Jazeera staff members we interviewed said that they have put Al Jazeera behind them and moved ahead with their careers, while others confided to us that they were contacted by Al Jazeera and were solicited to come back to Doha but declined the offer because it was not on their terms. A few staff who have left the network eventually came back to it.

This sense of loyalty, however, should not be overstated. While it was interesting to find out that none of the staff members who left Al Jazeera was resentful toward his or her former employer, it was more significant and more instructive to discover that there was no obvious trend for why people leave Al Jazeera. While dodging the question as to why he left Al Jazeera, one former staff member pointed out, and perceptively so, that the issue of turnover cannot be examined independently from larger considerations which relate to the culture of the media industry in the region. In an institution like the BBC where he used to work, there is always the possibility of moving ahead, of building a career, of aspiring to a higher position, of carrying on, and of belonging for more than just the period of time one spends working with the organization. The people-oriented agenda of the BBC — being public service oriented, its broadcasting is conceived in terms of public good and public betterment[9] — seeps into the very culture of the organization. Conversely, in the Arab world — where meritocracy, job stability, career ambition and long-term objectives are not always obvious — the turnover in the media sector is fairly high. The reigning mentality favors quick profit, fast achievement, short-term gains and temporary employment; in short, what tends to prevail is a "mercenary culture." Not only is the overall culture in the region receptive to such trends, but the fast-changing Arab mediascape favors and even promotes it. As such, job loyalty cannot be discussed independently of such factors as the succession of events in the Middle East, the proliferation of crises in the region, the taxing demands of 24-hour news broadcasting, the mushrooming of channels, the increase in competition and the shortage of local talent.

When it comes to compensation and in absolute terms, there is an overall perception in the network that Al Jazeera is one of the best-paying media companies in the region and that the benefits package it offers is competitive. One senior producer told us that he is happy about his compensation package and pretty content with the yearly increments he received. He noted that as inflation started to creep in and the prices of rent in Doha started to go up, Al Jazeera adjusted the benefits of its employees accordingly. In the future, though, he admitted, the rising cost of living in a country that is rapidly growing may be an issue.[10] Surely enough, when we visited the network early in 2005, the hot issue on the network's talk-back system was health care. With the added pressure on the government health system of a growing country, the debate revolved around the need to consider private health care providers.

In comparative terms, though, there is a felt discrepancy in the reward system; in fact, there is a perception that the reward system itself tends to be non-transparent to a certain extent. The many interviews we conducted suggest that the sense of equity in reward (and opportunity) is not shared by everyone. Naturally, the employees' lack of familiarity with the reward system may be a source of dissatisfaction.[11] There is a perceived sense of favoritism, particularly when it comes to the stars of the network and some of the figures who are prominent on screen. Although there is a scale for salaries and benefits, the discrepancies are sometimes huge and unjustified. The criteria the network uses for reward contribute further to the perceived sense of inequity. In fact, there is a perception that the reward system Al Jazeera uses is not always competence-based.[12] As one resentful editor lamented, personal qualifications and degrees are not adequately factored in the reward system, although used as criteria in the hiring process. The poles of power inside the network further contribute to the problem. There are notable practices which suggest that what is permissible for some people is not permissible for others. Likewise, some staff resent what they consider as preferential treatment. For example, it was noted that a program may have an assistant or researcher assigned to it where there is no critical need for such resources, while programs and individuals who may greatly benefit from such institutional support do not have access to it. Some other practices in the network, we were told, are based on personal preferences and personal relationships. As such, some of the decisions and practices in Al Jazeera lack the element of rationality. Naturally, such inequities, which instill a culture of favoritism in the organization, are disturbing for many of the staff. One female anchor who left Al Jazeera pointed out that "when considerations of beauty take preeminence over experience, intellect and distinction in determining compensation, the discrepancy in salary becomes more than a pecuniary matter; it strikes at the heart of one's own belief in what one is and what one thinks." Such practices are not without consequences. As management literature tells us, the negative emotional reaction which ensues from compensation systems that are deemed unfair or inequitable can have a damaging effect on inter-unit relationships and thwart participation in the work process in ways which could lead to lower utilization of knowledge and skills.[13]

Finally, the tendency to promote either individual or group performance is worth commenting upon. In an environment which requires close collaboration and team effort, rewarding users solely on individual bases can prove to be disruptive to the unit solidarity as well as the collective commitment to work.[14] Reward systems that emphasize group performance more than individual performance are likely to result in a higher utilization of their knowledge and skills. This is particularly true when the corporate culture or the nature of the work demands close cooperation in the workforce.[15] In the case of Al Jazeera, there is a culture of group performance in the news division more than the program division. In the former case, because of the nature of news production and news broadcasting, the team spirit is particularly important. The editor in chief of the news plays a big role in promoting the collaboration and team-work — and in fact tries to make every contribution matter. He routinely sends short notes of appreciation and emails of encouragement in a crafted language which makes them genuine. Likewise, when mistakes occur, he takes it upon himself to correct those mistakes quietly and discreetly with the concerned party. His approach is to make the staff he works with feel that he can follow everyone in the network — which, as he admits, is practically impossible. The outcome is a sense of trust that reigns and a true appreciation of what he conceives as "foot soldiers" who work hard behind the scenes.

IX.

The Knowledge Imperative

A business process is a coordinated and sequenced set of activities and associated resources that produce something of value to a customer. Organizations that structure their operations around business processes tend to better satisfy their customers. A process-based structure is a formalized process whereby resources are automatically reverted under the control of those responsible for delivering value to customers. Stated differently, a business process is a collection of activities that take one or more kinds of input to create an output of value to the customer.[1] As such, it has to provide value to a recipient, whether it be a person or an organization. In fact, the whole organization acts as a process focused on satisfying the customer's or client's requests whether it be an internal or external client. The former refers to employees inside the organization who add more value to the product or service as it makes its way to the final customer; the latter are the people or entities outside the organization purchasing products and services from the organization. A business process tends to be cross-functional in the sense that it cuts across many different departments and units. For example, a sales process entails contacting the customer, filling the order, shipping, invoicing and collecting payment. Furthermore, as business processes tend to cut horizontally across organizational functions (sales, research and development, engineering and manufacturing), power is transferred from these functions to processes.[2] For Schotles and Hacquerbord, the horizontal configuration shapes employee priorities on the job as follows: "If you ask someone in your work: 'who is important for you to please?' and he or she answers 'my boss,' that person experiences the organization as a chain of command. If the answer is 'the person in the next process, my internal customer,' then that person has a systems perspective."[3]

The attention to business process acquires an added significance when studying media organizations because of the nature and challenges of broadcasting. In a process-based structure, the media organization delivers value (whether it be programs or news) through a chain of value-added processes (such as logistics to secure the participation of guests or technical and IT support for a particular program) feeding into one another and ending with the ultimate customer, the viewer. Generally speaking, Al Jazeera can be said to have process-based structures. If a journalist is to work on a program, he or she does not need permission to have access to resources or to make decisions. For example, a program like *The Opposite Direction* operates in an independent and autonomous manner. The host of the program, Faisal Al Kasim, with the help of his research assistant, is responsible for virtually all aspects of the program. Al Kasim is in a position to make decisions and in fact has the last say in whatever matter pertains to his program, whether it be the topic of the episode, the content of the program, the selection of the guest or the accommodation of that guest.

The value of the process-based structure which characterizes Al Jazeera's operations becomes more evident when set against the backdrop of traditional TV broadcasters in the Arab world, who generally operate under the constraints of a long-standing history of heavy bureaucracy. Government-controlled media institutions in particular are generally subject to a top-down hierarchical management. In such a setting, virtually all decisions are dictated and managed to the smallest detail. Everything from selecting assignments, to acquiring basic human and technical resources for a program, to the scheduling and format of delivery are largely dictated by those in positions of power. Stories of journalists who were axed because they failed to toe the hierarchical line are abundant. An anecdote can further illustrate the extent of what may be loosely described as a culture of submission. Recently, one of the authors was solicited for an interview with a Dubai-based journalist who was investigating the role of the SMS phenomenon in fueling the proliferation of satellite channels in the region. At the end of the encounter, the interviewee was naturally inquisitive about the fate of the interview. To the question of when the ensuing report is expected to be published, the journalist answered without hesitation and with no reservation whatsoever that he had no idea because it was up to the editor in chief of the magazine to decide when, how and if at all the report would go to press. Seen from a management perspective, Al Jazeera stands in marked distinction from the heavy-handed bureaucracy which characterizes state media. To be accepted and implemented, the decisions, actions or mandates in government institutions are to come from the top, whether it be a head of a department or a director. In fact, initiatives that do not follow this structure or fall outside the conventions of the hierarchical system are looked down upon. Such a culture is alien to Al Jazeera, where reporters independently prepare reports and air them on prime-time news without being reviewed by a higher authority. In one instance, the reporter in a war zone took the initiative to air a tape which had been delivered to him while on air without seeking the approval of the powers that be. One of Al Jazeera's network staff we interviewed who was not otherwise enthusiastic about Al Jazeera's organizational model still credited it with great flexibility, autonomy on the job, and control over resources that are critical to the delivery of quality programs including the selection of guests, provisions for production, editing resources and editorial support.

This said, Al Jazeera does not fully rise to the level of a process-centered organization where the need to deliver high levels of customer service dictates ready access to resources. As it is, the existing process-based structure tends to be available for some and not for others and is rather regulated through the balance of power within the organization. While some network staff have full access to resources whenever requested because of their long history with the network, their established "meritocracy" and their achieved stardom, others — and especially those who have not broken through the ranks — are subject to several resource restrictions irrespective of their outstanding talent and proven abilities, thus affecting their performance and reducing the quality of their output. The issue of the disparities in rewards aside, the various interviews conducted with the network staff in the course of this research suggest that a major source of frustration is the unequal access to resources. In a genuine process-based structure, access to resources is generally mandated by market requirements (in this case, delivering services/programs to the customers/viewers) and not by the internal balance of power, which, interestingly enough, could be driven by market considerations in the first place. In other words, over time, some staff in the organization accumulate power by virtue of their critical position for market access and quality service delivery. The power these people develop gives them access to resources partly because the network's success depends on their own success. Needless to say, such a situation leads to a vicious circle.

Another aspect of the process-based structure is the enterprise-wide integration of organizational processes, which means that, if need be or required, the collaboration of several departments or units could be achieved seamlessly and in a transparent way to the recipient of the final service or output. So far, Al Jazeera is far from such a model. In fact, its different processes (i.e., programs and units) are more like stovepipes that do not intersect rather than flexible processes which, in need, would come together to augment and enhance the value that is being delivered. If anything, Al Jazeera is closer to a compound of fiefdoms run independently than to a collaboration-infused enterprise. This could partly explain the heavy redundancy in Al Jazeera's program offerings. For example, on a particular day, viewers are exposed extensively to the same issue pertaining to the situation in Iraq during prime-time news only to find themselves later in the evening watching an hour or an hour-and-a-half-long talk show program on the very same issue. If anything, the redundancy in and overlapping between Al Jazeera's programming shows poor planning. Without adequate planning, the network is bound to fall into the trap of repetitiveness which kills any drive for innovation — airing the same programs and adopting the same formats.

Clearly, the question as to whether Al Jazeera draws some of its strength and success from the process-based structure underlying its various value-adding processes or whether it is another hierarchical edifice with centralized control over resources that only those who are privileged have ample access to is not an easy question to answer. It is probably safe to characterize Al Jazeera as being a structure of loosely coupled processes operating in a fairly independent manner. It is obvious that some processes benefit from access to resources more than others, depending on the stature of the process owner, generally the program anchor, except maybe for the news division where the "newsroom owner" does not appear on the screen. This is also generally true about genuine customer-driven, hence process-based, organizations. However, the similarity starts to fall apart when one realizes the near absence of an integrative process which systematically brings together different combinations of processes to deliver greater value through a synergy effect between the various processes. Ultimately, the lack of an integrative process is likely to negatively affect the network's capacity to match increasingly sophisticated market and customer requirements and, in fact, risks opening the door for competitors — which are not lacking in the region — with better integrated processes to offer distinctly better products. It also insulates individual processes from contributing to the overall welfare of the network. In the long run, diverging process objectives may fuel conflict, foster unhealthy internal competition and undermine the achievements of the organization. Finally, unless Al Jazeera attends to the problems that plague the process-based structure underlying its various value-adding processes, it will remain at the mercy of the creativity and innovation of its star anchors and program hosts.

Tightly connected with process-based structures are integrated systems or integrated and seamless IT infrastructure which makes information (and knowledge) available and accessible throughout the organization. Information systems integration tends to tear down barriers between and among departments and organizational boundaries, and in doing so reduces duplication of effort. Data sharing and joint execution of business processes across functional areas allow individuals in one area to quickly and easily provide input into another area.[4] Workflow software is one of the potent technologies that have been specifically developed to support processes. Seen from this vantage point, e-commerce, for instance, is not simply a customer interface or merely a web presence which allows for and facilitates the interaction between customers, but a total restructuring of organizations into a set of interconnected processes which render real-time services to customers in a way which either minimizes or eliminates all human intervention. For example, as a virtual corporation, Amazon.com consists of a set of fully automated and integrated processes that are pre-programmed to deliver real-time services to online customers. Developing an IT infrastructure to support a process-based organization provides the basic layer for a comprehensive knowledge management infrastructure. However, the mere existence of such an information system infrastructure does not guarantee the existence of a knowledge-orientated organization; as such, it is a more of a pre-requisite than a determinant.

Until not long ago, knowledge — being the intellectual capital of an organization — was not explicitly recognized as a corporate asset. Recently, however, there has been a heightened interest in the production and management of knowledge within organizations. How an organization transforms knowledge embedded in routines and practices into valuable products and services has become a question that cannot be ignored. In fact, many companies are becoming increasingly keen on gaining a better understanding of what they know and how to use such an asset effectively. As Thomas Davenport and Laurence Prusak point out, how to manage and make effective use of knowledge and, further, how to gain a better understanding of what an organization knows are issues that can be hardly ignored: "what an organization and its employees *know* is at the heart of how the organization functions.... Knowledge itself is worthy of attention because it tells firms how to do things and how they might do them better."[5] Companies can no longer afford to disregard the importance of knowledge if they want to decisively improve performance.

Theoretically speaking, knowledge management is a concept that refers to the creation of a knowledge infrastructure whereby the organization can benefit from an institutional memory by facilitating, managing and sharing the knowledge the organization has accrued over time. Naturally, such knowledge, which is usually derived from problem solving,[6] is valuable because it can be transferred among employees (or possibly shared with business partners and even customers) and reused whenever the organization faces similar problems or comparable situations. As it is, a company can benefit tremendously from insights into its best practices, new ideas, creative synergies and breakthrough processes which information cannot yield.[7] For Gabriel Szulanski, the organization's ability to extract value from superior knowledge gives it a distinctive competitive edge: "The performance of a firm reflects its ability to re-use superior knowledge before competitors are able to reproduce it effectively. A firm is supposedly at an advantage relative to imitators because it has better access to templates or working examples of its own practices."[8] Maximizing the value of employees as intellectual assets requires a culture that values intellectual participation, facilitates individual and organizational learning, and exhibits a willingness to share knowledge with others — in short, one which promotes a knowledge management culture.

Seen from an IT infrastructure point of view, Al Jazeera benefits from an integrated system which gives its staff access to information. Thanks to a central system of information, employees work in an information-rich and information-open environment. However, judged against the professional standards in the media industry, Al Jazeera is far from being at the forefront of technological sophistication, particularly when it comes to actual physical systems in place. Ironically, it is significantly below what one would expect from such a leading network.

If anything, Al Jazeera is behind technology-wise; other than some basic technology that is necessary for modern TV broadcasting, Al Jazeera is rather archaic in its IT standards. A senior producer who has been with the network since its early years pointed out that the technology of Al Jazeera goes back to 1996–97, but he finds consolation in that the new building they were in the process of moving to has high-class media technology. When we inquired about any state of the art technology, especially IT, that helps integrate the different functions and processes in the organization, some network staff we interviewed were quick to acknowledge that they were no match for world standards or even for such regional competitors as Al Arabiya who came to the scene later with more advanced and more updated technology.[9] Surely enough, Al Jazeera's original newsroom is fairly modest, with a dozen pods or so, each with a computer and television set. On one of the walls stand 16 television monitors showing competing channels. On another wall, clocks show the hour in major world cities and not far from them an electronic chart displays satellite booking times. In contrast, Al Arabiya's newsroom is different and better equipped with sophisticated world maps software[10] and nifty editing and producing technology. The implication of that is notable not only in Al Arabiya's 3D look, which makes the screen more animated and less stiff, but also in its outcome. A case in point is the coverage of the 2004 U.S. presidential elections where Al Arabiya had better access to technology. Being part of a conglomerate which includes MBC 1, MBC 2, MBC 3 and MBC 4 and which has a standing contract with ABC News, Al Arabiya had access to information well ahead of its competitors. Associated Press wire had a deal with the U.S. networks to feed information to a system which provided estimates of the votes 3 hours prior to the official tally. Because of its arrangement with ABC News, Al Arabiya was able to acquire such information and to feed it to its viewers in ways which gave its coverage of the U.S. presidential elections a notable edge.

Granted that Al Arabiya has a "technological" edge over Al Jazeera, technology is not necessarily a source of weakness for the latter. One of the staff members who worked with Al Jazeera before moving to Al Arabiya headquarters in Dubai, where we interviewed him, does not see technology as a decisive factor in acquiring an edge in the regional media market. A comparative perspective can elucidate the point. For example, Al Arabiya is equipped with a LAN share system (Local Area Network) by AVID Technologies, whereby a number of computer edit worksta-tions are able to access, edit and share digital media (visual and audio media elements) that exist on a central multi-terabyte hard drive for the purpose of broadcast media production. Al Arabiya's staff are connected to a central server with access to a diverse range of still pictures and video sequences — with some of the visual material produced originally by Al Arabiya and other media elements acquired through access to external visual database "libraries" like APTN and Reuters — enabling staff edi-tors and producers to download visual materials directly onto their com-puters. At least prior to moving to the new building in summer 2005, such a technology was not readily available to Al Jazeera staff. Random and continual access to a wide range of video footage and other visual elements makes it possible to produce and disseminate news reports much faster, in an industry where time is of the essence. The pictures are down-loaded to and assembled on a PC or Macintosh workstation, then sent to the editing department for fine cutting of the overall sequence. Once cleared by quality control, the produced work is disseminated. Such a process ensures work flow while providing quality assurance.

Set in a pre–LAN share intranet (which is a fairly recent technology) era, Al Jazeera works in a less technologically sophisticated environment. In contrast to Al Arabiya's, Al Jazeera's editors and producers have to work directly with videotapes or other resource materials that are known and available in the in-house library (such as still images, audio elements and video visual elements). This *modus operandi* relies upon tape-based sources and is performed with the use of individual editing stations or non-linear workstations (i.e., one would digitize the material and work from a PC instead of working from a central database). Naturally, this means that one has slow and cumbersome access to a more limited data-base whereby one picks available images to use in making a point or sup-porting one. Rather than pull from originally produced footage from the field, the reporters would rely to a large extent on a stock footage.

However, the technological edge that Al Arabiya enjoys is neither significant nor substantial enough to make a real or long-lasting differ-ence. Time-wise, a news editor who has such a technology at his or her disposal would cut down on the time it takes to produce a report only slightly; but even so, one interviewee pointed out, the physical setup of Al Arabiya is such that the time that is recuperated is eventually con-sumed in the communication between the various departments since the editing suite is located on the first floor of the MBC building while the newsroom of Al Arabiya is located on the fourth floor. Not so in Al Jazeera; being more compact and less stretched out than MBC's headquarters with its impersonal sterile aura, the physical setup of Al Jazeera makes all departments within reach and their team accessible in such a way as to ensure both efficacy and efficiency. Although the task at hand may involve either running down the hall to locate a tape and find a particular shot or searching through a digitized version of the material, the work flow is neither cumbersome nor slow. The fact that Al Jazeera is relatively small and relationships are personal facilitates the task of the staff and ensures the workflow. Seen from this perspective, the advantage IT gives Al Arabiya is not a long-lasting one, nor for that matter is it a strategic one, particularly in an age where technology is fast changing. If Al Arabiya is more invested in technology it is, in part, because it was launched years after Al Jazeera made its debut. Surely enough, Al Jazeera's new locale, which is adjacent to the old building, is better equipped and more up-to-date. In the meantime, the old newsroom, which is being occupied by Al Jazeera International, has been equipped with a Vizrt HD system which will provide it with the latest technology for breaking news graphics, maps and template graphics.[11]

What is less certain, however, is the extent to which such technology can make a difference. So far, the most insistent problem has not been access to technology, but the use and appropriation of such technology. Even the most *avant garde* TV broadcasters in the Arab world are still not sufficiently picture oriented. In the words of Al Jazeera anchor Mohamed Krichene, "the visual culture is still limited and in fact overshadowed by the narrative tradition."[12] At the level of production, reports are often conceived in their inception as written text infused with voice-over and then animated with pictures to support the voice-over narration track. In other words, the picture is more often than not placed as an afterthought with a marginal relationship to the voice-over narration. Since this is the case, having access to a limited internal visual resource library puts one only at a slight disadvantage in comparison to subscribing to the visual resource library of an international press agency. In the latter case, the cost of subscriptions to a visual library is quite high, and when the pictures are used primarily to support voice-over they tend to be less than cost effective.

Even when the issue of value for money is overlooked, the problem remains one of perspective. In an interview with Chris Forrester, Mohammed Jassim Al Ali noted: "Our news sources are varied. The most important among them is our vast net of ... correspondents who operate in countries around the world. In addition, there are the international news agencies, such as Reuters, APTN, AFP, the Qatari News Agency and the Middle East News Agency."[13] When asked "If you are frequently sharing their news material, what makes you different from other Arab media?," Al Ali pointed out that "Al Jazeera puts a lot of weight on the statement and announcements of the authorities connected to the news — be they journalists, government officials or analysts. In most cases, the news department will extend airtime to better cover a news item via phone calls or DTLs [live commentary by satellite] and to reflect the various points of view about the topic in question."[14] Likewise, in a published interview, the general manager of Al Arabiya, Abdul Rahman Al Rashed, pointed out that the source of the news item is not an issue: "It does not matter who is the source for a tape or for a report — whether it is APTN, freelancers, our own stringers, or our full time correspondents."[15] One would argue, however, that engaging in on-location documentary production is significantly different from integrating material that is shot by a third party. In the latter case, the opinion in the voice of the storyteller is not necessarily the subject on camera, so that if the subject at hand is the tsunami, for instance, one is bound to feel a discrepancy between the victim in the report and what or who is on camera. There is a rift between the cameraman and the storyteller. The images are far less powerful than the voice-over, either because the producer bought the image rather than produced it or because he or she is using stock footage. Being superficial and secondary, the visuals do not push the story forward. More than anything else, the stories that are produced are audio-driven insofar as the audio element is the backbone of the program. A look at some of Al Jazeera's programs reveals that the dominant strain is talk shows which feature talking heads sitting in a studio. There is an awareness even within the network that the overwhelming majority of Al Jazeera's programs is talk rather than picture. As such, Al Jazeera is still driven by words more than by pictures, by narrative more than visuals. In fact, many of Al Jazeera's journalists admit that they do not think visually. Overall, Al Jazeera's programs tend to be more studio production than field reporting. In the case of live field reporting, the reporter tends to provide a general or obvious interpretation of an event that is already described by the anchor in the studio. In this respect, Al Jazeera comes off as particularly limited by producing journalistic programs that are studio-based and studio-driven, rarely enhanced by visual or other original materials acquired on location. Increasingly, Al Jazeera's staff are expected to improve their skills in this area. Thus, anchors used to presenting the news from the studio find themselves called upon to take part in training sessions on field reporting. Part of the process of capitalizing on the visual element and stimulating visual thinking, as Ahmed Sheikh points out, is to insist on reporters producing a standard script with visuals and narrative side by side.[16]

By and large, the visual element is not one of Al Jazeera's strengths. At the level of form, Al Jazeera's screen is sad and gloomy. In the words of one anchor, its news bulletins often sound more like military briefings than news broadcasts. Sometimes, the coverage of the events in Palestine or in Iraq amounts to death toll reports, with close-ups on images of destruction, death, bodies and violent confrontation. While the news itself cannot be different from what it is, the conception and presentation of the news can be dramatically improved. In fact, the décor, background and graphics seem to be in need of change. Compared to Al Arabiya, for instance, Al Jazeera comes off as too stiff. The problem, as a former Al Jazeera staff who moved to Al Arabiya points out, is that Al Jazeera is limited by its conception of itself. Because it broadcasts news, Al Jazeera focuses on content more than on looks. This poses noteworthy difficulties for producers who want to be creative or who would like to have visual or sound enhancement. For Al Jazeera, our interviewee noted, music has to be serious. As such, Al Jazeera is limited by the rigidity of the news. Any diversion would be discouraged as being "not Al Jazeera style." With Al Arabiya, this same producer is afforded the opportunity to be more creative and to work more creatively with the graphics department. If this is possible with Al Arabiya, it is because the latter inherited the culture of MBC — a channel which has accumulated considerable experience since the days it was based in London. The entertainment background of MBC and the creativity of its staff enabled it to escape the rigidity of news Al Jazeera finds itself in — although, as a producer who worked at Al Jazeera for a few years before ending up in Al Arabiya points out, being an all-news channel, Al Arabiya thrived within the existing structure of an entertainment channel like MBC with the end result being "a strange mix."

Interestingly enough, aspects of Al Arabiya's style, particularly when it comes to the visuals, are gradually making their way to Al Jazeera. One staff member we talked to reads in Al Jazeera's hiring of a senior producer from Al Arabiya — particularly during a period when it was positioning itself for change — and promoting him to the position of deputy chief editor a desire to emulate some of Al Arabiya's more visually conscious style. In mid–2005, Al Jazeera revamped its image by relaunching its news format and graphics — which coincided with its moving to a new and more technologically sophisticated newsroom in an adjacent building — aiming at ensuring speed, diversity and closeness with the viewers. The general manager of the channel explains the nature and scope of the changes: "There will be a new format, characterized by dynamism and effectiveness that will try to connect the viewer to the newsreader, and the newsroom to the field. It will try to present a beautiful, interactive and lively model. It will try to present better substance, a distinctive substance, and high credibility in a splendid, beautiful way."[17] Al Jazeera's slogan for the new phase, which aims at making the substance and especially the form in tune with the spirit of the age, is "a more beautiful image and better substance." Still, although the changes Al Jazeera has introduced to its look and program format suggest that it is aware of the need to capitalize on the visual element, which is a defining element in TV broadcasting, it has along way to go.

This of course affects the quality of Al Jazeera's programs. Al Jazeera is particularly weak in quality programs which have a "value added" such as documentaries, as these are more demanding and more expensive to produce. So far, home-produced documentaries are scarce on Al Jazeera's screen — which raises questions about the full-fledged documentary channel the network is starting. Even before the launch of the channel, Al Jazeera signed an agreement with BBC Worldwide for a package of 1000 hours of factual programming the aim of which, as the manager of the news documentary channel put it, is "to repeat the success of our main news channel with a strong selection of BBC titles on Al Jazeera documentary."[18] Content-wise, a documentary channel which does not emanate out of a commitment to and a tradition for producing its own quality documentaries may not have an edge when competition picks up. Eventually, as Hugh Miles points out, "all Arab satellite channels, including Al Jazeera, need to make more and import less of their programs."[19]

Seen from a different angle, Al Jazeera's modest IT infrastructure has direct implications on knowledge management, which relies on the existence of an underlying integrated IT infrastructure to concretely take hold in the organization. This not being the case, knowledge management is severely reduced although not fully nonexistent. Indeed, because of its peculiar history and its increasingly pointed sense of mission, Al Jazeera has developed a strong sense of identity or culture in spite of its relatively short history. The pervasiveness of such an organizational culture translates among other things into a shared frame of reference. How significant this common frame of reference is in generating, sharing and managing knowledge that has been accrued for organizational success is yet to be determined. A string of insistent questions come to mind here, the answer to which may provide insights into the degree of Al Jazeera's success in transferring and using knowledge internally: Does Al Jazeera have an institutional memory which capitalizes on the organization's know-how that is shared by everybody to know what problems occurred in the past and how to solve them? How does Al Jazeera capture knowledge and make it available to its employees? Does Al Jazeera have a knowledge infrastructure? To what extent does Al Jazeera help facilitate, manage and share the knowledge it has accrued over time? How can the new staff inherit the know-how Al Jazeera has accumulated? What does Al Jazeera do to help new recruits who join the network be on a par with their colleagues in the organization knowledge-wise? And finally, does Al Jazeera have a system in place that enables it to manage value-added information and knowledge, which are all the more crucial for an organization that feeds off and thrives on news and information?

When we asked a senior producer about his personal experience, he admitted that Al Jazeera has not made much use of the knowledge he has accumulated, but justified that on the grounds that Al Jazeera had other priorities and the fact that it is not stable yet. The network started off with a core group of well-trained and in some cases accomplished journalists. For the following two or three years, it did not hire new prominent faces, except perhaps for a handful of news readers. Although talent often moved horizontally as seasoned employees of Al Jazeera found themselves called upon to train their colleagues, overall Al Jazeera did not develop the culture of transferring knowledge. The recognition of knowledge and the use of it in the network are minimal, to say the least. But this is hardly surprising as documenting ideas is not all that common in an oral culture such as the one Al Jazeera operates in. So far, Al Jazeera has not quite developed an indigenous professional culture which capitalizes on the knowledge acquired from its years of news broadcasting, its top shows and its well-trained staff. Rather than generating ideas in an open "knowledge market," the network feeds off personal initiatives. Given that Al Jazeera tends to be more individual than group driven, particularly when it comes to programs, knowledge sharing is not all that common a practice nor is it a priority. People tend to build personal relationships inside the network with the primary aim of maintaining their own resource base. Accumulated knowledge, complemented with personal and influential relations, has been mostly geared toward reinforcing the fiefdoms created early on in the history of the network and insulating the "stovepipes" from one another. One gets a sense that some of the staff, particularly stars, have their own aspirations, which eventually may be at odds with the best interest of the network.

An examination of Al Jazeera's practices in its newly created Media Training and Development Center confirms these findings. There is a perception that the center, which is reportedly set up on a commercial basis but is not a profit-making one, is driven by business considerations more than knowledge imperatives. As Gordon Robinson points out, "unlike other programs which aim to improve the skills of people already working in the profession, the Al Jazeera center's courses are available to anyone who cares to fill out a form and pay the required fees."[20] Many of the trainers in the center are foreigners. In fact, the center has a mutual agreement with the Thompson Foundation for providing skilled trainers and consultants for its various courses. The network justifies its resorting to British media experts and international training organizations on the grounds that it does not want to give the impression that it is providing inculcation; as such, it prefers to draw on the BBC's expertise and infuse it with the know-how of its seasoned journalists. One of the interviewees reported that upon attending one of the training sessions in the center, he was startled at the modesty of the training provided. He and many other Al Jazeera employees who attended the training were skilled well beyond the training provided. What made matters worse and even caused resentment is that Al Jazeera brought a foreign trainer without making any effort to identify in-house competencies. Aside from possible political motivations not to use internal resources for training, these practices illustrate one thing — the absence of a systematic knowledge-transfer mechanism whereby potential suppliers and demanders of knowledge could be identified. Although on a few occasions Al Jazeera's Media

Training and Development Center did resort to Al Jazeera personnel for training journalists and media practitioners from other Arab countries, the pool of the network staff who offer such training is small and so far limited to star anchors. As such, most of the training is offered by staff from outside Al Jazeera. If anything, the intensive use of outside trainers, irrespective of the availability of the related knowledge within the network itself, is yet another indicator of Al Jazeera's lack of emphasis on knowledge management. In the final analysis, Al Jazeera has not fully capitalized on the transfer of knowledge it accumulated during its years of existence; nor has it drawn from the story of its success those elements and variables it could foster, develop and sell to aspiring media outlets in the region. Overall, knowledge management still remains basic and underdeveloped within the network.

Nevertheless, a close look at another initiative within Al Jazeera's network, namely Aljazeera.net, the online news portal that is immensely successful with internet users, suggests that knowledge is codified and shared both within and outside of the organization. It remains to be said, though, that although the quality of information produced by Aljazeera.net is acknowledged by the rest of the network staff, it seems to operate in isolation from the satellite TV channel. The impression we got is that of an unspoken competition between Aljazeera.net and Al Jazeera rather than one being a knowledge repository for the other. It is true that Al Jazeera and Aljazeera.net draw from each other. Indeed, journalists from the broadcasting station have the information generated by Aljazeera.net at their disposal and the information and knowledge content generated in the TV station are readily available on the web portal. However, the rapprochement stops there. There is no consistent attempt to make of Aljazeera.net the institutional memory of Al Jazeera itself—although this initiative offers a good promise for the future to become the knowledge vehicle and repository for the network. To the contrary, the two are separated physically, as each is hosted in a separate part of town, and culturally, as each has developed its own subculture. The current inhibitors for such development seem to be a clash of cultures that exist between the two units. During our visit to Aljazeera.net and our interaction with the staff there, we felt a resentment towards the TV station for a variety of reasons which were evident although not made explicit. The first is the perceived lower status of Aljazeera.net in comparison with the TV station. Aljazeera.net people argued that the quality of their services in many cases surpassed that of Al Jazeera satellite channel and that their editorial policy was more sound and professional. For instance, they questioned the redundancy in the TV program offerings and the relevance of some programs and their presenters. They also expressed a deep conviction that with the advancement in telecommunication, the future of Al Jazeera would be Aljazeera.net, which represents the first strides of Al Jazeera in this new broadcasting paradigm. Interestingly enough, when we asked staff members in the TV station about Aljazeera.net, they seemed to be overall positive though not enthusiastic. Many of them even shrug it off as non-essential for Al Jazeera's media enterprise. As such, their use of knowledge produced by Aljazeera.net seems to be mostly *ad hoc* and not part of a knowledge management strategy. For one TV anchor, Aljazeera.net is simply convenient and tangentially so. Asked about the relevance of Aljazeera.net, he ventured: "When you use stuff from Aljazeera.net, you don't have to worry about copyright issues." How much this constitutes a knowledge transfer is undoubtedly a tricky issue.

So far, Al Jazeera's ability to transfer knowledge internally seems to be more of a weakness than a strength of its internal management processes which can be consequential if not effectively addressed and overcome. Currently, it is hard to profile Al Jazeera's knowledge management efforts because these are either unmanaged or under-managed. The network's knowledge base is certainly not at the level of sophistication one expects from such an organization; Al Jazeera does not have a formal knowledge management structure but only the rudiments of such a structure. It is true that Al Jazeera values the experience, know-how and knowledge of its employees, and it is true that knowledge is often transferred through such informal channels as work environment socialization (inside and outside work); however, such individual initiatives to attend to the issue of knowledge management are hardly sufficient or adequate. Given the absence of an integrated IT infrastructure (or integrated information systems) and the loose coupling of a process-based structure, Al Jazeera is not well placed to develop a formal knowledge management strategy. Channeling and making better use of such knowledge requires more than a casual approach to organizational knowledge — in fact, knowledge management has to be consciously pursued and made part of the organization's strategy. If Al Jazeera is to maintain its position of leadership, sustain its competitive edge and expand in the future, it has to address this lacuna institutionally and systematically.

But this may not be easy to achieve, not because Al Jazeera's culture is not knowledge intensive, but because the culture within which Al Jazeera itself operates is not conducive to the identification and appropriation of acquired knowledge. When asked about the extent to which the network makes use of the knowledge that its more seasoned staff have accumulated throughout the years they spent with Al Jazeera, one of the senior network staff shrugged as a sign of helplessness and then went on to explain how he finds it a bit ironic for someone who has spent three decades in the country to be on a par with an unskilled worker brought from the Indian sub-continent only a few months back. "The system is such," he added, "that we simply do not have rights. Come to think of it, the system of sponsorship which is operative in this country as in the rest of the Gulf countries is a system of serfdom." In the Gulf region, the system is such that every person needs a sponsor to acquire a residence visa. Locals usually sponsor individuals or organizations who in turn act as the sponsors of workers, professionals or the members of their own family. Inherent in this system is a certain hierarchy which is often operative at the expense of meritocracy. An incident pertaining to a visa application in a neighboring Gulf country, the UAE, can help elucidate this point further although it is outside the context of media proper. Upon retrieving the application for a southeast Asian housemaid from the typing services offered by the Department of Naturalization and Residence in the Ministry of Interior, one of the authors realized that the part which is allocated for the level of education was filled out incorrectly. When pointing out to the clerk that she had typed in the wrong information, that she had done so without bothering to check the accuracy of the information, and that the maid in question was listed as having an elementary school diploma when in fact she had a two-year university degree, such a remark was met with a rebuke: "What do you expect us to write down for a maid? After all, it is only a formality!" It never occurred to the clerk at the desk that the application she was processing was indeed that of a maid but one who was overqualified. In a cultural environment where human talent is not duly acknowledged, the kind of disenchantment the Al Jazeera senior staff member experienced is not all that uncommon. What is uncommon, though, is for Al Jazeera not to ward off this *cul de sac*, particularly as it succeeded, at least to some extent, in shedding off some notable constraints as epitomized by the empowerment of its staff.

X.

Al Jazeera at the Crossroads

In stable environments, successful organizations share a vision of the future, value tradition and emphasize conformity. However, organizations operating in rapidly changing environments perform best when they value flexibility and change. At the same time, cultures are not static. For Schein, having a strong organizational culture and being change-oriented are not mutually exclusive. In today's fast-changing environment, organizations need a strong culture but at the same time one that is not all that pervasive in terms of prescribing particular norms or designating behavioral patterns. A dynamic culture is one where the leadership can adequately assess how the culture is performing and when to change it. In certain cases, the change in environment can lead the organization to redefine its mission, revisit its goals, and refine the means by which these goals can be achieved.

Media is a particularly dynamic industry. The pace of change in the media sector is fast at all levels from audiences to technology to employees. Naturally, new developments have implications which call for organizational changes and for adaptability measures to keep up with new trends and with competition. In *Managing Media Organizations*, John M. Lavine and Daniel B. Wackman articulately outline the challenges organizations have to be prepared to meet and cope with:

> We put considerable emphasis on building on strengths, especially the talents of the firm's staff, because those strong points are a unique resource. Other firms can purchase new technology or prepackaged materials, but only the leaders of a media company possess the blend of talents in their staff. Those strengths allow the leader to mobilize the staff to move in a new direction. If the executives' movements are wise and strategic, they will provide the organization or department with an advantage for a time. Eventually, competitors will figure out the direction of movement and the strengths; then they regroup to catch up. But

by the time that happens, the media managers will be busy building up new strengths and forging ahead in another direction for another advantage.[1]

Seen from this perspective, the organization's direction and its ability to adapt to environmental changes are of utter importance.

Al Jazeera is not immune to these changes. In fact, the pace of change in Arab media in general, and Arab satellite TV in particular, points to a number of questions with regards to the media organization under consideration: What is Al Jazeera's response to environmental developments? Is Al Jazeera's culture environmentally "adaptive" in the sense that it promotes learning and self-development or is it "disabling" in the sense that it insulates the organization from its environment? Does Al Jazeera's culture promote growth or lead to inertia? Do people in the organization share the same vision? Does Al Jazeera feel the need to redefine its mission? Does it have the organizational instinct to rethink its goals, revisit its strategies and reconsider its objectives as the need arises or as changes occur? And, more generally, how does the network position itself to prosper in the future?

Clearly, Al Jazeera's culture developed in response to a particular set of internal and external circumstances. At least in its formative years, Al Jazeera did not have the traditional elements one would expect to find in a successful organization. Several factors contributed to its organizational deficit. Understandably, no one expected Al Jazeera to burst onto the media scene or to rise to such prominence so fast and to have an impact that reverberates not just around the Middle East and North Africa but across the world. This resounding success took the network itself aback and surprised even its makers.

Al Jazeera's prominence notwithstanding, the future of the network could not be seen with certainty, leaving it contingent on the unfolding of events. At the same time, the uncertainty that characterized Al Jazeera all along has been one of the sources of its strength. Al Jazeera's awareness of itself as an alternative media outlet had made the pressure of "formal" strategic planning less acute. Its self-consciousness of the maverick image it projects often discourages it from engaging in classical strategic activities, which in turn helps free it from constraints of involvement with new developments in its environment while positioning it in such a way as to take advantage of the opportunities that may arise — all of which are noteworthy challenges when it comes to managing a media organization.

The specificity of Al Jazeera particularly in terms of viewer base, market and finances can hardly be overlooked. Being a pioneer in the field of Arab news broadcasting and operating in what is otherwise a new niche in a virgin mediascape, Al Jazeera had no competitors for a few years. There was no competition for audiences, at least not in the way one expects in Western media, nor for that matter was financial solvency and profit margin a pressing issue. As noted earlier, the *de facto* boycott that was imposed on Al Jazeera, discouraging major regional and international companies from advertising their products with it, has made its financial situation peculiar to say the least, relying for the most part on subsidies from the Qatari government. Nearly a decade later, the network continues to thrive on government subsidies. Not only was Al Jazeera not confronted with a pressing need to shore up financial performance, but even if it did, its controversial coverage has proven to be less than reassuring for hesitant potential advertisers who fear that Al Jazeera's shaky relationship with Arab governments could affect or harm their business interests. Although no figures are available, anecdotal evidence suggests that the network has been running annual deficits since its inception despite its lean work force and its sources of revenue, modest as these may be. Paradoxically enough, this peculiar and precarious situation has made research about Al Jazeera's audiences in particular and information about the broader environment in which it operates less insistent than the less-than-optimistic financial picture warrants. There is certainly a receptive audience for Al Jazeera, but determining how much audience share Al Jazeera has is a tricky issue. It is believed that Al Jazeera has no feedback on viewers beyond speculations that it has a massive audience estimated to amount to tens of millions of viewers. Even so, the often quoted raw figure of 40–60 million viewers is hardly helpful for advertising agents and their clients as these numbers do not say much about who is watching what at what time. Naturally, such variables affect Al Jazeera's goals, its direction, and its management.

Not surprisingly, the network's phenomenal rise has been marked by a certain unevenness which has gradually become more acute. During the first six or seven years of its existence, Al Jazeera was concerned with professional considerations rather than administrative matters, which meant that insufficient attention was paid to institutional and organizational issues. As such, things were loosely managed. Because there was no elaborate frame for paperwork to be processed nor was there an editorial policy in place, the staff dealt with issues and situations as they came up. Some staff did not even have a job description when they were hired. Likewise, there was no formal training; in some instances, the network staff used to train each other or benefit from on-the-job learning. At least the first and second batches of staff who were hired between 1996 and 1998 had a diverse experience and benefited from interaction and rotation. One staff member we interviewed recounts how she was able to move both laterally and horizontally in the organization, taking on field reporting, field production, and special projects before ending up as a senior producer. This was feasible at the time because of the manageable size of Al Jazeera. As the demands of such tasks became too much to handle, some of the senior staff found themselves stretched too thin. For example, as the network started to make headway, the news editor in chief found himself now and then called upon to act as an administrator on top of the responsibility of overseeing the news room during times when the whole world started to take notice of what Al Jazeera is broadcasting. As the going got tough, it was simply too hard for him to keep up with the demands of the job, particularly as some of the tasks he was performing fell outside his formal job duties.

If anything, these practices point to institutional shortcomings. As one senior staff member put it, "the secret behind Al Jazeera's success was not the institution; there was an administration and there were prerogatives, but there was no institution in the full import of the term." Seen from a cultural perspective, Al Jazeera has some of the symptoms that plague organizations in the Arab world and hold them back. For one thing, Al Jazeera is an organization that is set in an Arab environment which does not strongly believe in institution building. In this sense, Al Jazeera, as one staff member laconically put it, "is modeled on a political organization and not a business organization." There are some differences between the two. Being under the watchful eyes of viewers with high expectations, Al Jazeera could not afford the lethargy of Arab regimes who continue to pay lip service to political reform. The unflinching rise and development of Al Jazeera along with the ever-present controversy surrounding it made it difficult to continue to manage Al Jazeera the way it had been managed all along. There was a pressing need for the organization to institutionalize itself. In fact, there was a general awareness of the need to stabilize Al Jazeera and to ensure the continuation of its experience. Thus the need arose for drafting a code of ethics and a code of professional conduct. It became also indispensable to form an editorial board. Likewise, because of its international obligations, Al Jazeera felt the need to expand and better manage its bureaus worldwide as it felt the need to create specialized departments. There was also a need for better communication and interaction with the international community and a need to separate Al Jazeera's administration from its editorial division. In short, Al Jazeera felt, more than any time before, the need for an institutional framework that guides and directs its operations. There was a realization that for Al Jazeera to endure, it had to be reconceived and to dramatically change at various levels — the institutional, organizational, financial and editorial levels; that is, the way it conceives of itself, the way it structures its operations, the way it finances itself and the way it works.

Partly because it was overwhelmed and partly because its controversial coverage of the war in Afghanistan and the invasion of Iraq has kept it on the defensive, Al Jazeera focused its energy on trying to defend and assert itself. As doubts about the survival and sustainability of Al Jazeera started to recede, giving way to a feeling that the network was there to stay, an introspective look became more insistent than ever. The unevenness which marks the development of Al Jazeera has become acute to the point that it can no longer be ignored or brushed aside. The coming to eminence of Al Jazeera as an international news broadcaster has come with certain expectations. In fact, Al Jazeera has come to be held to high standards. Naturally, because it has pitched itself as an international channel, viewers and analysts alike tend to use the same yardstick to measure it with as they use with such leading international news broadcasters as CNN and the BBC. Increasingly, Al Jazeera finds itself called upon to reach international standards at the level of the institution to match those of the profession. In the words of one network staffer, Al Jazeera took it upon itself "to enhance the revolution in the Arab media and to bring it up to standards with the Western media."[2] There was a strong awareness that Al Jazeera succeeded thanks to its media content and not its organizational structure. Within Al Jazeera itself, there was a growing unease about the network's lack of a developed administrative system and of a proper structure which would help turn this Arab media organization into a full-fledged institution.

But these are not the only reasons behind Al Jazeera's organizational deficit. During the short years of its existence, Al Jazeera has relied heavily on the good will, enthusiasm and faith of its staff. Its success has strongly enhanced its ability to motivate and mobilize the staff, who were entrusted to act in the best interest of the network, partly aided by the absence of rigidity and undue bureaucratic constraints within the network. One of the staff members we interviewed pointed out the extent to which the absence of red tape contributed to the efficacy of managing the network. He emphasized "the ease and speed with which decisions are made within Al Jazeera" particularly in the first few years of its existence. Contributing to such flexibility is a culture of informality and spontaneity" that is enhanced by a let's-do-it *modus operandi* which Mohammed Jassim Al Ali has ingrained in Al Jazeera. To the extent that Al Ali adopted a management style which is sensitive to the vision set by Qatar's political leadership while capitalizing on the resources at his disposal (both human and financial), the kind of leadership he brought to Al Jazeera has gone a long way toward fostering a culture that gives the network a clear edge. Naturally, the way Al Jazeera has been run and the way it evolved helped undermine the development of a culture of planning and the institutionalization of the organization as much as the lack of red tape and the improvisational approach that have found their way to the network have helped Al Jazeera move forward and in fact move ahead.

The cultural artifacts reinforce the perception of an institutional deficit within Al Jazeera. When visiting the network, one gets a feeling that things are provisional. Some departments are in the midst of moving while others are anticipating a move. Outside the network headquarters itself, new departments are being created at various locations in Doha. In terms of physical artifacts, one is struck by how humble Al Jazeera's locale is. The first thing one comes across when entering Al Jazeera's compound is the security office at the main gate. This comes off as shabby and run-down, with archaic or rudimentary admission procedures which do not suggest that there is an efficient and reliable system in place. Upon clearing security at the main gate, the thing that strikes one the most is the run-down and decrepit parking lot. The setup of the facilities around the network is also eye-catching. Both the cafeteria and the mosque are set in a tent that is adjacent to the main building. Further down to the right is yet another tent for meetings which people at the network refer to as the Loya Jorga, in reference to Afghanistan's national assembly, as it is often used for open and heated debates. Across from the main building is a set of mobile-home type prefabricated offices which the employees themselves refer to as "refugee camps." Although minor, these details are telling and in fact significant. When coupled with certain trends in the network, the locale gives the impression not simply that many things at Al Jazeera are provisional, but that the provisional is there to last and become perpetual.

From the start, Al Jazeera was never given the opportunity to grow and evolve naturally. The fact that the network was continuously under scrutiny embroiled its leadership in the management of everyday business at the expense of developing the structural. Thriving in a quasi-unplanned way, Al Jazeera came short of being an institution in the full import of the term; it had neither the standards nor the structures one would expect from such an organization. What contributed greatly to the success of Al Jazeera is not its structural capability but the organic nature which was fostered by Al Ali. For some time, this has been a source of strength for the network; however, as the years went by, institutionalization became more important than ever for success. The unfolding of events, the eruption of crises and the succession of wars, particularly after September 11, kept Al Jazeera in perpetual motion and pre-determined its priorities. With the expansion of Al Jazeera's staff from some 400 in 2000 to some 1400 in 2005, with nearly 800 in Al Jazeera's headquarters in Doha and more than seventy correspondents in over 30 offices scattered all over the world, it was hard to ignore the organizational needs of the network. There was a realization that Al Jazeera urgently needed to attend to its "organizational vacuum," particularly as certain practices, decisions and challenges made questionable the extent to which business as usual could be carried out in the absence of formal structures and institutionalized guidelines on issues ranging from salary scale to internal guide policy to professional standards to style of news and programs. The awareness of the need to change among the people who work in the network was matched with a desire to change on the part of the higher echelons of Al Jazeera's hierarchy. The politics of change aside, with the increasing awareness of the need to develop Al Jazeera and to take it to the next stage, change was inevitable.

These developments, which led up to "the self critical months that followed the invasion of Iraq,"[3] coincided with the coming to the scene, in October 2003, of Waddah Khanfar, Al Jazeera's former Baghdad bureau chief and correspondent, who succeeded Mohammed Jassim Al Ali as Al Jazeera's managing director after a short interim period during which the management of the network was entrusted to a veteran newsman. In June 2003, and for a period of four months or so, Al Jazeera named Adnan Al Sharif, a British citizen of Palestinian origin, as acting general manager replacing Al Ali, who had managed the station since its inception in 1996 until he was "removed" amid reports that Saddam Hussein's intelligence service had infiltrated the Qatari network in an effort to influence its coverage and accusations made by the head of the once U.S.-backed Iraqi National Congress, Ahmed Chalabi, that some Al Jazeera journalists were working for Iraqi agencies and that Al Ali himself visited Iraq before the U.S.-led invasion and met with Saddam Hussein.[4]

Al Sharif's beginning was with Qatar's radio and TV in the 1970s. After some two decades, he moved to the BBC's Arabic service and on to the BBC Arabic-language TV in 1994, which was funded by the giant Saudi Arabian Mawarid Group's subsidiary, the Rome-based Orbit Communications Corporation. In 1996, the partnership with Saudi Arabia collapsed over editorial independence. The latter's failure to tame the BBC left a pool of BBC-trained journalists and auxiliary staff members jobless. Coming during a time when a media initiative had been simmering in the mind of Qatar's new leadership, which was eager to forge an identity for Qatar that was distinct from that of neighboring Saudi Arabia, as an Al Jazeera staff member put it, the tip from Adnan Al Sharif about the ill fate and sudden demise of the BBC Arabic-language TV channel and the staff to be laid off fell on receptive ears. Al Sharif had been with the network since the beginning — in fact, he joined during the study and planning phase (being one of three people entrusted with setting up Al Jazeera) and was a potential candidate for the position of general manager, which he indeed held, albeit only temporarily, during the few weeks which preceded the launching of the channel. According to one source, "Al Sharif had been expected to become Al Jazeera's first director, but was dropped in favor of Al Ali, a Qatari national. He served as head for just one month before the channel was launched, but left for London when he was discarded and took up a job with the BBC's Arabic service, returning to Al Jazeera as news anchor in 2000."[5]

For some of the staff members we talked to, Adnan Al Sharif's tenure was "uneasy" while for others it was "problematic," even "disastrous." Word has it that his appointment was controversial and was met with some objections from some members of the board. Some of the changes he brought about or decisions he took were whimsical and without proper consultation. He also antagonized many network staff. There was a perception that he wanted to do away with programs, many of which were hosted by leading figures who had been with the network from day one. He introduced some restrictions which, although they did not last long, caused much resentment. In one instance, he did away with the travel indemnity Al Jazeera staff have benefited from all along. This was met with a lot of resistance as it smacked of a bureaucratic instinct which was at odds with the spirit of Al Jazeera and the resourcefulness its staff have been used to. When Al Jazeera's correspondent Tayseer Allouni was arrested and detained in Spain, many of the staff felt that their manager put them and the network in an awkward situation. The news presenter on duty was asked to hang a button bearing Tayseer Allouni's picture on his lapel. For some time, Al Jazeera anchors appeared on screen wearing Allouni's face on a badge with "Free Tayseer" printed on it as they delivered the news. Some felt that such a decision, which was taken without proper consultation, compromised the independence and objectivity of the channel during times when all eyes were on Al Jazeera. Still, the incident that probably invited resentment the most and later on broke the camel's back was the decision to hire a female news broadcaster, along with her personal hairdresser, at a salary that was significantly higher than what an accomplished news anchor in the network made. Naturally, this incident created a problem of inequity which resulted in a strong sense of unease among some network staff who felt that there was no consideration for pay scales, longevity of service or seniority. Ironically, this female anchor was later sacked in obscure conditions during the tenure of Adnan Al Sharif, causing sympathy even among those who previously resented her hiring as they felt undervalued considering the offer she received.

As much as Al Sharif's tenure as a general manager was problematic, it had a positive outcome of sorts as it made the institutional lacunae within Al Jazeera more obvious than ever before. For some of the network staff we interviewed, the tenure of Adnan Al Sharif was not a bad thing for Al Jazeera precisely because it accelerated change. For better or for worse, the appointment of Waddah Khanfar was a relief for many of Al Jazeera's staff. He was perceived as young, dynamic, energetic and open-minded. When Khanfar came on board as the new managing director, one staff member told us, he was full of life and everybody wished him success and in fact wanted him to succeed. Being also an outsider, so to speak, he brought in much-needed new blood, particularly after the uneasy transition period with the interim general manager.

While for some network staff the rationale for appointing Waddad Khanfar, a Jordanian of Palestinian descent,[6] is not all that evident, for others it is not as arbitrary as it may seem. His background is peculiar, to say the least. After receiving his bachelor's degree in mechanical engineering in Jordan, Khanfar pursued postgraduate studies in philosophy for two years, focusing on aesthetics. Later, he moved to South Africa during its political transformation, where he got a degree in international studies before joining the University of South Africa's African studies program. His thesis, which he never defended, was a contextual study of the Anglo-Saxon and Anglo-American model of democracy and democratization and its applicability in Africa. It was also in South Africa that he began his career with Al Jazeera in 1999, serving first as a correspondent and then bureau chief there before moving to India in 2001. On the eve of the war in Afghanistan, Al Jazeera did not have much direct access to the northern territories in Afghanistan, as these were controlled by the Northern Alliance. Khanfar used New Delhi as a base to cover the war in Afghanistan and cultivate a relationship with the Northern Alliance, given the latter's strong diplomatic presence in and support from India, which was uneasy with the Taliban long before the United States launched its War on terrorism. For S. Abdullah Schleifer, the role Khanfar played during the postwar era was particularly instrumental in sustaining the presence and credibility of Al Jazeera:

> When the Taliban regime began to collapse and the Northern Alliance forces swept into Kabul, Al Jazeera's presence in the Afghan capital in 2001 was bedeviled by problems.... The Kabul bureau had been hit by U.S. fire and Al Jazeera's correspondent and Kabul Bureau chief Taysir Allouni had been compromised in the eyes of many journalists and diplomats, not to mention the Northern Alliance, as a partisan of the Taliban cause. Khanfar took over the Kabul Bureau and restored working relations with the new authorities.[7]

During the invasion of Iraq, Khanfar covered the war from the north, where he reported exclusively on the Kurds. With the fall of Baghdad and the collapse of Saddam Hussein's regime in 2003, Al Jazeera found itself confronted with a *déjà vu* scenario and Khanfar found himself called upon to play a role similar to the one he played in Afghanistan, particularly as Al Jazeera came increasingly under attack for its coverage of the war and its alleged clandestine relationship with the Iraqi intelligence. Khanfar became Al Jazeera's Bahgdad bureau chief, a position which allegedly called for establishing a relationship with the potential Iraqi leadership, including the pre-war opposition, and improving relations with the American authorities. The fact that Khanfar was among a select group of journalists who got to interview Paul Bremer, the then U.S. civil administrator of Iraq, gives some credence to these views. Still, others find these speculations unfounded. In his book on Al Jazeera, for instance, Hugh Miles dismisses the claim that Khanfar's appointment was meant to fortify the relationship between the network and the U.S. forces in Iraq as a conspiracy theory.[8] The fact that Al Jazeera continued to be subjected to harassment from the authorities in Iraq during Khanfar's tenure as a bureau chief and later as a network manager, including threats, attacks and imprisonment, does not give credence to the rapprochement or trust-building thesis; nor does it suggest that Khanfar was very successful in getting the Iraqi and American governments to trust Al Jazeera again. If anything, Al Jazeera saw its banishment from Iraq during much of Khanfar's tenure as the network's managing director, suspending Al Jazeera's coverage of any official activities of the Iraqi Governing Council for some time and eventually banning it when it refused to change its editorial policy. In fact, in August 2004, Iyad Allawi's government closed Al Jazeera's Baghdad bureau and banned the network from operating in Iraq.[9]

For Iason Athanasiadis, the "appointment of new boss Waddah Khanfar at the Qatar headquarters comes amid mounting revelations that Al Jazeera's top management chose not to air several Osama bin Laden tapes; pulled from its news websites caricatures the White House deemed offensive; and removed its former general manager following U.S. complaints to the Emir of Qatar about the channel's coverage of the war in Iraq."[10] Increasingly, Khanfar's name came to be associated with change — although some of the changes undertaken under his directorship, particularly in relation to the expansion of Al Jazeera, go back to Al Ali's days.[11] According to an AFP communiqué, Al Jazeera's board decision to appoint Waddah as the new managing director "is part of an administrative and professional drive and means that Al Jazeera will now adopt a more moderate and professional policy."[12]

In the first few months after assuming his new duties at Al Jazeera headquarters in Doha, Khanfar developed a visible and interactive relationship with the rest of the staff. During this period of backgrounding, he interacted with almost every single employee in Al Jazeera inside and outside the newsroom. He could be seen everywhere and in fact spent considerable time in the cafeteria mingling with virtually everyone in the organization and establishing a rapport with Al Jazeera's diverse staff. When first appointed as a general manager, Khanfar gave the impression that he was both accessible and interactive; he also brought with him hope and energy. Many of the network staff rallied behind him. With the lapse of his grace period, the looming of new ideas about the future of Al Jazeera, the seeping of new management style and the coalescence of new practices and preferences, a mood of distancing started to insulate the management from the network staff. A year or so into his new position, the managing director started to be engulfed in his new position and to be seen less and less, becoming at times even hard to access. Soon differences between Khanfar's management style and that of his predecessor became evident, leading to some unease among many of the network staff.

In some instances, the ensuing unease was more of an anxiety which comes with change. As Al Jazeera started to edge toward institution building, some unease ensued. Some of the network staff who saw Al Jazeera evolve and were part of its coming of age could not quite see it operate outside its traditional *modus operandi*. For these people, such changes meant that the identity of Al Jazeera as well as the mindset of the people affiliated with it were starting to change. As one producer put it, "Al Jazeera was ours; we made it what it is; we made it to be this collective entity. With its expansion, however, we are no longer able to take credit for it. We do not feel we belong, at least not the way we used to. We no longer hang out in Al Jazeera for hours when we are off duty. We started to work and leave." For another staff member, with the new face of Al Jazeera and the emergence of regional competitors, "the dream vanished." When there was no viable outlet in the Arab mediascape to rival Al Jazeera, the network seemed relentless and unsurpassed. With the coming to the scene of Al Arabiya, along with the institutionalization of Al Jazeera and the coming to being of a slightly different culture within the institution, things started to change. The zeal and enthusiasm which had long been held by Al Jazeera's staff started to give in to more realistic expectations.

In other cases, the unease that sank in among some network staff emanated out of genuine concerns about the new state of affairs. Broadly speaking, some of the interviewed staff felt that the network has been going through an undeclared crisis of leadership. Part of the problem as some of the staff see it is upper management. To start with, there is no clear understanding among staff members of how decisions at the highest level are made within the network. The rationale for some of the appointments is not all that clear, either. Sometimes, personal relationships tend to take precedence over institutional frameworks. People within the network do not have a clear understanding of who influences what, how the new board of editors came to be assembled or what the rationale for appointing the new managing director is. Likewise, there is a perception that management decisions are not always objective. In some cases, the employees do not relate to some decisions because the rationale behind them is not all that obvious. Overall, the lack of involvement of the staff in the ongoing changes and the lack of information about the specifics of the whole process of change points to problems of involvement and transparency in decision making processes. There is a sense that the vision of the managing director and that of the board is not clearly and fully conveyed to the members of the organization, making a number of them feel not part of these developments.

Although Al Jazeera hired an international consulting firm to restructure the network, there is a feeling among some of the network staff that these initiatives are not driven by a genuine desire for change and that they are more signs of prestige than real change. The prevailing feeling is that the ongoing restructuring of the organization is in accordance with a model that is imposed from outside rather than one that emanates from within or is developed in-house. In fact, there is a strong perception among the staff members we interviewed that discernable changes were demanded from above. When asked how Al Jazeera's refined vision and the ensuing changes came about, Waddah Khanfar pointed out that "they have emerged from an open and honest debate which involves the editorial board and the upper administration. Not everybody was involved, but the vision reflects debates and convictions."[13] Surely, not everybody was on board. An anchor woman we talked to had no clue about the changes nor was she much concerned about the restructuring Al Jazeera has been going through — although she admitted that the network is not secretive about the envisaged changes. Similarly, a news editor we interviewed was aware that international consulting firms have been brought in to look into what Al Jazeera does and how it does it, but did not know much beyond that. Likewise, a senior producer in the newsroom admitted that there is no clear understanding of the changes but added apologetically that this is the case "just because they did not happen yet." Some of the staff who were interviewed were aware of a new structure of the organization posted on a board not far away from the office of the managing director, but did not seem to have a good grasp of it or even relate to it. In this respect, the lack of involvement of the average person in Al Jazeera is particularly noteworthy. Overall, the staff are aware that there is an ongoing restructuring but do not have a clear sense of the scope, substance and extent of this change, nor has there been a serious attempt on the part of the administration to bring their input to bear. For John M. Lavine and Daniel B. Wackman, such a lack of involvement can have implications on the staff's commitment: "Especially in the media, where people all across the firm have expertise and work with the messages that are developed, it is a waste of mental resources not to tap each employee's best input. Yet, unless they are asked to contribute, staff members seldom volunteer. And if they do not get involved, their commitment may be lacking. That could result in a death knell for turning an idea into successful reality, which is fatal in a media form."[14] If Al Jazeera's vision does not always trickle down to the lower echelons of the network, one staff member pointed out, it is not necessarily because the rest of the network does not subscribe to such a vision, but because they are sometimes disempowered, a feeling which leads to disengagement.

Beyond the issue of involvement, there is a problem of disorientation. Although some of the interviewed staff admit that they are proud to be part of Al Jazeera, they have reservations about the practices, orientation and development of the network. They argue that the image people have about Al Jazeera does not always match what really goes on inside the network. Seen from an insider's perspective, Al Jazeera is not the "perfect institution" it gives the impression it is. If anything, it is plagued with contradictions. There is even a perception among some of Al Jazeera's staff that the network is in a state of disarray, regression and even disintegration. In this respect, the resignation in 2005 of Al Jazeera's official spokesman and its link with regional and international media, Jihad Ballout, and his decision to join its chief competitor, Al Arabiya, is indicative of the concerns some of the staff have *vis-à-vis* the change the network has embarked on. The resignation came amid talks about a diversion of views between Al Jazeera and its spokesman pertaining to certain policies adopted by upper management.[15] In an interview with *Al Sharq Al Awsat*, Ballout conceded that "matters reached a point where there was a difference in opinion regarding how to perform the tasks that [he] consider[s] essential in [his] media work.... There was simply a difference in defining the priorities regarding the approaching phase on mid-term and long-term bases."[16] While significant in and of itself, the decision of the man who spent years passionately and tirelessly defending Al Jazeera's editorial policies and corporate choices to relocate is noteworthy because it echoes the desire of some of the frustrated network staff we interviewed to move out if they can find better opportunities.

Adding to the complexity of the problem is Khanfer's profile. Some staff members we interviewed in Doha expressed doubts about Khanfar not on personal grounds but on professional grounds. In their view, a good correspondent does not necessarily make a successful manager. One staff member explained that "in order to succeed, a general manager of a media organization must have developed a full understanding of how the news division works, which is not the case here." As long as Khanfar does not understand the fundamentals of media, he added, it will be a challenge for him to either succeed or last. Unlike Al Jazeera's previous manager, Khanfar did not come from a media background; in comparison to Al Ali, as one interviewee put it, Khanfar comes off as lacking the "instinct for the profession." Soon the differences in management with his predecessors started to become evident for the network staff.

Al Ali's long and diverse experience has helped him acquire a deep understanding of the media environment and prepared him well for his new position. Being an insider who came to know every little detail about TV production, Al Ali had a good and rounded understanding of how a media organization functions technically. He started as a floor manager at age 18 and worked his way up, gradually going from assistant producer to producer to director to assistant to head of programs to head of Qatar TV before being transferred to Al Jazeera when it was launched. In the early days of Al Jazeera, Al Ali benefited from Qatar TV and leaned on some of its "cadre" who were brought on board with higher salaries. Before long, he improved the system he brought along and adapted it to the needs and specificity of Al Jazeera. Under Al Ali, management was a matter of pragmatism. In terms of his management style, Al Ali worked closely with key people and departments. Financial and administrative affairs, the news, the programs, and the satellites, among other important departments, reported to him directly. In terms of the nitty-gritty of Al Jazeera's work, Al Ali did not interfere much; instead, he delegated duties. However, he contributed considerably to the areas that had to do with production, shooting, images and stage direction — all of which he knew well given his long and considerable experience and expert knowledge. He had a keen and perceptive eye on what was going on inside the newsroom, but intervened only when need be, and when he did, he tried to fix things on the spot.

Under Al Ali, the management of Al Jazeera had a personal touch to it, making it a face-to-face conversational organization. While revered, Al Ali was also very approachable. He had an open-door policy and the network staff felt comfortable talking to him and working with him. At least in the first few years of its existence, Al Jazeera was relatively small and Al Ali knew everybody by name. When it came to the newsroom staff, he knew even details about their families — enough to inquire after their kids by name. The only thing he refrained from doing is socializing with his staff outside Al Jazeera headquarters, except for very few members he knew well since his early days with Qatar TV. Not only did Al Ali have a good rapport with his crew, but he also knew how to deal with the "stars" of Al Jazeera and in fact win them over. Overall, Al Ali operated in a friendly way and managed to run things smoothly, in part thanks to the good esteem Al Jazeera staff had for him.

This rapport with the network staff is significant particularly for those of the view that Al Jazeera is such that it can be entrusted neither to a technocrat nor to a manager. Under the directorship of Al Ali, Al Jazeera was constituted of a small and intimate group and operated more like a family business. This sense is hardly lost on those who visit Al Jazeera's headquarters. The network, Hugh Miles concurs, "is small enough to possess a sense almost of family loyalty ... [as] the staff are closer to one another than in other news organizations."[17] This management style has several advantages, including the consolidation of authority, the speed with which decisions can be made, the speed with which the staff can identify sources of strength and weakness, and the flexibility it affords to the staff. For example, when a Gulf Air plane crashed in Bahrain in 2000, Al Jazeera immediately covered the event and then moved on to air its regular programs, only to receive a call from a viewer inquiring why Al Jazeera did not cover the event. To this inquiry, Al Jazeera pointed out that it already did before any other Arab channel and then carried on with its regular programs. This incident prompted a short meeting between Al Ali and the news editor in chief, the outcome of which was the decision to introduce a script which reads "Breaking News" on the screen. The next step was to request a format for such an item from the graphics department. It did not take long to do that and in fact the next day, this feature was operative on Al Jazeera's screen.

This same initiative, we were told, takes a month or so to materialize in Al Arabiya, as it has to go through the marketing division which controls the look of the screen, the graphics division which would produce the script, and the technical division which would put things on screen. Every step in the process is subject to paperwork, which is not the case in Al Jazeera. In the latter case, only big tasks require paperwork, and even so the supporting paperwork which eventually follows is not a prerequisite for getting the job done. The interpersonal relationship and human interaction within the network give the word of mouth credence and efficacy. In the words of one staff member, "the guarantees are there." As such, Al Jazeera comes close to a family business, with trust and connection being inherent to its management style. Because the network is small enough to foster family atmosphere and because the staff members tend to be closer to one another than in typical news organizations, as Miles put it,[18] the sense of intimacy that has developed in Al Jazeera gives work relationships a personal touch which facilitates the task of the staff a great deal. Although not everyone is committed to the network with the same degree, the sense of belonging and connection is widespread. In fact, high social capital has been one of Al Jazeera's strengths — although that may be declining — leading to greater cohesion of action and enhancing the sense of participation and membership.[19]

At times, though, the intensely social work environment that prevailed under Al Ali's leadership had a side effect, if not a negative impact, leaving the fault line between the personal and the professional blurrier than one wishes it to be. One former staff member noted how the human resources department often treated personal information with no confidentiality, so much so that the newsroom may know of a raise or a reward a particular journalist has gotten even before the concerned party is aware of it. The incident is all the more interesting because it captures a moment of entanglement between the culture of the organization and that of the region. The same reporter added that the whole atmosphere in Qatar, being a small country where people know each other, is suffocating, for "in Doha, one not only works in Al Jazeera, but one's life revolves around Al Jazeera." With respect to the aforementioned incident, the problem is not only that interpersonal relationships are such that there is no sense of privacy, but also that such behavior within the network goes largely unpunished.

Al Ali may not have management skills in the corporate sense of the term; what he has instead is the instinct for media and the know-how to run a media organization. Relying on the wisdom comparable to that of a tribe leader rather than on standards and procedures, Al Ali comes off more as a "missionary leader who is keen on seeing Al Jazeera succeed." Surely enough, one staff member told us, "Al Ali's management had its own shortcomings and its own lacunae, but it was far from being controversial. Because of his experience and his keenness on not succumbing to any ideological allegiance, Al Ali was both respected and revered," and most of Al Jazeera staff who worked under his supervision speak favorably of him. There is a common feeling that Al Ali had a strong presence and a charisma which distinguished him and enabled him to exhibit a sense of leadership which was appreciated. When he makes a decision, we were told, he hardly ever goes back on it or reconsiders it without first going back to the concerned party. Al Ali was also appreciated for his common sense and good judgment. He displayed the ability to be considerate and the characteristic of rewarding good efforts. In sum, as an empowered Qatari with a technical base and charisma, Al Ali came to an unstructured group, several members of which were steeped in BBC standards of journalism, and spontaneously instilled patterns and norms of behavior and embedded assumptions in the various routines of the organization that became the culture of Al Jazeera.

Waddah Khanfar's leadership seems to be different from Al Ali's charismatic leadership. This is hardly because Khanfar is not a local or a member of the board of directors, as is the case with his predecessor. Rather, Khanfar found himself managing an organization that had reached a new growth stage, particularly as its circumstances, its make-up, its aspirations and its status have changed. With Khanfar, the management of the network started to take a more structured approach aimed at keeping up with the increasing organizational complexity of Al Jazeera. As it became larger, Al Jazeera started to undergo a process of differentiation, symptoms of which include functional differentiation, geographical decentralization, and differentiation by product and hierarchical level. Gradually, the old pattern, which was to a large extent based on interpersonal relationships, started to give way to an organizational structure based more on formal management principles which are called for by the high expectations, increased size and added resources (human and otherwise) of the organization. Khanfar's coming the scene meant also the introduction of a terminology that has so far been alien to Al Jazeera — guidelines, order, structure, code, organization, among other concept words. It soon became clear that, under its new management, Al Jazeera is embarking on momentous changes, introducing a system and providing pointers for an organizational model that has been organic, loose, informal and idiosyncratic.

XI.

Surviving Change

In an interview with the authors, the general manager of Al Jazeera noted that "in a way, Al Jazeera's bread and butter consist of news. The other programs are important but they complement the news rather than compete with it. For the news to be credible and professionally handled, they have to obey certain standards and be produced in accordance with set guidelines. Whence the importance of having a sound structure in place."[1] Accordingly, Al Jazeera set out to institutionalize editorial decisions, recruitment, foreign offices, employee affairs, financial affairs and administrative affairs. In fact, it set a number of policies and structures in place, drafted binding documents and improved a number of processes. To start with and in an attempt to institutionalize editorial policies, Al Jazeera put in place for the first time a five-member editorial board, composed of senior staff members and journalists, to ensure that the news is not left to the whim of key individuals or a particular editor and that decision-making is not an individual prerogative, but a group effort in accordance with set policies. Likewise, Al Jazeera set up an internal quality control department which monitors the programs it screens and measures how its output lives up to the principles it has set for itself. The editorial board receives daily reports about Al Jazeera's programs which are then discussed with the presenter of the program in order to avoid certain practices in the future or simply to give the program hosts feedback about their programs.

Al Jazeera also drafted a code of ethics — a document which took some four months to put together and which in the words of Khanfar has become "a constitution."[2] The code of ethics outlines the network's professional beliefs, delineates its standards and notes its keenness on distinguishing between what is news and what is opinion and analysis. In order to ensure that its staff abide by the code of ethics, Al Jazeera also published a code of professional conduct. Furthermore, and in order to implement its policy of "professionalism," Al Jazeera established Al Jazeera Media Training and Development Center, which would allow it to distinguish itself, to retain its leadership position and to forge a school of journalism altogether. The aim of the center is not only to provide Al Jazeera's staff with the necessary training and "the best methodologies and techniques of media work"[3] but also to increase awareness of the media, promote communication between media organizations and keep abreast of media developments.[4] The center's initiative is not limited to the field of journalism; it also covers the expertise of media technicians and other professional activities. To provide the best possible professional training, Al Jazeera has drawn on international media organizations including the Thomson Foundation and Getrac for Training and Consultancy.[5] Through the center, Al Jazeera is aspiring to develop and raise skills in the media sector, exchange expertise and raise the performance level of media practitioners. In order to meet the expectations of the organization, it was made mandatory for staff to participate in training sessions. There is also a performance or aptitude assessment system for assessing what employees have gained in terms of skills — which is used in yearly increments.

At the level of structure, Al Jazeera established methods of planning. The tangible changes Al Jazeera introduced include the setting up of a committee for program planning and the creation of a unit for news planning, a non-academic body which seeks to follow important events, predict new developments and prepare dossiers beforehand. Likewise, Al Jazeera created a unit to monitor Al Jazeera programs for quality control whereas, in the past, problems, lacunae or incidents were dealt with at the level of the editor in chief if and when these were noticed.

In terms of institutional development, Al Jazeera has become increasingly aware of the need to focus more on the customers. In the past, Al Jazeera catered to its audience almost instinctively insofar as it developed a populist tone or inclination which distinguished it from regional competitors who opted for a more sober tone. More recently, with the loss of "its monopoly on Arab satellite news," with no decisive market share lead, and with the "intense competition [which] has reduced whatever ability Al Jazeera once had to single-handedly shape opinion in the Arab world,"[6] the network has become more scientifically interested in its consumer base. In the words of the general manager, Al Jazeera has become particularly interested in "taking the pulse of [the] audience — of the greater public — scientifically. So far, Arab media are indifferent to this so [Al Jazeera] must develop these methods of research and planning, of strategic thinking, a school of thought in the Arab world based on rational understanding of what media is all about, how to develop media along such lines, yet keep it rooted in the Arab world."[7] One such initiative is the launching of a Center for Studies and Polling which aims at providing Al Jazeera with the kind of research and information it needs, producing field surveys and assessment studies and evaluating audience responses. Part of the problem, as Khanfar further explains, is that the polling culture is anathema to the Arab world. The way Al Jazeera is coping with this problem is to conduct polls for basic programs on the internet and monitor the feedback it receives from viewers, either in the form of email or fax correspondences, and forward such input to the appropriate divisions or programs. Another initiative is the creation of the Research and Studies Unit in Aljazeera.net, which both covers certain issues and dossiers for the journalists of the channel and provides material for the general public. Al Jazeera is also seeking to create links with universities and study groups through its newly established International Relations Office. The international media forums Al Jazeera hosted in 2004 and 2006 on "Changing Media Perceptions: Professionalism and Cultural Diversity" and "Freedom of Expression and Media Responsibility," respectively, are also the sort of initiative which capitalizes on the spirit of the new institutional changes. These changes could lead the network to have an introspective look at its practices and to engage journalists from the international media community on issues ranging from covering crises to the role broadcasters should play in spreading political reform throughout the Arab world to whether media's mission should be to inform or to reform. In a subsequent workshop organized in conjunction with UNESCO, which brought together government media officials from all over the Arab world, Al Jazeera set out to probe the issue of new ways of managing media organizations.[8]

However, while in theory the changes Al Jazeera has embarked on are admirable, in practice, they have problematic aspects at the level of implementation. One senior staff member we interviewed complained that some of the changes that have been introduced may be well intended but remain to a large extent ineffective. As an example, he pointed out that there is no real quality control nor is there an effective mechanism for enforcing standards. A case in point is the use of the terminology used to report the death of Al Jazeera's own reporter in Iraq. Until the issue became a source of controversy, Al Jazeera did not have a position or a stand on the use of the word "martyr." After the war in Afghanistan, Al Jazeera consciously made the decision not to use the word "martyr," which has been the subject of controversy. And so Al Jazeera's editorial line has honored those decisions up until the death of one of its reporter, Tarek Ayyoub, on the eve of the fall of Baghdad, when Al Jazeera's bureau was hit by a missile. Needless to say, this was a sensitive moment for the channel and for Ayyoub's colleagues who were reporting his death. The assistant news editor in chief who was on duty then recounts how he was deeply touched by the death of his colleague to the point of having tears in his eyes. Yet, professionally speaking, he had to refer to the incident as "the death of Tarek Ayyoub." He even took a reporter off the air because his voice was a bit emotional when reporting the event, and aired a documentary instead lest the professional standards of the network be compromised. Later in the day, when the news editor in chief reported to Al Jazeera headquarters, he chose to refer to Tarek Ayyoub as a martyr. Not only was the difference in editorial line confusing, as Ayyoub was reported as being killed in the morning news only to be labeled as a "martyr" in the afternoon bulletin, but this was also a significant departure from the editorial policy of Al Jazeera which even in the minds of some network staff is ridden with contradictions. While those who die in bloody clashes or those victims who fall in Iraq were simply called dead, Tarek Ayyoub was labeled a martyr.

Even more controversial is the case of Tayseer Allouni — one of Al Jazeera's star reporters. Allouni is a Spanish citizen of Syrian origin whose name came to eminence during the coverage of the war in Afghanistan when Al Jazeera was for some time the only foreign news organization with reporters in Taliban-controlled Afghanistan. Allouni was in fact Al Jazeera's bureau chief in Kabul and its mouthpiece during the war. Later on, he was arrested in Spain and charged with being a member of Al Qaeda network. Eventually, Allouni was sentenced to seven years in jail by a Spanish court "which deemed that he had not just cultivated Al Qaeda contacts as he pursued bin Laden, but had actively collaborated with them" — although some network staff feel that "the whole trial was, from the very beginning, politically motivated."[9] During his detention, the channel mounted a media campaign to free him, issuing communiqués, devoting a few programs to him, providing updates about his case in their news bulletins and even getting news anchors for some time to wear badges with his picture on their lapels while reading the news. For a senior network staff who has a high esteem for Allouni and who valued him both as a person and as a colleague, the handling of the case of Allouni was not well thought out, leaving Al Jazeera walking the thin edge of the wedge: "For Al Jazeera to endorse his case is a risk it should have never taken because eventually, if Allouni is pronounced guilty of having ties to Al Qaeda network, the channel's credibility is tarnished and its objectivity and professionalism are put into question. We are after all a media organization and we should stick to that." If anything, the way Al Jazeera dealt with Allouni's case suggests that the fault line between what is political and what is professional is thin. When seen in light of the espionage allegations surrounding Al Jazeera and its relation with the former Iraqi regime, Allouni's case, as Hugh Miles points out, is not insignificant: "If Al Qaeda had penetrated Al Jazeera ... it would be a serious blow to the channel."[10]

Other practices suggest that not much has changed. When an episode of Ghassan bin Jeddou's program *Open Dialogue* on the crisis in Lebanon in the aftermath of the assassination of former prime minister Rafik Al Hariri was set in Martyrs' Square in Beirut, where a demonstration by the opposition was held, the element of independence could have already been sacrificed as the choice of the setting was already a statement in and of itself. This is far from being an isolated event. During the siege of Fallujah, to take another example, one of Al Jazeera's star reporters, Ahmad Mansour, was taken to task for engaging in what has been described as the Hollywoodization of the news. His coverage of the fighting in and updates from the besieged Iraqi city of Fallujah was emotional. Pointing out that the American bombing of Fallujah was arbitrary, he would send appeals to the international community live on the air to intervene and save Fallujah. For one staff member, who pointed out that Al Jazeera is not Al Manar, the mouthpiece of Hizballah, such initiatives or practices are clearly in violation of responsible journalism. Another staff member complained that Al Jazeera's coverage of the assassination of Sheikh Amed Yassine, the spiritual leader of Hamas, and Dr. Abdul Aziz Al Rantissi, Hamas's subsequent leader, made it sound more like an Islamist channel than anything else.

It is true that the management created a quality control department made up mostly of a team brought from Aljazeera.net and entrusted with producing reports based on well-defined criteria and in accordance with a detailed grid, but these seem to have hardly any effect or impact. One staff member dismissed the whole initiative as nothing more than "lip service," pointing out that there is hardly any follow-up or actions ensuing from those reports. In the absence of professional conscience among the journalists themselves, he explained, genuine and committed follow-up becomes a real institutional shortcoming with ramifications for the organization. And in fact, there are other noteworthy institutional lacunae which are not in synch with the proclaimed change. One interviewee in particular recounts how some hiring practices under the current managing director, Waddah Khanfar, raise serious questions. In 2005, we were told, Al Jazeera hired a number of new staff in a way which diverges from old practices, particularly when it comes to the way the hiring was conducted and the make-up of the new recruits. In response to the need to hire about 20 new staff members, there was an initial plan to recruit journalists from various locations in the Arab world. The understanding was to seek out an equal number of talent from the Levant, Jordan, Egypt, and possibly North Africa — which is in line with Al Jazeera's diverse make-up. Accordingly, a small team, including a senior staff member from the editorial board, set out to Cairo, one of the interview sites. In response to an advertisement, Al Jazeera received an overwhelming number of applications. For six openings, Al Jazeera was swamped with some 7,000 applications which, in the initial screening, were reduced to around 500. It took some twenty hours of work to select 200 applicants who were then required to sit for an exam, which led to the interviews of 100 short-listed applicants. Eventually, the hiring committee which was dispatched to Egypt for recruiting purposes made a recommendation to hire three news readers.

However, not long after the process was over and to the committee's surprise, it turned out that the general manager himself flew to Cairo on a recruitment mission along with a newly hired deputy news editor in chief of Egyptian nationality. The trip was so discreet that even some members of the editorial board, including the news editor in chief, had no prior knowledge of plans for such a recruitment *en masse*. The outcome of this trip was the hiring of 13 new Egyptian staff members who obviously did not go through the same stringent process of selection and interview the others that were recommended were subjected to. Ultimately, getting the chairman of the board to approve the hiring of these new recruits was a mere formality. As one interviewee put it, knowing how "benign" and how "unconcerned with details" Sheikh Hamad is, he would immediately approve the general manager's request to hire these people. However, for the staff members who went through nearly 7,000 applications during their recruitment trip, there was a sense of dismay and even resentment. It just did not make sense to them to go through a process which required tens of hours of work and cost close to 100,000 Qatari Riyals only to find out that there was a parallel process which seemed to be based on personal decisions and influenced by certain favored members in the network. The issue is not so much "the Egyptianization of Al Jazeera" whereby, as one staff member put it, "an Egyptian would favor, hire and promote an Egyptian"—something not uncommon in the Gulf region—but the departure from practices which many perceive as defining moments in the history, culture and identity of Al Jazeera—namely the sociological diversification of its Arab journalists and the pursuit of a practice which ensures that the recruited network staff are diverse enough and representative enough of Arab nationalities.[11] For one staff member, such practices stand in marked distinction to the tradition Al Ali fostered. Behind the latter's success, we were told, "lie two important factors—developing an instinct for the job and refusing to espouse a particular ideology."

Practices such as these call all the more attention to themselves when they are not isolated incidents. As one senior staffer recounts, Khanfar appointed a head of the newsroom, only to realize a few months later that "he is probably not the perfect fit for the position." Although retained in his position as editor in chief, we were told, he was sidelined and in fact made somewhat redundant. For the position of deputy news editor in chief, Al Jazeera hired a senior producer who, incidentally, had left Al Jazeera for Al Arabiya when the latter was first launched. The new deputy chief editor is perceived as being given a free hand to operate. One of the staff members we talked to believes that he has a say when it comes to setting the agenda of the news. The move to hire a senior producer from Al Arabiya and bring him to Al Jazeera in his capacity as deputy editor in chief was not well received, as the new appointment sidelined four senior producers in the channel who could have been promoted to such a position, not to speak of the fact that they are either insiders or pioneers. As a result, we were told, a couple of staff who were affected in one way or another by such an appointment or who would be working closely with the newly appointed deputy chief editor considered such a move as desperate as working for the faltering American-backed channel Al Hurra — which from a not-so-uncommon Middle Eastern or Arab perspective amounts to selling out one's soul precisely as the vision, politics, agenda and even audience of Al Hurra stand in counterdistinction to those of Al Jazeera, among other Arab broadcasters.

However, another staff member we interviewed gave little thought to the whole matter, pointing out that the case of the news editor in chief is *déjà vu*. Under the directorship of Al Ali, three Arabs filled that position. Naturally, for a network that specializes in news broadcasting, the position of news editor in chief is an important and sensitive one. When launched in 1996, Al Jazeera appointed the Jordanian Sami Haddad as its news editor in chief. Haddad is a former presenter, broadcaster and current affairs editor with BBC Arabic Radio at the BBC and a BBC Arabic Television veteran. In Doha, he served as editor in chief for a year or so before relocating to Al Jazeera's London office to host a current affairs program called *More Than One Opinion* where political and social issues are openly debated by experts and officials with questions phoned in or faxed by viewers. Before leaving, Doha Haddad recommended Salah Nejm to succeed him in the position of news editor in chief. For some of the network staff we interviewed, such a recommendation was far from being objective. In terms of qualifications or experience, we were told, there were more qualified candidates within the existing Al Jazeera staff. One particular interviewee who worked with Al Jazeera during its early years recounts how, during his tenure, the news editor in chief at that time hired a number of newsroom staff from the Levant region (mainly producers and news editors) who were perceived to have an affinity with his own inclinations. In order to ensure the continuation of his editorial inclinations in Al Jazeera, he recommended an editor in chief who could be easily swayed. According to this same staff member, "the succeeding news editor in chief was by no means an outstanding candidate for the position as there were many network staff in the newsroom who were more seasoned. The managing director favored him and promoted him to the position of news editor in chief because of considerations of loyalty. It was desirable after all to have someone who would be willing to toe the line. Later on, the newly appointed news editor himself started to promote other staff members who were not necessarily the best and most deserving."

Even if these shortcomings are overlooked, there are other problems which plague Al Jazeera. At least up to the invasion of Iraq, Al Ali was proven to be the right person for building, developing and leading Al Jazeera. Interestingly enough, Al Ali has not only instilled an organizational culture which has proven to have an enduring impact, but has also left behind him certain subcultures. Clearly, there are discernable subcultures within the network which can be schematically articulated in the following dichotomies: upper management versus staff, staff who appear on screen versus staff who work behind the scene, staff versus line, young staff who are technology-oriented versus older staff who are technology-averse, Aljazeera.net versus Al Jazeera channel, Aljazeera.net in Arabic versus Aljazeera.net in English. However, none of these subcultures is creating a friction that is more pointed and more felt within Al Jazeera than that ensuing from the rift between the culture of news and programs and between BBC veterans or pioneers and those who joined the network later.

It is evident that the culture of news is different from the culture of programs. The former revolves around "foot soldiers" while the latter revolves around "stars." Likewise, the identity, standards and expectations are different. While news is more on the professional side, with an emphasis on professionalism, programs are more fluid. Program-wise, Al Jazeera is embroiled in what one member of the staff described as "a run-away," with little kingdoms erected here and there. Having gotten a royal treatment from the beginning and then having expanded their privileges, the stars of Al Jazeera are on a pedestal, a situation which is breeding considerable resentment. At the same time, the flagship programs are a sensitive issue as they have contributed a great deal to the reputation of Al Jazeera. This left the network with two poles: the general manager who controls most of the operations in the network, and the programs which are centered around influential figures who are riding high on the path of stardom and who allegedly have political connections. In a published interview, Yousri Fouda, host of the investigative program *Top Secret*, admitted that "some of the flagship programs of Al Jazeera still seem to be acting out a stance of condescending maturity.... I am a little concerned about Al Jazeera and I am worried that they are stuck. It is partly linked to the flexibility of Al Jazeera, in which the live interview shows are on their own, not reporting back to a higher level of editorial management."[12] However, since Al Jazeera inaugurated its change agenda at the beginning of summer of

2005, the presence of some stars on screen is becoming less felt and at least two prominent programs have been occasionally hosted by newer figures and the time period for leading talk show programs has been reduced from 90 minutes to an hour, giving room to newer and shorter programs to be launched and the opportunity for less prominent journalists to host programs. According to Al Jazeera, the move was aimed at breaking the rigid distinction and the barriers between the news and programs by fostering a more fluid relationship and a sense of continuity between the two in the mind of the viewers. Still, the culture of stardom is deeply entrenched in Al Jazeera and may be difficult to undo or change.

Reinforcing the above dichotomy is yet another distinction between the so-called pioneers and the newcomers. The former group draws its legitimacy from being with the network from the start. It is made up, in great part, of BBC veterans who were hired by Al Jazeera when the BBC Arabic service fell out with its Saudi partner over editorial independence. Overall, the core group of journalists which moved to Doha is perceived as having contributed immensely to Al Jazeera — in fact, of having been the motor of Al Jazeera's success. In many ways, such a narrative has been internalized, so much so that nearly a decade after its launching, some of the BBCers that were interviewed still draw on this factor as a legacy of Al Jazeera's success. For its part, Al Jazeera's keenness on retaining this core group of journalists is matched by the latter's own keenness to remain part of Al Jazeera. For the viewers, such a pool of pioneers who come from the BBC means high standards and professional journalism, while for the network itself it means the existence of a tradition of meritocracy whereby only talented staff make it to the network. Naturally, seniority in the network gives this group recognition and even influence and sets it apart from staff who were hired at later stages, particularly after Al Jazeera established itself. There is clearly a degree of unease between the two strains. The old staff see in the new staff a potential threat to their eminence, legitimacy and interests, while the new staff feel that the pioneers' culture, which is largely predicated on a BBC complex as one staff member described it, is a hindrance to the emergence of new figures and the realization of the potential many of the new staff have. Admittedly, upper management is aware of this rift or gap between these two sub-cultures within the organization, the risk of having protected small kingdoms within the network, and the need to bring in fresh blood — although not much is currently being done to attenuate its effects.

160

From a business perspective, the most insistent problem remains that of the organization's ability to evolve and grow. Asked about the challenges which face Al Jazeera, Waddah Khanfar outlines four areas that need attention: maintaining its leadership position, safeguarding the margin of freedom Al Jazeera has benefited from since its inception, transmitting Al Jazeera's vision to the Arab world, and daring to come up with a new form and a new vision without being afraid of renewal and innovation because the biggest danger for any organization is to fall prey to itself and to be subject to internal confinements.[13] The latter point is particularly important. For one thing, no serious organizational study or institutional research has been conducted to help the network evolve. Overall, there is a notable dearth of in-house research and, in fact, no genuine interest in outsourcing research. A media researcher with Pan Arab Research Center (PARC), a Dubai-based independent media research center affiliated with Gallup International which conducts studies for major media companies in the region, noted that Al Jazeera was a former client but has not commissioned any study with them for quite some time. Although PARC drafted many proposals for Al Jazeera's consideration, none of these came through. When following up on these proposals, PARC came to know that Al Jazeera made a strategic decision to invest in research and development and to produce in-house studies. But such an initiative has limited implications. Although the network has set up an international media relations office with a center for studies and polling, its very understanding and perception of research remain limited at best. Furthermore, Al Jazeera hardly has the infrastructure, knowledge, tradition and credibility necessary to carry out institutional research at a time when its very journalistic instincts and media practices are perceived as controversial.

If anything, these instances point to the limits and strategic vulnerability of Al Jazeera. It is true that Al Jazeera is currently ahead of its competitors in the region and has a competitive edge, but it may quickly lose that edge if it becomes complacent and falls into the winner's curse whereby one stops innovating and starts enjoying its success. A channel like Al Jazeera which operates in an environment that lacks the sources of innovation and renewal faces a serious strategic threat of regressing and eventually losing its competitive edge. Al Jazeera does not seem to invest and develop sources of innovation and knowledge generation through acquisition of knowledge and strategic alliances with sources of innovation and through instituting creativity within the organization through the fusion of media talent of different perspectives, qualifications, and backgrounds. Establishing and sponsoring serious media research projects and consortia that would perform basic and applied research that would eventually result in a reliable and continuous flow of new ideas, themes and programs are essential initiatives for Al Jazeera to maintain its edge and to widen the gap with its closest competitors. At present, these sources of innovation for Al Jazeera appear to be non-existent not only in Qatar but virtually in the whole region — one that suffers from a flagrant lack of media research centers, top notch academic media programs, and political, cultural and financial support for artistic creativity as well as talent recognition, fostering and promotion.

XII.

Innovation and Expansion

In tandem with the attempt to institutionalize and restructure itself, Al Jazeera has also been expanding its media services both regionally and internationally. In fact, Al Jazeera has embarked on a massive expansion aimed at the consolidation of existing strengths and application of acquired competencies in ways which allow it to rebrand and reposition itself as a global network rather than simply a pan–Arab channel. In a reflective statement on Al Jazeera's strategic goals, the managing director, Waddah Khanfar, provides a glimpse on how Al Jazeera sees itself and how it is positioning itself in a congested global media environment: "We are expanding globally because for us the competition is not Al Arabiya. They may have been set up to compete with us, but for the competition (and I say this in the collegial spirit of friendship and cooperation) it is BBC World Service and CNN International because we see ourselves as a global broadcaster on the merits of our coverage and the fullness of our vision."[1] The goal of Al Jazeera is to transform itself from a news channel for Arab viewers to a full-fledged network able to compete internationally with leading global media organizations to vie for a global audience. In order to formalize its expansion from a channel to a network, Al Jazeera appointed Waddah Khanfar as the director general of the network in addition to the position he has been holding since 2003 as a managing director of Al Jazeera Satellite Channel. Al Jazeera announced that the creation of the new position of director general for the entire network was "a step to promote the institutional structure of the Network and improve integration."[2]

Al Jazeera's acquired strengths provide a powerful basis for its expansion to a full-fledged network. Using the knowledge and know-how it has accumulated, the network can create other channels in a cost-effective way, benefiting from the infrastructure it has in place and capitalizing on its brand name. Likewise, Al Jazeera's ability to repurpose may be fundamental to its strategic success. In fact, in its few years of existence, Al Jazeera has proven itself capable of creating new products and remarketing old ones. Al Jazeera's ability to expand is evidenced not only in its new programs and products, but also its new concepts. In 2001, Al Jazeera launched an Arabic website, in 2003 added an English-language website and in 2004 it started its mobile service — a fairly novel approach to news dissemination in the Middle East, utilizing GSM technology to transmit news and information via SMS and WAP with the intention further down the line to have its services include both text and multimedia messaging service (MMS).

Al Jazeera has also invested in a variety of specialized channels. In 2003, it launched Al Jazeera Sports Channel. Two years later, it launched two new round-the-clock sports channels, Al Jazeera Sports Plus 1 and Al Jazeera Sports Plus 2, which offer live coverage of prime world-renowned tournaments such as the Spanish football league. The latter two channels are different from the former one insofar as they are encrypted — a move that is more motivated by the need to meet international legal and technical requirements than by the desire to generate revenue. In fact, the decision to charge a nominal annual subscription fee for these two sports channels was impelled by the tendency of Al Jazeera's free signals to Arab viewers on Nilesat and Arabsat to spill over to some Western countries and to encroach on the ability of some Western channel providers to generate revenue on live coverage of these sports events.

In the same year, Al Jazeera launched yet another first in Arab broadcasting — Al Jazeera Live, a specialized media service similar to C-Span in the USA, airing live — with neither anchor people nor editing process — conferences, meetings, discussions and other significant gatherings covering political, social, cultural, and economic issues and events of relevance. For Al Jazeera's Gassan bin Jeddou, the new service will "bring out everything that ... takes place behind closed doors to the masses. The news channel cannot convey everything and focus on the live broadcasts of official news conferences which carry some political stance. However, we violated this rule when we carried the recent Lebanese demonstrations [in the aftermath of the assassination of Prime Minister Rafiq Al Hariri]. This drew our attention to the fact that we need to make use of the materials we can acquire through live broadcasts."[3]

In 2005, Al Jazeera launched a new children's channel in conjunction with Qatar Foundation for Education, Science and Community Development, which is headed by the Emir's wife, Sheikha Moza Bint Nasser Al Misned. Not unlike MBC 3, the Saudi Arabic-language cartoon channel which belongs to the same group which owns Al Jazeera's competitor Al Arabiya, the new channel — which is expected to produce 40 percent of its programs — combines "edutainment" with respect for traditional values and teaching tolerance. According to an AFP communiqué, "the goal of Al Jazeera's youth channel is to teach modern values such as open-mindedness and tolerance to Arab children age three to 15 and their families."[4] Likewise, the network opened a documentary channel and has concrete plans to start a business channel which capitalizes on Al Jazeera's news channel and cater to a largely untapped market niche in satellite broadcasting. During its Second International Forum, which was held in 2006, Al Jazeera signed a cooperation agreement with Telesur, the Latin American television which was launched by Argentina, Bolivia, Cuba and Venezuela, for cooperation in training and the exchange of footage and logistics. Previously, Al Jazeera signed an agreement with Indian TV for sharing content.[5] It also announced, on the same occasion, a new service in Urdu through simultaneous translation, in advance of plans to offer similar services in French, Spanish and Turkish. Aljazeera.net is also expanding its services to provide multi-language editions of its site, namely in French, Spanish, Urdu and Turkish.[6] Likewise, Al Jazeera is setting up kiosks in front of its offices worldwide to record comments, which will subsequently be edited and broadcast. There is even talk about an Al Jazeera magazine. Word also has it that Al Jazeera is forming a partnership with a British travel firm to sell hotel accommodation and other tourist services to its audience in the Middle East.[7] A year after it launched its international television production festival, Al Jazeera announced in 2006 its decision to bequeath $1.4 million to sponsor a major new initiative to fund independent television and film production to encourage talented young producers. Finally, on the occasion of its tenth anniversary, Al Jazeera announced plans to launch a daily newspaper.[8]

Although Al Jazeera is spreading its wings and developing new media projects and initiatives, these may not necessarily be viable projects which can bring additional income. As one former staff member put it, so far the network has not developed sources of income to develop itself. With few exceptions, Al Jazeera's new projects raise a number of questions. For example, financially speaking, a documentary channel will require immense funding with no guarantee of returns. Likewise, Al Jazeera Live, the new specialized media service that airs live conferences, meetings, discussion and other high-profile events may not live up to its promise given the quality and frequency of the material to be covered in the Arab world.

But these are not the only projects Al Jazeera has in line. More globally significant is probably the much-publicized Al Jazeera International, an English-language news service the network launched in 2006. This is the first Arab media outlet to transmit news in English twenty-four hours a day for what is perceived as "a ready audience," some of which is located in North America and Britain, but the bulk of which lies in Asia, which has a sizable Muslim population and is teeming with English-speaking viewers.[9] However, the fact that the channel is well positioned to gain quick popularity in such countries as Pakistan, Indonesia and Malaysia does not make it a Muslim channel, nor is that something the network's management is after.[10] The idea of Al Jazeera International is not so much to be a mirror image of its Arabic-language sister where news, commentaries and current affairs programs are dubbed into English using live translations, but an English channel that is managed by a Western team, staffed with native English speakers for the on-air jobs, caters to an international market and has its own specificity but which nonetheless operates in accordance with Al Jazeera's code of ethics and aspires to be professional in the full import of the term. Its purpose is to report global news and to provide a Middle Eastern perspective. Comprising initially some 300 staff members, Al Jazeera International has news centers in Doha, Kuala Lumpur, London, and Washington. The senior management team includes former executives from Hill and Knowlton, and the BBC such as managing director Nigel Parsons, a veteran British television journalist and producer who previously worked at the television arm of Associated Press. Al Jazeera International also appointed as its head of news Steve Clark, who was a former MBC manager and former executive producer at Sky News, and as head of programs Paul Gibbs, who oversaw programming for the BBC and Discovery Channel in Europe. It has also hired Sky News presenter David Foster, BBC reporter Rageh Omar, and CNN anchors Riz Khan and Veronica Pedrosa.

Such an expansion, as Hugh Miles points out, comes "at a time when the mainstream American television news channels are in the hands of an even smaller number of media companies [as] there are only five independently owned national television news outlets in America,"[11] and especially during a time when American news is increasingly homogenous. As it recasts itself for a global audience, Al Jazeera is in a position to capitalize on the perceived need for alternative media outlets during a historical juncture in Middle Eastern and world history. Financially, Al Jazeera International can prove to be a source of income for Al Jazeera provided the targeted audience is properly addressed.

Naturally, not everyone is optimistic about the prospects of success for Al Jazeera International. While some observers fear that if Al Jazeera were to broadcast in a language other than Arabic it would lose its edge, others who question the extent to which Al Jazeera can get across its message to the world in a non–Arab voice by non–Arabs find such an initiative anathema to the very identity of Al Jazeera. Still, others have doubts about Al Jazeera's ability to compete with giant Western media conglomerates with better resources and a longer tradition, particularly when it has always catered to a niche of Arab viewers. Some observers are also pessimistic about Al Jazeera's ability to secure nationwide distribution in North America, which can prove to be a hurdle in the United States — assuming that American viewers want another international news channel.[12] These considerations notwithstanding, for Parsons, who believes that "what will probably begin with 'curiosity viewers' is likely to snowball and help into opening new markets," the prospects for success are assuring.[13]

The expansion of Al Jazeera, as S. Abdallah Schleifer points out, intersects with and benefits from Qatar Foundation, the educational pet project of the Emir's wife, which hosts branch campuses of leading American universities. In fact, the studios of Al Jazeera's children's channel are hosted in Qatar Foundation's educational city and the channel is conceived from the outset as an autonomous Qatar Foundation initiative. Likewise, Qatar Foundation's Doha Debates, which are hosted by Tim Sebastian and aired on the BBC, are an obvious resource to Al Jazeera International as news material (since they are conducted in English) and to Al Jazeera Live as debates to be broadcast live in their entirety.[14] Internally, Al Jazeera has also set in place a lecture series where a speaker is invited every month while capitalizing on existing events and conferences in Doha to make use of and engage guests.

From an operational standpoint, the new and envisaged channels Al Jazeera is launching are cheaper to set up and run than the original Arabic-language channel as they will benefit from an existing infrastructure, a network of bureaus in place and a repository of know-how. From a business perspective, such an expansion could also have positive implications. A network the identity of which no longer has strict political overtones and especially one which has a wide reach could attract advertising money which in turn could enhance its independence. As Waddah Khanfar put it, "once we have a network ... we should be able to offer alternatives to the advertising community which until now has largely looked the other way for political reasons, despite our overwhelming superiority in demographics. At the same time, we are thinking of this programming as income generating.... We expect we will be recognized as such by advertising agencies, because this niche is beyond regional politics and their unfortunate effects."[15]

Some of the envisaged changes also include putting Al Jazeera on the stock market. In fact, Qatar is considering privatizing the network and issuing an IPO. An Emiri decree stipulated that Al Jazeera would be converted to "a privately owned 'company of participation' ... [which] would most likely be owned by shareholders in the Arab world"[16]—i.e., a domestic and Gulf Cooperation Council IPO rather than an international one. To that end, Al Jazeera commissioned a feasibility study for privatizing the network and possibly floating its shares on the Doha stock exchange so long as this does not interfere with its editorial independence. There is even a perception that the recent changes in Al Jazeera's board of directors have been undertaken with the intention of facilitating the conversion of the network into a private shareholding company. It is also alleged that Qatar's initiative to privatize the network is partly motivated by the desire to turn Al Jazeera into a media institution that meets international standards of professionalism and partly by the desire to spare Qatar external pressure to rein in Al Jazeera. The Bush administration in particular has repeatedly criticized Al Jazeera's "biased" coverage of foreign policy and military actions in the Middle East and has specifically asked Qatar's foreign minister, Sheikh Hamad bin Jassim, "to take steps to professionalize the station, and to adapt and adopt practices that other responsible news organizations do," and Qatar has indeed pledged to get Al Jazeera to review its coverage.[17] It is believed that the measure to privatize Al Jazeera and to possibly float its shares on the local stock market will not only relieve the government of Qatar from public affairs problems, but also bring in more diversity and reassert the need for the network to be financially viable.

However, some of Al Jazeera's staff fear the changes in financing may lead to a loss of editorial freedom and may eventually muzzle the network. Likewise, there is a sense that such a move may relieve Al Jazeera from political pressure only to lead it to succumb to commercial pressure emanating from the expectations of its prospective shareholders or investors who, in general, tend to be antagonistic to what the organization does. As Steven Weisman points out, "with such a big audience but a lack of profitability, it is not clear who might be in the pool of potential buyers or how a new owner might change the editorial content."[18] There is fear that the mainstream commercial success Al Jazeera aspires to may be achieved at the expense of the unique character which has put this Qatari network at the forefront of pan–Arab satellite broadcasting.[19] Regardless of the outcome, changing the ownership paradigm of Al Jazeera is likely to have effects on its organizational structure, processes and culture.

For Corey Pein, the impending privatization of the network does not necessarily guarantee its solvency:

> Al Jazeera has long planned to go public, thinking financial independence would further boost its status in the eyes of the wider world. Channel executives are optimistic about prospects for survival without tens of millions of dollars in annual subsidies, and estimate the size of the Arab advertising market at $500 million. On the other hand, a Congressional Research Service report from July 2004 advised that the U.S. government could kill Al Jazeera by pushing for its privatization; the report's author ... puts the ad market at no more than $180 million — not enough to support a private news channel. And the Saudis already encourage advertisers to boycott the Qatar-based muckrakers; presumably, they would redouble their efforts if they thought they could finally finish off a newly privatized and financially vulnerable Al Jazeera.[20]

Hugh Miles concurs; in his view, so long as the Saudis maintain the embargo on advertising, Al Jazeera is not commercially attractive.[21] One would assume that Saudi Arabia may have drawn the lesson from the past and may be inclined to change its strategy toward Al Jazeera, going by the old adage "if you can't beat them, join them." In this respect, the United States is not the only party which may benefit from the privatization of Al Jazeera; no less anxious about such plans for privatizing the network, Rupert Cornwell explains, is neighboring Saudi Arabia, which has always considered Al Jazeera a thorn in its side: "Assuming privatization goes ahead, the station is likely to be listed on Qatar's stock market, where most of its shares would be available only to citizens of member countries of the Gulf Cooperation Council (GCC). This would allow Saudi Arabia, the richest GCC member and prime source of media funding across the region, to gain a major stake in Al Jazeera."[22] So far, the network's executives are banking on Al Jazeera International to yield enough profit to keep them in business.[23]

XIII.

The Road Ahead

The findings of this research suggest that Al Jazeera's "success" cannot be credited to objective factors and certainly cannot be attributed to its organizational model. In fact, Al Jazeera is far from being an organization in the full business import of the term. If anything, Al Jazeera has many of the symptoms that plague Arab organizations. Even a cursory look at such objective factors as vision, strategy, leadership, empowerment, reward system and knowledge management suggests that Al Jazeera does not live up to the image it has acquired over the years of being at the forefront of Arab news media. Although these organizational problems may not be threatening or detrimental to the survival of Al Jazeera, they are nonetheless risk factors which cannot be overlooked if the network is to maintain its privileged status in an already congested Arab mediascape.

A convenient starting point is Al Jazeera's success factors. It is obvious that Al Jazeera could not have been where it is now were it not for the margin of freedom it has been enjoying all along. However, as much as the margin of freedom represents an impetus for Al Jazeera to be at the forefront of Arab broadcasting, and as much as the freedom of the press remains anathema to the Arab world, it is not a sustainable competitive edge in the mid or long term. For one thing, the gap between Al Jazeera and other regional media outlets in this area is starting to narrow down gradually. In fact, a minimum threshold of freedom of speech is becoming a *sine qua non* for the success of any news media outlet in the region. As Olfa Lamloum observes, "the creation of Al Arabiya shows that, even for a channel that is under the thumb of the Saudis, in terms of satellite news, there is a pre–and a post–Al Jazeera era. It is no longer possible to engage in credible broadcasting without rejecting taboos, crossing certain red lines, and adopting a multiple perspective even if the field of such diversity or pluralism remains selective."[1] Not only have the norms and standards of the industry changed but also the expectations of the Arab viewer have changed as well. Even state media have come to realize that the kind of mind-numbing news, reports and programs which used to pass off as journalism not long ago are becoming an insult to the intelligence of the Arab viewer.

Adding to changes in the mindset of the viewer and the developments in the industry itself is the increasingly pressing demand for reform in the Middle East. In the aftermath of the September 11 attacks, the Arab world has been subjected to a political change agenda in order to bring the region up to speed with the rest of the "free" world. Increasingly, espousing political reform in what the Bush administration refers to as "the greater Middle East" is becoming more of an imperative than a choice — although whether change should come from within or be imposed from the outside remains a matter of debate, if not a bone of contention. The impact of such changes will be undoubtedly reflected in the media sector. The push for democratization in the Middle East is likely to force the emergence of competing media organizations with a sizable margin of freedom. These changes are not without effect for a channel like Al Jazeera. While the margin of freedom is likely to be increasing everywhere else, it is more likely to stagnate in the case of Al Jazeera, if not recede, having already a high ceiling. One would assume, for instance, that Al Jazeera may be cautious and even reluctant in the future to take risks of the kind involved in the case of Tayseer Allouni, its star reporter during the war in Afghanistan who was accused of having ties to Al Qaeda network, if it does not want to be implicated in the wrongdoings of international politics. One would also think that the freedom to come close to issues that are alien to the U.S. agenda in the region can no longer be taken for granted. Already, Al Jazeera is more tame than it used to be.

Although Al Jazeera is toning down the Fox News-type of populist appeal that has often stigmatized it during the coverage of certain crises, it still comes off as the channel of Arab discontent, giving an outlet to people's anger and frustration about a Middle East that is going through troubled times. In a way, Al Jazeera went for the obvious — the less than comforting state of affairs in the Arab world. To the extent that Arabs were for a long time deprived of freedom of expression, publicly discussing Arab politics is an achievement in and of itself. By making the unthinkable possible, Al Jazeera has also opened the door for new channels in the region. However, for any channel to distinguish itself in the future, including Al Jazeera, it has to go beyond mere talk. So far, Al Jazeera does not seem to be providing much beyond engaging in what Fatema Mernissi calls "the art of polemics,"[2] which used to strike a chord with its viewers in the past but is unlikely to do so in the future.

To what extent the role of media is to go the extra mile is also subject to debate. What can be asserted, though, is that reality is such that viewers are already being saturated with *déjà vu* Arab politics and will end up expecting more or will tune out of news channels altogether. This may pose a real challenge for Al Jazeera in more than one way. Internally, the network does not seem to have the intellectual capital to develop itself and aspire to a more involved or higher-end role. Although well trained, most of Al Jazeera's on-screen journalists do not come off as either particularly deep or notably intellectual. Even the leading figures in the network come off more as ideologically inclined than intellectually stimulating. The network may take particular pride in its initial pool of BBCers, but Al Jazeera is no BBC. Suffice it here to note the prestige that comes from being affiliated with the BBC, partly because the channel is in a way an institution that has benefited tremendously from the country's elite (and with it the connection to the upper stratum of British life) and absorbed their talent. Particularly as the British empire came to be dissolved, a venue like the BBC became an alternative career choice for young graduates who would otherwise have joined the foreign or colonial services and a natural choice for creative talent from Commonwealth countries.[3] Not so with Al Jazeera which, incidentally, is more populist than elitist. If the network is to go beyond the reputation it has acquired for ruffling feathers and to envisage a role for itself that is less controversial and more constructive, it has to seek wider institutional support. It has to fall back on a wider system of creativity, including scholars, specialists and freelancers, and to capitalize on centers for research and studies which can tackle issues in systematic and profound ways, provide in-depth analysis and even offer possible solutions. Sadly, such research and studies centers are either missing in the Arab world or when they exist are likely to be controlled by government agendas.

So far, Al Jazeera has lacked a system that weaves innovation into what it does best, and even if there are sources of innovation, they are not tapped into. Ironically, some of the units Al Jazeera has created with the change it has embarked on to address some of these lacunae, such as the research and studies unit, smack more of public relations endeavors than of a supporting creative system. When we interviewed staff in the said unit, hardly anybody suggested that the main mission of the Center should be to weave innovation and creativity into the network's offerings. Rather it was perceived as an instrument for Al Jazeera to transfer its professional standards to others — which in many ways is based on assumption that the network has reached a level of maturity which makes it a standard in the profession. Ironically, where Al Jazeera has partially succeeded in fostering creativity, namely within Aljazeera.net, its news web portal, the rampant feeling among those involved with the portal unit is of great marginalization and little consideration of their efforts by Al Jazeera Channel. Yet again, Al Jazeera not only lacks institutions of creativity to support its endeavors but is also unable to connect with its surrounding creative system whenever it exists. When the authors offered to connect Al Jazeera with their university environment as a means of tapping into the intellectual resources of the region, the response was that the network was eager to hold training for media students on the university premises, for a fee of course.

Even if the implications of an increased margin of freedom in Arab media and the prospects for further capitalizing on such a margin of freedom to provide quality programs is provisionally overlooked, Al Jazeera remains plagued by a number of problems. To start with, its relationship to its patron/sponsor is as much a liability as it is an asset. Al Jazeera was made by an Emiri decree and could be effaced in the same manner — although this is a remote scenario. Assuming Al Jazeera continues to be a vibrant media force in the region, its covert political dimension makes it somewhat fragile. Adding to the complexity of the situation is Al Jazeera's continued inability to be self-supportive. Over a decade after its launching, Al Jazeera still relies on government funding, which eventually may affect its proclaimed independent status. Being the pet project of the Emir and governed by a board that is headed by a member of the ruling family renders decision-making and agenda-setting (in the political import of the term) at the highest level less objective and less transparent than they would otherwise be. Clearly, Al Jazeera cannot be conceived outside of or independently from the set of political constellations which engulf it. In the past, this has put severe strains on it and tainted its credibility as the foreign policy of the Qatari government seems at odds with the network's proclaimed mass appeal. One can surmise that the situation will become worse with a possible normalization of relations between Qatar and Israel, something that will be hard for the network to ignore if it wants to keep an acceptable credibility level with the Arab masses.

At the level of the organization itself, there are several problem areas which Al Jazeera will eventually have to address if it is to maintain its competitive edge. To start with, there is less enthusiasm inside the network than before; people do not feel as much empowered as they used to; the level of commitment to the mission of Al Jazeera is not as strong as it was in the first few years of the network's history. For many network staff, Al Jazeera is not as inspiring as it used to be; it is no longer the same passionate organization which ignites the fire of employee commitment, to borrow James Lucas's words,[4] which is tantamount to saying that the feeling of "belonging" and "commitment" are increasingly less pointed. In terms of reward, although the level of dedication and commitment within Al Jazeera is fairly high, there are signs that the kind of intrinsic reward which has been a source of motivation for many network staff is not as strong as it used to be. Likewise, while not precluded, advancement and internal promotion, particularly to visible positions, is not systematic. Although currently not insistent, the problem of meritocracy or equitable opportunity is somewhat critical. The combination of untapped talent within the organization, favoritism and clan mentality, which are gradually developing and are reinforced by certain hiring practices, may be detrimental to the organization if not properly addressed. Furthermore, and because Al Jazeera has come to be a brand name for Qataris, Qatarization or nationalization may seep in the organization in a burdensome way as more locals aspire to join the network. Adding to this is the lack of transparency and objectivity that marks some human resources practices and which is undermining loyalty in a regional environment where competition for talent is becoming increasingly fierce. When considering that knowledge is not appropriately and sufficiently harnessed within Al Jazeera, the loss of talent, while currently not alarming, may prove to be problematic in the future, particularly because, state media aside, the Arab world has not developed a strong media tradition.

With the changes Al Jazeera has been undergoing in the post–Al Ali era, there is a perception common among many network staff that the culture of Al Jazeera is deteriorating, so to speak. What is more lamentable according to some of the staff members we talked to is that certain practices and trends which have benefited Al Jazeera considerably are being effaced. In recent years and with the change of agenda, Al Jazeera seems to be undoing the organic culture which the organization has known all along without providing a viable alternative. Even some of the changes Al Jazeera has embraced are perceived as deceptive in many respects. Whether it is setting up an editorial board, starting a research and studies unit or drafting a code of ethics, Al Jazeera seems to be instituting little more than formal processes. In other words, the process of institutionalization Al Jazeera has embarked on has been reduced to "formalization." Even so, such formalization remains anathema to the culture of Al Jazeera.

As Al Jazeera expands to be a group of media corporations and units rather than just a news network, its growth is likely to lead it to develop a more conservative instinct in line with the overall interests and inclinations of the group. In addition, the management structure itself will change and affect the Arabic-language news channel upon which Al Jazeera's reputation has been built. The Arabic-language news channel may end up being merely a cog in a network made out of numerous divisions. Since this is the case, Al Jazeera is likely to turn into an impersonal organization with impersonal relations, which may lead in turn to a change of culture that can undermine what the network does best. The other noteworthy risk is probably privatization. If and when Al Jazeera goes public, the imperatives of profit will naturally be on the table, which may force the network to change. Finally, there is some degree of unease in the network because of a felt discrepancy between what Al Jazeera aspires to do and hopes to achieve, on the one hand, and what it can do given the way it currently operates, on the other hand. The zeal, ambition and aspiration of the network are not in synch with its modest organizational abilities and its management style. As one staff member put it, Al Jazeera's ability to plan and its desire to expand are ahead of and in fact hindered by its ability to execute and deliver.

Having said that, one should not fall into the trap of depicting Al Jazeera as a failing venture. To the contrary, no matter how it evolves in the future, Al Jazeera will go down in history as a turning point in the history of the Arab people, not only as a free medium of expression but first and foremost as an enterprise for rebuilding the self-confidence and dignity of the humiliated Arab masses. It has been speaking forcefully on their behalf, bypassing the perceived apathy of the Arab leaders and opening a channel to those who reflected popular feelings to talk directly to "the other." Despite its populist outlook, it has probably participated in the dialogue of civilizations more than any other forum. Viewers are growing tolerant to listening to "the other" and to issues that they would have rejected outright in the not so distant past. Al Jazeera might have even used its acquired credibility with the people to push for a dialogue that many were not ready to engage in.

A few years back, MBC, then running as a single channel, hailed it as a scoop to air a recorded interview with then President Bill Clinton. Nowadays, highly placed politicians and other noteworthy people are vying for airtime on Al Jazeera, and as a result on the other Arabic-speaking networks. Only bin Laden can afford the luxury of surging on the air any time he wishes to speak out. Maybe that is why Al Jazeera is often referred to by its detractors as bin Laden TV....

Chapter Notes

Preface

1. Edgar H. Schein, *Organizational Culture and Leadership,* 2nd edition (San Francisco: Jossey-Bass, 1992), p. 196.

2. Schein, *Organizational Culture and Leadership,* pp. 11–12.

3. For Schein, culture is not a single belief or assumption, but a set of interrelated, though not necessarily consistent, beliefs and assumptions. An organization's core assumptions find their way into many aspects of the organization. Schein (*Organizational Culture and Leadership,* p. 12) identifies two categories — internal integration and external adaptation. Internal integration would seek to develop consensus on the common language to be used in the organization; the group boundary definition, sense of identification amongst the members and criteria for inclusion; the criteria for allocating status, power and authority; and the criteria for allocating reward and punishment. Conversely, an analysis of external adaptation would focus more on the sense of mission, shared purpose, goal and strategy which can create a sense of responsibility and lead to organizational commitment and loyalty. To put this more plainly, a study of an organization's external integration pays attention to the internal dynamics of the network and emphasizes the element of consistency among its members, particularly in the assumptions they hold; it probes the organization's life which its members take for granted as a result of socialization and everyday experience in the organization (i.e., what makes culture cohesive). An analysis of an organization's external adaptation focuses more on the network's mission and its relation to its external environment (i.e., what happens outside). Naturally, the culture of an organization can be a source of power but it can also be a negative influence, particularly when it constrains strategic activity and places limits on organizations. The culture of an organization tends to be a potential constraint on strategy insofar as an organization's strategic processes can extend, at least theoretically, only as far as the culture permits.

4. For example, while insightful, Schein's early formulations are integrative insofar as the organizational culture is described as being shared by all members of the culture in an organization-wide consensus. In his later work, though, Schein stresses the need to take heed of the asymmetry of the culture of an organization.

5. Edgar H. Schein, "Sense and nonsense about culture and climate," in *Handbook of Organizational Culture and Climate,* ed. Neal M. Ashkanasy, Celeste P.M. Wilderom and Mark F. Peterson (London: Sage Publications, 2000), p. xxv.

6. Organizational culture researchers distinguish subcultures on the basis of occupation, hierarchy level and previous organizational affiliations, among other criteria. For more on subcultures within organizations, see Mary Jo Hatch, *Organizational Theory: Modern, Symbolic and Postmodern Perspectives* (Oxford: Oxford University Press, 1997), pp. 225–30.

7. Mats Alvesson, "The Culture perspective on organizations: Instrumental values and basic features of cultures," *Scandinavian Journal of Management* 5, no. 2 (1989): pp. 132–35.

8. Alvesson, "The Culture perspective on organizations," pp. 134–35.

9. Alvesson, "The Culture perspective on organizations," pp. 131–32.

10. Schein, "Sense and non-sense about culture and climate," p. xxvi.

11. Schein, "Sense and non-sense about culture and climate," p. xxvi.

12. Hugh Miles, *Al Jazeera: The Inside Story of the Arab News Channel that is Challenging the West* (New York: Grove Press, 2005), p. 5.

13. Corey Pein, "Is Al Jazeera ready for prime time?" *Salon.com*, 20 April 2005, <http://www.salon.com/news/feature/2005/04/22/aljazeera/print.html>.

14. Lorne Manly, "Translation: Is the whole world watching?" *New York Times*, 26 March 2006.

15. Miles, *Al Jazeera*, p. 11.

16. "How the BBC is Run." <http://www.bbc.co.uk/info/running/>.

Introduction

1. Philip Fiske de Gouveia, *An African Al Jazeera? Mass Media and the African Renaissance* (London: The Foreign Policy Center, 2005), p. 14.

2. Howard Tumber and Jerry Palmer, *Media at War: The Iraq Crisis* (London: Sage Publications, 2004), pp. 69–73; Robert Fisk, "America increasing pressure on Al Jazeera TV," *The Independent*, 30 July 2003.

3. David Hirst, "Qatar calling: Al Jazeera, the Arab TV channel that dares to shock," *Le Monde Diplomatique*, 8 August 2001.

4. Fayad E. Kazan, *Mass Media, Modernity and Development: Arab States of the Gulf* (Westport, CT: Praeger, 1993), pp. 91–93.

5. See Marc Lynch, *Voices of the New Arab Public: Iraq, Al Jazeera, and Middle East Politics Today* (New York: Columbia University Press, 2006), pp. 37–40.

6. Marwan Kraidy, "Transnational television and asymmetrical interdependence in the Arab world: The growing influence of the Lebanese satellite broadcasters," *Transnational Broadcasting Studies*, no. 5 (Fall/Winter 2000), <www.tbsjournal.com/Archives/Fall00/Kraidy.htm>.

7. Naomi Sakr, *Satellite Realms: Transnational Television, Globalization and the Middle East* (London: IB Tauris Publishers, 2001), pp. 3–8.

8. Muhammad I. Ayish, "The changing face of Arab communication: media survival in the information age," in *Mass Media, Politics and Society in the Middle East*, ed. Kai Hafez (Cresskill: Hampton Press, 2001), pp. 111–36.

9. Kai Hafez, "Mass media in the Middle East: Patterns of political and societal change," in *Mass Media, Politics, and Society in the Middle East*, ed. Kai Hafez (Cresskill: Hampton Press, 2001), p. 7.

10. Hirst, "Qatar calling."

11. Mohamed Zayani, *Arab Satellite Channels and Politics in the Middle East* (Abu Dhabi: Emirates Center for Strategic Studies and Research, 2004), pp. 7–19.

12. Sakr, *Satellite Realms*, p. 39.

13. Douglas Boyd, "Saudi Arabia's international media strategy: Influence through multinational ownership," in *Mass Media, Politics, and Society in the Middle East*, ed. Hafez Kai (Cresskill: Hampton Press, 2001), pp. 56–57.

14. Gaëlle Le Pottier, "The emergence of a pan–Arab market in modern media industries," in *Transnational Connections and the Arab Gulf*, ed. Madawi Al-Rasheed (London: Routledge, 2005), pp. 111–27.

15. Stephen Schwartz, "Losing the hearts and minds of Arabs," <http://www.islamicpluralism.org/articles/2005a/losingtheheart.htm>. El Nawawy, Mohammed, "U.S. public diplomacy in the Arab world: the news credibility of Radio Sawa and Television Al Hurra in five countries," *Global Media and Communication* 2, no. 2 (2006): pp. 183–203.

16. Eric Pfanner, "In shift, BBC to start Arabic TV channel," *International Herald Tribune*, 26 October 2005, <http://www.iht.com/articles/2005/10/25/news/bbc.php>; "Bush House of Arabia: The BBC takes on Al Jazeera," *The Economist*, 29 October 2005.

Chapter I

1. "Middle East communications and internet via satellite," *Spotbeam Communications Ltd.* (October 2002), <http://www.mindbranch.com/page/catalog/product/2e6a73703f706172746e65723d31303326636f64653d523133312d303038.html>.

2. Hugh Miles, "What the world thinks of Al Jazeera," *Transnational Broadcasting Journal* 14 (Spring 2005), <http://www.tbsjournal.com/miles.html>.

3. Jon B. Alterman, "The challenge for Al Jazeera International," *Transnational Broadcasting Studies* 14 (Spring 2005), <http://www.tbsjournal.com/alterman.html>.

4. Quoted in Hugh Miles, *Al Jazeera: The Inside Story of the Arab News Channel that is Challenging the West* (New York: Grove Press, 2005), p. 405.

5. Greg Dyke, "Impact of global news channels on international relations," in *Arab Media in the Information Age* (Abu Dhabi: ECSSR, 2006), pp. 399–416.

6. Olivier Da Lage, "The politics of Al Jazeera or the diplomacy of Qatar," in *The Al Jazeera Phenomenon: Critical Perspectives on New Arab Media*, ed. Mohamed Zayani (London: Pluto Press, 2005), pp. 49–65.

7. Louay Y. Bahry, "The new Arab media phenomenon: Qatar's Al Jazeera," *Middle East Policy* 8, no. 2 (June 2001): pp. 89–90.

8. Samuel Abt, "For Al Jazeera, balanced coverage frequently leaves no side happy," *International Herald Tribune*, 16 February 2004.

9. Muhammad Ayish, "Arab television goes commercial: A case study of the Middle East Broadcasting Center," *Gazette* 59, no. 6, pp. 473–94.

10. "Middle East communications and internet via satellite."

11. See Gassan bin Jiddou's interview with Sheikh Hamad bin Khalifa Al Thani, *Open Dialogue*, 28 October 2006, <http://www.aljazeera.net/NR/exeres/0B720564-C6FC-4D71-A5FE-9615F63E388C>.

12. Bahry, "The new Arab media phenomenon," p. 89.

13. John F. Burns, "Arab TV gets a new slant: Newscasts without censorship," *New York Times*, 4 July 1999.

14. Marc Lynch, "Watching Al Jazeera," *The Wilson Quarterly* 24, no. 3 (Summer 2001): p. 36.

15. See Faisal Al Kasim, "Crossfire," *Harvard International Journal of Press/Politics* 4, no. 3 (1999): 93–97.

16. Hazem Saghieh, "Al Jazeera: The world through Arab eyes," *The Muslim News* 17 (June 2004), <http://www.muslimnews.co.uk/pda/news.php?article=7600>.

17. Olfa Lamloum, *Al-Jazira, miroir rebelle et ambigu du monde arabe* (Paris: La Découverte, 2004), p. 20.

18. James Drummond, "Qatari broadcaster emerges as key channel of communication," *Financial Times*, 9 October 2001, p. 4.

19. Mary Ann Weaver, "Revolution from the top down," *National Geographic* 203, no. 3 (2004): p 84.

20. The second and third Gulf Wars refers, respectively, to the war between the American-led allied forces and Iraq in the aftermath of the Iraqi invasion of Kuwait in 1991 and the American invasion of Iraq in 2003. The first Gulf War was that which took place between Iraq and Iran between 1980 and 1988.

21. Faisal Bodi, "Al Jazeera tells the truth about war," *Guardian*, 28 March 2003, <http://www.guardian.co.uk/print/0,3858,4635417,00.html>.

22. "BBC signs news exchange agreement with Al Jazeera," <http://www.bbc.co.uk/pressoffice/pressreleases/stories/2003/01_january/15/al-jazeera.shtml>.

23. According to Information & Technology Publishing <http://www.ITP.net>, these sites are: *Albawaba.com, Aljazeera.net, Arabia.com, Maktoob.com* and *Ahram.org.com*.

24. "Aljazeera.net breaks the 5 million daily visitor threshold," *Aljazeera.net*, 28 September 2005, <http://www.aljazeera.net/NR/exeres/4AA8D374-4367-446E-8317-0039F9FF73F2.htm>.

25. Lamloum, *Al-Jazira*, p. 12.

26. AFP dispatch, No. 271450, 27 April 2004.

27. Jeffery Tayler, "The Faisal factor," *The Atlantic Monthly* (November 2004).

28. Amir Taheri, "News is not the only things on the agenda: Is Al Jazeera an independent news organization?" *Sunday Telegraph*, 26 December 2004.

29. Waddah Khanfar, "Statement," World Electronic Media Forum in Geneva, 9–12 December 2003, <http://www.wemfmedia.org/documents/speech_khnafar.PDF>. See also Antony Lowesenstein, "Al Jazeera awakens the Arab world," 9 June 2004, <www.smh.com.au/articles.2004/06/09/1086749772562.html?oneclick+true#>; and Waddah Khanfar, "Why did you want to bomb me, Mr. Bush and Mr. Blair?," *The Guardian*, 1 December 2005, <http://www.guardian.co.uk/usa/story/0,12271,1654762,00.html>.

30. Khanfar, "Statement."

31. Robin Wright, "Al Jazeera puts reform into focus," *The Washington Post*, 8 May 2005, p. A1.

32. Wright, "Al Jazeera puts reform into focus," p. A1.

Chapter II

1. Waddah Khanfar, "Credibility of specialized news channels: Competing for viewers," lecture delivered at the tenth ECSSR Annual Conference on Arab Media in the Information Age, Abu Dhabi, 9 January 2005.

2. Ian Richardson, "The failed dream that led to Al Jazeera," <http://www.richardson-media.co.uk/al%20jazeera%20origis.html>.

3. Hugh Miles notes that "Al Jazeera has employees from various religions, including Jews." Miles, *Al Jazeera*, p. 354.

4. Alastair Campbell, "I was wrong about Al Jazeera," *The Guardian*, 15 September 2004.

5. Richardson, "The failed dream that led to Al Jazeera."

6. Mike Boyer, "Al Jazeera's brand name news," *Foreign Policy*, April 2005, <http://www.foreignpolicy.com/story/cms.php?story_id=2822&print=1>.

7. "Al Jazeera's Adnan Sharif: An interview with Chris Forrester," October 2003, <http://www.worldscreen.com/interviewsarchive.php?filename=1003sharif.txt>

8. "Arab satellite television and the problems of the nation," *Arabs and Satellite TV* (Beirut: Center for Arab Unity Studies, 2004), p. 165.

9. Miles, *Al Jazeera*, p. 356.

10. "Arab satellite television and the problems of the nation," p. 165.

11. "The world through their eyes," *Economist*, 26 July 2005. See also Mariah Blake, "From all sides: In the deadly cauldron of Iraq, even the Arab media are being pushed off the story," *Columbia Journalism Review* 43, no. 6 (March/April 2005): pp. 16–19, <http://www.cjr.org/issues/2005/2/onthejob-blake.asp>.

12. A Congressional Research Service report notes that "although the government in 1995 lifted formal censorship of the media, journalists tend to exercise a degree of self-censorship [and in fact] Al Jazeera devotes less airtime to coverage of Qatari affairs." See Jeremy M. Sharp, "Qatar: Background and U.S. relations," Congressional Research Service Report for Congress, 17 March 2004, <http://fpc.state.gov/documents/organization/33741.pdf>.

13. "Qatar," *The World Fact Book*, <www.cia.gov/cia/publications/factbook/geos/qa.html>.

14. "Qatar," *The World Fact Book*.

15. Mohammed El Oifi, "Influence without power: Al Jazeera and the Arab public sphere," in *The Al Jazeera Phenomenon: Critical Perspectives on New Arab Media*, ed. Mohamed Zayani (London: Pluto Press, 2005), pp. 66–79.

16. Olivier Da Lage, "The politics of Al Jazeera or the diplomacy of Doha," in *The Al Jazeera Phenomenon*, p. 52.

17. William A. Rugh, *The Arab Press: News Media and Political Process in the Arab World* (Syracuse: Syracuse University Press, 1979).

18. Da Lage, "The politics of Al Jazeera or the diplomacy of Doha," p. 55.

19. El Oifi, "Influence without power," p. 71.

20. See Avi Jorisch, *Beacon of Hatred: Inside Hizballah's Al Manar Television* (Washington, D.C.: Washington Institute for Near Eastern Studies, 2004).

21. Khaked Al Hroub, "Talking books," *Index on Censorship* 33, no. 2 (2004), p. 184.

22. It is worth noting a poll prepared for Worldcasting by the Middle East television survey organization IPSOS-STAT which points out a decline of Al Jazeera's popularity among its viewers. See Alvin Snyder, "Al Jazeera novelty wearing thin," *Middle East Times*, 25 January 2006, <http://metimes.com/articles/normal.php?StoryID=2006 0125-075509-5624r>. See also "Al Arabiya wins the bet," *Al Hayat*, 17 February 2005, p. 21.

Chapter III

1. Dorothy Leonard-Barton, *Wellsprings of Knowledge: Building and Sustaining the Sources of Innovation* (Boston: Harvard Business School Press, 1995), pp. 4–5.

2. See Lucy Küng-Shankleman, *Inside the BBC and CNN: Managing Media Organizations* (London: Routledge, 2000), pp. 103–04, 135–36, 170–74.

3. See Küng-Shankleman, *Inside the BBC and CNN*, p. 103.

4. See Küng-Shankleman, *Inside the BBC and CNN*, pp. 103–04, 135–36, 170–74.

5. "Arab attitudes towards political and social issues, foreign policy and the media," <http://www.bsos.umd.edu/sadat/pub/Arab%20Attitudes%20Towards%20Political%20and%20Social%20Issues,%20Foreign%20Policy%20and%20the%20Media.htm>.

6. See Lydia Saad, "Al Jazeera: Arabs rate its objectivity," *Gallup Poll Tuesday Briefing*, 23 April 2002, and Richard Bukholder, "Arabs favor Al Jazeera over state-run channels for world news," *Gallup Tuesday Briefing*, 12 November 2002.

7. Although some praise Al Jazeera for its keenness on presenting balanced views, when it comes to objectivity, it is less likely to be singled out. While the network's reputation for objectivity is strong when compared to other channels, it is probably the weakest area with less than half of the respondents in some Arab countries and a slight majority in the other countries perceiving Al Jazeera as objective.

8. The focus groups in question were conducted by one of the authors in Sharjah, UAE (7 March 2003), Manama, Bahrain (3 December 2003), and Beirut, Lebanon (13 January 2003).

9. "Middle East communications and internet via satellite."

10. Leonard-Barton, *Wellsprings of Knowledge*, p. xi.

11. Paul J.H. Schoemaker, "How to link strategic vision to core capabilities," *Sloan Management Review* 34, no. 1 (Fall 1992), pp. 75–76.

12. Schoemaker, "How to link strategic vision to core capabilities," p. 75. See also Leonard-Barton, *Wellsprings of Knowledge*, p. 4.

13. Leonard-Barton, *Wellsprings of Knowledge*, p. xi.

14. See Küng-Shankleman, *Inside the BBC and CNN*, pp. 172–73.

15. See Küng-Shankleman, *Inside the BBC and CNN*, pp. 172–73.

16. Barbara Demick, "The CNN of the Arab world, Al Jazeera, attracts big audiences and official ire," *Inquirer*, 5 March 2000.

Chapter IV

1. John M. Lavine and Daniel B. Wackman, *Managing Media Organizations: Effective Leadership of the Media* (New York: Longman, 1988), pp. 145–46.

2. Lavine and Wackman, *Managing Media Organizations*, p. 145.

3. Efraim Turban, Ephraim McLean and James Wetherbe, *Information Technology for Management: Making Connections for Strategic Advantage* (New York: John Wiley and Sons, Inc, 1999), pp. 136–38.

4. See Turban, McLean and Wetherbe, *Information Technology for Management*, pp. 136–38, and J. Cash et al., *Building the Information Age Organizations: Structures, Control and Information Technologies* (Burr Ridge, IL: R.D. Irwin, 1994).

5. Lavine and Wackman, *Managing Media Organizations*, p. 182.

6. Lavine and Wackman, *Managing Media Organizations*, p. 17.

7. Rugh, *The Arab Press*.

8. See Muhammad I. Ayish, "Political communication on Arab world television," *Political Communication* 19 (2002): pp. 139–44.

9. In the Arab world, media are usually feared and kept under control because they can potentially undermine the authority of the state and the legitimacy of the regime in power. Information is heavily guarded because it is believed that the flow of information can hinder the government's control and can even be a destabilizing force. The hierarchical organizational model followed by state media (which goes back to an era when media were a state monopoly) reflects and perpetuates the high degree of state control over information.

Chapter V

1. John R. Schermerhorn, James G. Hunt, and Richard N. Osborn, *Organizational Behavior* (New York: John Wiley, 2000), p. 8. See also Jerald Greenberg and Robert A. Baron, *Behavior in Organizations: Understanding and Managing the Human Side of Work* (Upper Saddle River, NJ: Prentice Hall, 2000), p. 506.

2. Robert B. Reich, "The Company of the future," *Fast Company* (November 1988), p. 124.

3. Lavine and Wackman, *Managing Media Organizations*, p. 91.

4. Schermerhorn, Hunt, and Osborn, *Organizational Behavior*, p. 8.

5. "Al Jazeera's Adnan Sharif."

6. "Al Jazeera Satellite Channel: The vision and mission," <http://www.aljazeera.net/NR/exeres/C9999251-E03C-41AA-9F21-5A27E80EC1D0.htm>

7. "Al Jazeera Channel: A historical perspective," Organization Document (2002), p. 1.

8. "Al Jazeera Channel: A historical perspective," p. 1.

9. "Al Jazeera Channel: A historical perspective," p. 1.

10. "Al Jazeera Channel: A historical perspective," p. 1.

11. "Al Jazeera Channel: A historical perspective," p. 2.

12. "Al Jazeera Channel: A historical perspective," p. 2.

13. "Al Jazeera Channel: A historical perspective," p. 1.

14. "Al Jazeera Channel: A historical perspective," p. 2.

15. "Al Jazeera's Adnan Sharif."

16. Peter Feuilherade, "Al Jazeera debates its future," *BBC News*, 13 July 2004, <http://news.bbc.co.uk/go/pr/fr/-/1/hi/world/middle_east/3889551.stm>.

17. Waddah Khanfar, interview with the authors, Doha, 7 April 2005.

18. "Six years after its inception, Al Jazeera imposes itself on the Arab media scene," Organization Document (2002), p. 2.

19. "Al Jazeera Channel: A historical perspective," p. 1.

20. "Al Jazeera Channel: A historical perspective," p. 2.

21. "About Al Jazeera," <http://english.aljazeera.net/NR/exeres/5D7F956E-6B52-46D9-8D17-448856D01CDB.htm>.

22. "Al Jazeera Channel: A historical perspective," p. 2.

23. "Al Jazeera code of ethics," <http://english.aljazeera.net/NR/exeres/07256105-B2FC-439A-B255-D830BB238EA1.htm>.

24. "Al Jazeera Channel: A historical perspective," p. 1.

25. Jeremy M. Sharp, "The Al Jazeera News Network: Opportunity or challenge for U.S. foreign policy in the Middle East?" *Congressional Research Service Report for Congress*, 23 July 2003, <hhtp://fpc.state.gov/documents/organization/23002.pdf>.

26. Faisal Al Kasim, "*The Opposite Direction*: A program which changed the face of Arab television," in *The Al Jazeera Phenomenon: Critical Perspectives on New Arab Media*, ed. Mohamed Zayani (London: Pluto Press, 2005), p. 101.

27. "Six years after its inception, Al Jazeera imposes itself on the Arab media scene," p. 1.

28. "Middle East communications and internet via satellite."

29. "Six years after its inception, Al Jazeera imposes itself on the Arab media scene," p. 1.

30. "About Al Jazeera."

31. "Al Jazeera code of ethics,"

32. "About Al Jazeera."

33. "Al Jazeera code of ethics."

34. "Al Jazeera Channel: A historical perspective," p. 2.

35. "About Al Jazeera."

36. "Al Jazeera Channel: A historical perspective," p. 2.

37. "About Al Jazeera."

38. "About Al Jazeera."

39. "Middle East communications and internet via satellite."

40. "Al Jazeera code of ethics."

41. "Al Jazeera code of ethics."

42. "Six years after its inception, Al Jazeera imposes itself on the Arab media scene," p. 1.

43. S. Abdallah Schleifer and Sarah Sullivan, "Interview with Mohammed Jassim Al Ali," *Transnational Broadcasting Studies* 7 (Fall/Winter 2001), <http://www.tbsjournal.com/Archives/Fall01/fall01.htmll>.

44. Khanfar, interview with the authors.

45. Michael Dobbs, "Qatar TV station: A clear channel to Middle East," *Washington Post*, 9 October 2001, p. C1.

46. "Al Jazeera Channel: A historical perspective," p. 1.

47. "Al Jazeera code of ethics."

48. Schleifer and Sullivan, "Interview with Mohammed Jassim Al Ali."

49. Jihad Ballout, interview with the authors, 5 February 2002.

50. "Al Jazeera Channel: A historical perspective," p. 2.

51. "About Al Jazeera."

52. Evan Dyer, "Al Jazeera television," *CBC News Online*, 14 March 2003, <http://www.cbs.ca/news/iraq/players/aljazeera.html>.

53. "Six years after its inception, Al Jazeera imposes itself on the Arab media scene," p. 2.

54. "Al Jazeera Channel: A historical perspective," p. 2.

55. Alterman, "The challenge for Al Jazeera International."

56. See Suleiman Al Shammari, *The Arab Nationalist Dimension in Al Jazeera Satellite Channel: A Case Study of The Opposite Direction* (Doha: Dar Al Sharq, 1999), p. 45.

57. Al Kasim, "The Opposite Direction," p. 97.

58. "Al Jazeera Channel: A historical perspective," p. 5.

Chapter VI

1. Schein, *Organizational Culture and Leadership*, p. 1.

2. Lavine and Wackman, *Managing Media Organizations*, p. 229.

3. Edward J. Szewczak and Coral R. Snodgrass, *Managing the Human Side of Information Technology: Challenges and Solutions* (Hershey, PA: Idea Group Publishing & Information Science Publishing, 2002), pp. 38–40.

4. Sharp, "Qatar: Background and U.S. relations."

5. Sharp, "Qatar: Background and U.S. relations."

6. See David Hirst, "Qatar calling: Al Jazeera, the Arab TV channel that dares to shock," *Le Monde Diplomatique*, 8 August 2001.

7. Kenneth Katzman, "The Persian Gulf states: Post-war issues for U.S. policy, 2003," Congressional Research Service Report for Congress, 14 July 2003, <http://fpc.state. gov/documents/organization/22873.pdf>.

8. Mohamed Mekki Ahmad, "Qatar abolishes the Ministry of Health Care," *Al Hayat*, 6 May 2005, p. 1, 6.

9. Sheikh Hamad bin Thamer Al Thani, "Interview with Abdallah Schleifer and Sarah Sullivan," *Transnational Broadcasting Studies* 7 (Fall/Winter 2001), <http://www.tbs journal.com/Archives/Fall01/Jazeera_chair man.html>.

10. "Country reports on human rights practices: Qatar," released by Bureau of Democracy, Human Rights and Labor, 4 March 2001, <http://www.state.gov/g/drl/ rls/hrrpt/2001/nea/8292.htm>.

11. "Country reports on human Rights practices: Qatar," released by Bureau of Democracy, Human Rights and Labor, 28 February 2005, <http://www.state.gov/g/ drl/rls/hrrpt/2004/41730.htm>.

12. Lamloum, Al-Jazira, p. 66.

13. Denis Siefert, "Al Jazira: 'Une revanche sur l'agressivité de la narration occidentale'— un entretien avec Olfa Lamloum," *Idées*, 16 September 2004, <http://www. politis.fr/article1063.html>.

14. Miles, *Al Jazeera*, p. 323.

15. "Qatar pledges Al Jazeera review," *BBC News*, 30 April 2004, <http://news. bbc.co.uk/2/hi/middle_east/3674287.stm>.

16. "Al Jazeera's Mohammed Jassim Al Ali: An interview with Chris Forrester," *World Screen News* (January 2002), <http:// www.worldscreen.com/interviewsarchive.ph p?filename=jazeera.txt>.

17. Brian Wheeler, "Al Jazeera's cash crisis," *BBC News*, 4 July 2003, <http://news. bbc.co.uk/go/pr/fr/-/1/hi/business/ 2908953.stm>.

18. Abdul Fattah Fayed, "Five billion Dollars is the size of spending on advertising in the Gulf region for this year," *Al Hayat*, 22 March 2006, p. 12.

19. Miles, *Al Jazeera*, p. 337.

20. See Gordon Robinson, "The rest of Arab television," Middle East Project Paper (Los Angeles: USC Center on Public Diplomacy, June 2005), p. 5., <http://uscpublic diplomacy.com/pdfs/Robinson_-_Rest_ Of_Arab_Television_June05.pdf>.

21. Miles, *Al Jazeera*, p. 340.

22. See Jeremy M. Sharp, "The Middle East Television Network: An overview," Congressional Research Service Report for Congress, 9 February 2005, <http://www. usembassy.it/pdf/other/RS21565.pdf>. See also Edward Djerejian, "Changing minds, winning peace: A new strategic direction for U.S. public diplomacy in the Arab and Muslim world," Report of the Advisory Group on Public Diplomacy for the Arab and Muslim World, 1 October 2003, <http://www.state. gov/documents/organziation/24882.pdf>.

23. "Country reports on human Rights practices: Qatar," 28 February 2005.

24. "Qatar reshuffles Al Jazeera TV

board," Associated Press, 22 November 2003, <http://www.aljazeerah.info/News%20archives/2003%20News%20archives/November/22%20n/Qatar%20Reshuffles%20Al-Jazeera%20TV%20Board.htm>.

25. Thomas Hylland Eriksen, *Small Places, Large Issues: An Introduction to Social and Cultural Anthropology*, 2nd edition (London: Pluto Press, 2001), p. 95.

26. Bahry, "The new Arab media phenomenon," pp. 88–99.

27. Miles, *Al Jazeera*, p. 425.

28. Miles, *Al Jazeera*, p. 22.

29. "Car bomb targets theatre in Qatar," *BBC News*, 20 March 2005, <http://news.bbc.uk/go/pr/fr/-/1/hi/world/middle_east/4365039.stm>.

30. "Qatar," *The World Fact Book*.

31. Mark Bixler, "Backgrounder Qatar: Reformist state a key base for U.S. in Persian Gulf," *The Atlanta Journal and Constitution*, 27 December 2002, <http://www.globalsecurity.org/org/news/2002/021227-Qatar01htm>.

32. Sharp, "Qatar: Background and U.S. relations."

33. Sharp, "Qatar: Background and U.S. relations."

34. In September 2005, Qatar Airways signed a deal with Airbus in the presence of the head of the French government, Dominique de Villepin, and the Qatari Foreign Minister, Sheikh Hamad bin Jassim bin Jabr Al Thani, to purchase 60 A350 planes with a total value of over 10 billion dollars. See Rhanda Takhi Eddine, "Qatar Airways purchases 60 Airbus planes," *Al Hayat*, 11 September 2005, p. 11.

35. "Gulf neighbors hope to heal rift," *BBC News*, 11 June 2004, <http://news.bbc.co.uk/go/pr/fr/-/1/hi/world/middle_East/3797893.stm>

36. William Wallis, "Qatar politics: Citizenship ordeal spotlights human rights record," *Financial Times*, Economist Intelligence Unit, EIU Views wire, 18 May 2005. See also "The decision affects the entire sub-tribe: 3500 people resort to Saudi Arabia after their Qatari citizenship was revoked," *Alarabiya.net*, 20 April 2005, <http://www.alarabiya.net/article.aspx?v=12355>, and "A Qatari sub-tribe is collectively deprived of its citizenship for supporting the Emir's father," *Al Arabiya*.net, 30 March 2005, <http://www.alarabiya.net/article.aspx?v=11736>. For a Qatari version of the story, see Ahmad Mansour's interview with Sheikh Hamad bin Jassim bin Jabr Al Thani, *More than One Opinion*, 22 June 2005, <http://www.aljazeera.net/NR/exeres/931FD653-1275-423E-BABA-84E59A1203D5.htm>.

37. See "Qatar reinstates citizenship to those who settled their status," *Al Hayat*, 2 February 2006, p. 4.

38. Jeremy M. Sharp, "Qatar: Background and U.S. relations."

39. "Qatar," *The World Fact Book*.

40. For an assessment of Qatar's economic development, see Moin A. Siddiqi, "Qatar economic report: The tiny emirate of Qatar is on track to become the Gulf's new super energy power," *Middle East*, no. 332 (March 2003): pp. 46–49. See also Rhanda Takhi Eddine, "Qatar exports natural gas to consumers in the East and the West," *Al Hayat*, 27 April 2005, p. 11.

41. The list of Qatar's potential customers includes even the United States. See Mohamed Mekki Ahmad, "The project of exporting gas to the U.S. gets underway," *Al Hayat*, 25 September 2005, p. 11.

42. Sharp, "Qatar: Background and U.S. relations."

43. Katzman, "The Persian Gulf states."

44. Bixler, "Backgrounder Qatar: Reformist state a key base for U.S. in Persian Gulf."

45. Miles, *Al Jazeera*, p. 10.

46. Campbell, "I was wrong about Al Jazeera."

47. Sam Cherribi, "From Baghdad to Paris: Al Jazeera and the veil," *Harvard International Journal of Press/Politics* 11, no. 2 (2006): 121–138.

48. Quoted in Miles, *Al Jazeera*, p. 354.

49. Sharp, "Qatar: Background and U.S. relations."

50. Katzman, "The Persian Gulf states."

51. John R. Bradley, "Will Al Jazeera bend?," *Prospect* (April 2004): p. 48.

52. Taheri, "News is not the only things on the agenda."

53. See Da Lage, "The politics of Al Jazeera" and El Oifi, "Influence without Power."

54. Samantha M. Shapiro, "The war inside the Arab newsroom," *New York Times*, 2 January 2005, <http://www.nytimes.

com/2005/01/02/magazine/02ARAB.html?ex
=105725966&ei=1&en+da3e80ce3fdee22e>.

55. Barbara Demick, "The CNN of the Arab world, Al Jazeera, attracts big audiences and official ire," *Inquirer*, 5 March 2000.

56. Mohannad Al Haj Ali, "Al Jazeera faces Bush's alleged threat: Media and power as weapons," *Al Hayat*, 30 November 2005, p. 17; Alan Cowell, "Bush spoke of attacking Arab news channel, British tabloid says," *The New York Times*, 23 November 2005, <http://www.nytimes.com/2005/11/23/international/europe/23britain.html>; "Report: Bush talked of bombing Al Jazeera," *The New York Times*, 22 November 2005, <http://www.nytimes.com/aponline/international/AP-Britain-Iraq.html>.

57. Nasser Karimi, "Tehran suspends Al Jazeera operations in Iran," Associated Press *Worldstream*, April 18, 2005.

eral manager on its 9th birthday," <http://www.aljazeera.net/NR/exeres/4B050A74-2DE5-4E69-A2B3-432E9A367587.htm>.

11. Küng-Shankleman, *Inside the BBC and CNN*, p. 68.

12. Khaled Al Hroub, "Behind the Western mask," *International Herald Tribune*, 19 November 2004, <http://www.iht.com/articles/2004/11/18/opinion/edhroub.html>.

13. Lavine and Wackman, *Managing Media Organizations*, pp. 191–92.

14. Lavine and Wackman, *Managing Media Organizations*, p. 191.

15. "Al Jazeera denies responsibility for unfitting statements on Sistani," *Al Hayat*, 16 December 2005, p. 4, and "Iranian Foreign Ministry calls the Qatari ambassador to protest 'Al Jazeera's harmful statements' about Al Sistani," *Al Hayat*, 19 December 2005, p. 3.

Chapter VII

1. Lamloum, *Al-Jazira*, p. 141.

2. See for instance Beysna Al Sheikh, "Akram Kouzam suspects Russian Intelligence Services behind Al Jazeera's decision to end his contract," *Al Hayat*, 20 December 2005, p. 21.

3. S.H. Appelbaum, D. Herbert, and S. Leroux, "Empowerment: power, culture and leadership: a strategy or fad for the millennium," *Journal of Workplace Learning* 11, no. 7 (1999): p. 91.

4. Turban, McLean, and Wetherbe, *Information Technology for Management*, pp. 138–40.

5. Turban, McLean, and Wetherbe, *Information Technology for Management*, pp. 138–40.

6. C. Hardy and S. Leiba-O'Sullivan, "The power behind empowerment: Implications for research and practice," *Human Relations* (April 1998): pp. 451–83.

7. Miles, *Al Jazeera*, p. 345.

8. Naomi Sakr, "The impact of commercial interest in media content," in *Arab Media in the Information Age* (Abu Dhabi: ECSSR, 2006), p. 87.

9. Mahmoud Abdulhedi, interview with authors, 8 December 2004.

10. See "The speech of Al Jazeera's gen-

Chapter VIII

1. Sunil J. Ramlall, "Measuring human resource management's effectiveness in improving performance," *Human Resource Planning* 26, no. 1, pp. 51–63.

2. B. Eves and M. Olson, "User involvement and MIS success: A review research," *Management Science* 30, no. 5 (May 1984): pp. 586–603. See also P. Tait and I. Vessey, "The effect of user involvement on system success: A contingency approach, *MIS Quarterly* 12, no. 1 (March 1988): pp. 91–108.

3. E.E. Lawler III, "Strategic design of reward systems," in *Strategic Human Resource Management*, ed. N. Tichy, C. Formbrun, and M. Devanna (New York: John Wiley and Sons, 1983).

4. Lawler, "Strategic design of reward systems."

5. Shapiro, "The war inside the Arab newsroom."

6. Fatema Mernissi, "The satellite, the prince and Sheherazade: The rise of women as communicators in digital Islam," *Transnational Broadcasting Studies*, no. 12 (Spring 2004), <www.tbsjournal.com/mernissi.htm>.

7. Al Qardawi has been ranked among the top 100 leading public intellectuals by *Foreign Policy* and *Prospect Magazine*. See "The Prospect/FP top 100 public intellectu-

als," *Foreign Policy* (September/October 2005), <http://foreignpolicy.com/story/cms.php?story_id=3249>.

8. Küng-Shankleman, *Inside the BBC and CNN*, p. 210.

9. Küng-Shankleman, *Inside the BBC and CNN*, p. 132.

10. "Expatriates in Qatar feel the weight of Inflation," *Al Hayat*, 18 October 2005, p. 3.

11. For a discussion of the open versus secretive reward system, see R.H. Kilmann, *Managing beyond the Quick Fix: A Completely Integrated Program for Creating and Maintaining Organizational Success* (San Francisco: Jossey-Bass, 1989) and S.J. Carrol, "Handling the need for consistency and the need for contingency in the management of compensation," *Human Resources Planning* 11, no. 3 (1988): pp. 191–96.

12. For a discussion of competency-based versus performance-based rewards, see J.L. Pearce, "Why merit pay doesn't work: implications from organization theory," in *New Perspectives on Compensation*, ed. D.B. Balkin and L.R. Gomez-Mejia (Englewood Cliffs, NJ: Prentice Hall, 1987) and E.E. Lawler III, *High Involvement Management: Participative Strategy for Improving Organizational Performance* (San Francisco: Jossey-Bass, 1994), p. 8.

13. Carrol, "Handling the need for consistency and the need for contingency in the management of compensation," pp. 191–96.

14. Carrol, "Handling the need for consistency and the need for contingency in the management of compensation," pp. 191–96.

15. L.R. Gomez-Mejia and T.M. Welbourne, "Compensation strategy: an overview and future steps," *Human Resource Planning* 11, no. 3 (1989): pp. 173–89.

Chapter IX

1. Turban, McLean and Wetherbe, *Information Technology for* Management, pp. 116–17.

2. Omar A. El Sawy, *Redesigning Enterprise Processes for e-Business* (Boston: McGraw-Hill, 2001), pp. 16–18.

3. P. Scholtes and H. Hacquebord, "Beginning the quality transformation," *Quality Progress* (July 1988): pp. 28–33.

4. Turban, McLean and Wetherbe, *Information Technology for Management*, pp. 371–72.

5. Thomas H. Davenport and Laurence Prusak, *Working Knowledge: How Organizations Manage What They Know* (Boston: Harvard University Press, 1988), p. x.

6. Turban, McLean and Wetherbe, *Information Technology for Management*, pp. 456–57.

7. Davenport and Prusak, *Working Knowledge*, p. xii.

8. Gabriel Szulanski, *Sticky Knowledge: Barriers to Knowing in the Firm* (London: Sage Publications, 2003), p. 16.

9. A newspaper article noting that "power failed in part of the Qatari capital on Thursday, interrupting news broadcasts by the popular pan–Arab satellite TV channel Al Jazeera" is suggestive about Al Jazeera's infrastructure. See "Power outage disrupts Al Jazeera," *The Jerusalem Post*, 2 December 2004.

10. "Mapping the Arab world: How curious world maps gave al Arabiya the edge," December 2004, <http://www.curioussoftware/userprofiles/alarabiya.html>.

11. "New Al Jazeera International global news center to rely on Vizrt," *Primedia Business Magazines and Media*, 24 August 2005.

12. "Arab satellite television and the problems of the nation," p. 152.

13. "Al Jazeera's Mohammed Jassim Al Ali."

14. "Al Jazeera's Mohammed Jassim Al Ali."

15. S. Abdallah Schleifer, "A dialogue with Abdul Rahman Al Rashed," *Transnational Broadcasting Studies* 14 (Spring 2005), <http://www.tbsjournl.com/al-rashed dialogue.html>.

16. S. Abdallah Schleifer, "Al Jazeera update: More datelines from Doha and a code of ethics," *Transnational Broadcasting Studies* 13 (Fall 2004), <http://www.tbsjournl.com/aljazeera_schleifer.html>.

17. "Qatar's Al Jazeera TV relaunches news format," *BBC Monitoring World Media*, 16 June 2005.

18. "Al Jazeera takes 1000 hours of BBC programming," BBC Worldwide Press Release, 26 February 2004, <http://www.bbc.co.uk/pressoffice/commercial/worldwidestories/pressreleases/2003/02_february/al_jazera.shtml>.

19. Miles, *Al Jazeera*, p. 337.

20. Gordon R. Robinson, "Tasting Western journalism: Media training in the Middle East," Middle East Project Paper (Los Angeles: USC Center on Public Diplomacy, May 2005), p. 7, <http:www.uscpublicdiplomacy.com/pdfs/Robinson_Tasting_Western_Journalism_May05.pdf>.

Chapter X

1. John M. Lavine and Daniel B. Wackman, *Managing Media Organizations: Effective Leadership of the Media* (New York: Longman, 1988), p. 96.
2. Quoted in Miles, *Al Jazeera*, p. 302.
3. S. Abdallah Schleifer, "Al Jazeera update."
4. For a detailed account of these allegations, see Miles, *Al Jazeera*, pp. 289–94.
5. "Saddam's agents infiltrated Al Jazeera TV," *Sify.com*, 3 June 2003, <http://sify.com/news/international/fullstory.php?id=13163009>.
6. See Miles, *Al Jazeera*, p. 318.
7. S. Abdallah Schleifer, "Stop press: Al Jazeera gets new manager," *Transnational Broadcasting* Studies 11 (Fall/Winter 2003), <http://www.tbsjournal.com/Archives/Fall03/stop_press.html>.
8. Miles, *Al Jazeera*, p. 319.
9. See Mariah Blake, "From all sides: In the deadly cauldron of Iraq, even the Arab media are being pushed off the story," *Columbia Journalism Review* 2 (March/April 2005), <http://www.cjr.org/issues/2005/2/onthejob-blake.asp>.
10. Iason Athanasiadis, "Trailblazing Al Jazeera loses its edge," *Asia Times*, 4 November 2003, <http://www.atimes.com/atimes/Middle_East/EK04AK01.html>.
11. S. Abdallah Schleifer, "Interview with Mohammed Jassim Al Ali," *Transnational Broadcasting Studies* 10 (Spring 2003), <http://tbsjournal.com/Archives/Spring03/jasim.html>.
12. "Jordanian becomes director of the Qatari Al Jazeera TV," *Jordan Times*, 26 October 2003.
13. Waddah Khanfar, interview with the authors.
14. Lavine and Wackman, *Managing Media Organizations*, pp. 114–15.

15. "Jihad Ballout from Al Jazeera to Al Arabiya," *Al Bawaba*, <http://www.albawaba.com/en/countries/UAE/188184>.
16. Faisal Abbas, "Question and answer with Al Arabiya's Jihad Ballout," *Al Sharq Al Awsat*, 9 September 2005, <http://aawsat.com/english/news.asp?id=1619&section=5>.
17. Miles, *Al Jazeera*, pp. 344–45.
18. Miles, *Al Jazeera*, pp. 344–45.
19. On social capital, see Don Cohen and Laurence Prusak, *In Good Company: How Social Capital Makes Organizations Work* (Boston: Harvard Business School Press, 2001).

Chapter XI

1. Waddah Khanfar, interview with the authors.
2. Waddah Khanfar, "Credibility of specialized news channels: Competing for viewers."
3. Waddah Khanfar, "The Future of Al Jazeera.," *Transnational Broadcasting Studies* 12 (Spring 2004), <http://www.tbsjournl.com/khanfar.htm>
4. "Al Jazeera." *Middle East* (October 2004): p. 50–54.
5. "Al Jazeera." *Middle East*, p. 50–54.
6. Marc Lynch, "Watching Al Jazeera," p. 38.
7. Khanfar, "The Future of Al Jazeera."
8. "Broadcasting management training started in Qatar with IPDC support," <http://portal.unesco.org/ci/en/ev.php-URL_ID=19801&URL_DO=DO_TOPIC&&URL_SECTION=201.html>.
9. Giles Tremelett, "When a reporter got too close to the story," *The Guardian*, 3 October 2005, <http://media.guardian.co.uk/site/story/0,14173,1583259,00.html>.
10. Miles, *Al Jazeera*, p. 313.
11. See El Oifi, "Influence without power," p. 71.
12. S. Abdallah Schleifer, "Interview with Yosri Fouda," *Transnational Broadcasting Studies* 11, (Fall/Winter 2003), <http://www/tbsjournal.com/Archives/Fall03/Yosri_Fouda.html>.
13. Khanfar, interview with the authors.

Chapter XII

1. Khanfar, "The Future of Al Jazeera."
2. "Director general for Al Jazeera Satellite Network appointed," Al Jazeera Press Release, 23 March 2006.
3. "TV Beirut bureau chief on rationale behind Al Jazeera Live channel," *BBC monitoring Middle East-political, BBC Worldwide Monitoring* (originally published in Arabic in *Al Safir*, 14 April 2005).
4. "Al Jazeera starts kids channel — with a difference," *Agence France Press*, 9 September 2005.
5. "Indiantelevision.com's interview with Al Jazeera MD Waddah Khanfar," 2 September 2004, <http://www.indiantelevision.com/interviews/y2k4/executive/wadah_khanfar.htm>.
6. Feiruz Zayani, "Al Jazeera Channel," *Kawalees*, 18 June 2005, <http://aljazeera.net/NR/exeres/2706A397-E5A8–46DA-853C-005C7E7316CD.htm>.
7. Kai Ryssdal and Stephen Beard, "Al Jazeera forms partnership with British travel agency," *Market Place*, Minnesota Public Radio, 16 August 2005.
8. "Al Jazeera celebrates its tenth anniversary," <http:www.aljazeera.net/NR/exeres/236F4584-EA4D-4C7E-B18E-F1A0612499E5.htm>.
9. Miles, *Al Jazeera*, pp. 404–13.
10. "Al Jazeera plans to set alternative agenda," *China Daily (North American Edition)*, 6 July 2005, p. 7.
11. Miles, *Al Jazeera*, p. 413.
12. Miles, *Al Jazeera*, p. 406.
13. "Qatar: Al Jazeera to launch sport channel," *BBC Monitoring World Media*, 17 August, 2005.

14. S. Abdallah Schleifer, "Al Jazeera update."
15. Khanfar, "The Future of Al Jazeera."
16. Steven R. Weisman, "Under pressure, Qatar may sell Al Jazeera station," *The New York Times*, 30 January 2004.
17. "Qatar pledges Al Jazeera 'review.'"
18. Weisman, "Under pressure, Qatar may sell Al Jazeera station." See also Mohamed Mekki Ahmad, "Al Jazeera is to be privatized," *Al Hayat*, 22 January 2005, p. 2, and "Qatar is keen on selling Al Jazeera," *Al Hayat*, 31 January 2005, p. 4.
19. Feuilherade, "Al Jazeera debates its future."
20. Pein, "Is Al Jazeera ready for prime time?"
21. Miles, *Al Jazeera*, p. 425.
22. Rupert Cornwell, "U.S. accused of plan to muzzle Al Jazeera through privatization," *The Independent*, 15 February 2005.
23. Miles, *Al Jazeera*, p. 425.

Chapter XIII

1. Lamloum, *Al-Jazira*, p. 105.
2. Fatema Mernissi, "How to seduce Arab minds," <http://www.mernissi.net/books/articles/cyber_islam_1.html>.
3. Küng-Shankleman, *Inside the BBC and CNN*, p. 67.
4. James R. Lucas, *The Passionate Organization: Igniting the Fire of Employee Commitment* (New York: AMACOM, 1999).

Bibliography

Abbas, Faisal. "Question and answer with Al Arabiya's Jihad Ballout." *Al Sharq Al Awsat*, 9 September 2005, <http://aawsat.com/english/news.asp?id=1619&section=5>.

"About Al Jazeera." <http://english.aljazeera.net/NR/exeres/5D7F956E-6B52-46D9-8D17-448856D01CDB.htm>.

Abt, Samuel. "For Al Jazeera, balanced coverage frequently leaves no side happy." *International Herald Tribune*, 16 February 2004.

Ahmad, Mohamed Mekki. "Al Jazeera is to be privatized." *Al Hayat*, 22 January 2005, p. 2.

_____. "Qatar abolishes the Ministry of Health Care." *Al Hayat*, 6 May 2005, pp. 1, 6.

_____. "The project of exporting gas to the U.S. gets underway." *Al Hayat*, 25 September 2005, p. 11.

"Al Arabiya wins the bet." *Al Hayat*, 17 February 2005, p. 21.

Al Haj Ali, Mohannad. "Al Jazeera faces Bush's alleged threat: Media and power as weapons." *Al Hayat*, 30 November 2005, p. 17.

Al Hroub, Khaked. "Talking books." *Index on Censorship* 33, no. 2 (2004).

_____. "Behind the Western mask." *International Herald Tribune*, 19 November 2004, <http://www.iht.com/articles/2004/11/18/opinion/edhroub.html>.

"Al Jazeera celebrates its tenth anniversary." <http:www.aljazeera.net/NR/exeres/236F4584-EA4D-4C7E-B18E-F1A0612499E5.htm>.

"Al Jazeera celebrates its tenth birthday." *Open Dialogue*, 28 October 2006. <http://www.aljazeera.net/NR/exeres/0B720564-C6FC-4D71-A5FE-9615F63E388C>.

"Al Jazeera Channel: A historical perspective." Organization Document (2002).

"Al Jazeera code of ethics." < http://english.aljazeera.net/NR/exeres/07256105-B2FC-439A-B255-D830BB238EA1.htm>.

"Al Jazeera denies responsibility for unfitting statements on Al Sistani." *Al Hayat*, 16 December 2005, p. 4.

"Al Jazeera plans to set alternative agenda." *China Daily (North American Edition)*, 6 July 2005, p. 7.

"Al Jazeera Satellite Channel: The vision and mission." <http://www.aljazeera.net/NR/exeres/C9999251-E03C-41AA-9F21-5A27E80EC1D0.htm>

"Al Jazeera starts kids channel — with a difference." *Agence France Press*, 9 September 2005.

"Al Jazeera takes 1000 hours of BBC programming." BBC Worldwide Press Release, 26 February 2004, <http://www.bbc.co.uk/pressoffice/commercial/worldwidestories/pressreleases/2003/02_february/al_jazeera.shtml>.

"Al Jazeera." *Middle East* (October 2004), pp. 50–54.

"Al Jazeera's Adnan Sharif: An interview with Chris Forrester" (October 2003), <http://www.worldscreen.com/interviewsarchive.php?filename=1003sharif.txt>.

Bibliography

"Al Jazeera's Mohammed Jassim Al Ali: An interview with Chris Forrester." *World Screen News* (January 2002), <http://www.worldscreen.com/interviewsarchive.php?file name=jazeera.txt>.

"Aljazeera.net breaks the 5 million daily visitor threshold." *Aljazeera.net*, 28 September 2005, <http://www.aljazeera.net/NR/exeres/4AA8D374-4367-446E-8317-0039 F9FF73F2.htm>.

Al Kasim, Faisal. "Crossfire." *Harvard International Journal of Press/Politics* 4, no. 3 (1999): pp. 93–97.

_____. "*The Opposite Direction*: A program which changed the face of Arab television." In *The Al Jazeera Phenomenon: Critical Perspectives on New Arab Media*, edited by Mohamed Zayani, pp. 93–105. London: Pluto Press, 2005.

Al Shammari, Suleiman. *The Arab Nationalist Dimension in Al Jazeera Satellite Channel: A Case Study of The Opposite Direction*. Doha: Dar Al Sharq, 1999.

Al Sheikh, Beysan. "Akram Khouzam suspects Russian intelligence services behind Al Jazeera's decision to end his contract." *Al Hayat*, 20 December 2005, p. 21.

Al Thani, Sheikh Hamad bin Thamer. "Interview with Abdallah Schleifer and Sarah Sullivan," *Transnational Broadcasting Studies* 7 (Fall/Winter 2001), <http://www.tbs journal.com/Archives/Fall01/Jazeera_chairman.html>

Alterman, Jon B. "The challenge for Al Jazeera International," *Transnational Broadcasting Studies* 14 (Spring 2005), <http://www.tbsjournal.com/alterman.html>.

Alvesson, Mats. "The Culture perspective on organizations: Instrumental values and basic features of cultures," *Scandinavian Journal of Management* 5, no. 2 (1989).

Appelbaum, S.H., D. Herbert, and S. Leroux. "Empowerment: power, culture and leadership — a strategy or fad for the millennium." *Journal of Workplace Learning* 11, no. 7 (1999).

"Arab attitudes towards political and social issues, foreign policy and the media." <http://www.bsos.umd.edu/sadat/pub/Arab%20Attitudes%20Towards%20Political%20and%20Social%20Issues,%20Foreign%20Policy%20and%20the%20Media.htm>.

"Arab satellite television and the problems of the nation." *Arabs and Satellite TV*. Beirut: Center for Arab Unity Studies, 2004.

Athanasiadis, Iason. "Trailblazing Al Jazeera loses its edge." *Asia Times*, 4 November 2003, <http://www.atimes.com/atimes/Middle_East/EK04AK01.html>.

Ayish, Muhammad I. "Arab television goes commercial: A case study of the Middle East Broadcasting Center." *Gazette* 59, no. 6 (1997): 473–94.

_____. "Political communication on Arab world television." *Political Communication* 19 (2002).

_____. "The changing face of Arab communication: media survival in the information age." In *Mass Media, Politics and Society in the Middle East*, edited by Kai Hafez, pp. 111–36. Cresskill: Hampton Press, 2001.

Azran, Tal. "Resisting peripheral exports: Al Jazeera's war images on U.S. television." *Media International Australia Incorporating Culture and Policy* 113 (November 2004): 75–86.

Bahry, Louay Y. "The new Arab media phenomenon: Qatar's Al Jazeera." *Middle East Policy* 8, no. 2 (June 2001).

Ben Belgacem, Habib. "Communication, mondialisation et monde arabe." *EurOrient* 11 (2002): 113–38.

Benhalla, Fouad. *Le Choc de la communication globale: Pouvoirs et sociétés arabes face au défi*. Parris: Éditions Publisud, 2005.

Bin Jeddou, Gassan. "Al Jazeera on its tenth anniversary." *Open Dialogue*, 28 October 2006, <http://www.aljazeera.net/NR/exeres/0B720564-C6FC-4D71-A5FE-9615F63E388C>.

Bondokji, Neven. "Peace-building media in the Middle East: The case of Al Jazeera and Al Arabiya." *Conflict in Focus* 13 (June 2006): 2–4.

"Bush House of Arabia: The BBC takes on Al Jazeera." *The Economist*, 29 October 2005.

"BBC signs news exchange agreement with Al Jazeera." <http://www.bbc.co.uk/pressoffice/pressreleases/stories/2003/01_january/15/al-jazeera.shtml>.

Bixler, Mark. "Backgrounder Qatar: Reformist state a key base for U.S. in Persian Gulf." *The Atlanta Journal and Constitution*, 27 December 2002, <http://www.globalsecurity.org/org/news/2002/021227-Qatar01htm>.

Blake, Mariah. "From all sides: In the deadly cauldron of Iraq, even the Arab media are being pushed off the story." *Columbia Journalism Review* 43, no. 6 (March/April 2005): pp. 16–19, <http://www.cjr.org/issues/2005/2/onthejob-blake.asp>.

Bodi, Faisal. "Al Jazeera tells the truth about war." *Guardian*, 28 March 2003, <http://www.guardian.co.uk/print/0,3858,4635417,00.html>.

Boyd, Douglas. "Saudi Arabia's international media strategy: Influence through multinational ownership." In *Mass Media, Politics, and Society in the Middle East*, edited by Hafez Kai, pp. 56–57. Cresskill: Hampton Press, 2001.

Boyer, Mike. "Al Jazeera's brand name news." *Foreign Policy*, April 2005, <http://www.foreignpolicy.com/story/cms.php?story_id=2822&print=1>.

Bradley, John R. "Will Al Jazeera bend?" *Prospect* (April 2004): p. 48.

"Broadcasting management training started in Qatar with IPDC support." <http://portal.unesco.org/ci/en/ev.php-URL_ID=19801&URL_DO=DO_TOPIC&&URL_SECTION=201.html>.

Bukholder, Richard. "Arabs favor Al Jazeera over state-run channels for world news." *Gallup Tuesday Briefing*, 12 November 2002.

Burns, John F. "Arab TV gets a new slant: Newscasts without censorship." *New York Times*, 4 July 1999.

Campbell, Alastair. "I was wrong about Al Jazeera." *The Guardian*, 15 September 2004.

"Car bomb targets theatre in Qatar." *BBC News*, 20 March 2005, <http://news.bbc.co.uk/go/pr/fr/-/1/hi/world/middle_east/4365039.stm>.

Carrol, S.J. "Handling the need for consistency and the need for contingency in the management of compensation." *Human Resources Planning* 11, no. 3 (1988): pp. 191–96.

Cash, J., et al. *Building the Information Age Organizations: Structures, Control and Information Technologies*. Burr Ridge, IL: R.D. Irwin, 1994.

Cherribi, Sam. "From Baghdad to Paris: Al Jazeera and the veil." *Harvard International Journal of Press/Politics* 11, no. 2 (2006): 121–138.

Cohen, Don, and Laurence Prusak. *In Good Company: How Social Capital Makes Organizations Work*. Boston: Harvard Business School Press, 2001.

Cornwell, Rupert. "U.S. accused of plan to muzzle Al Jazeera through privatization." *The Independent*, 15 February 2005.

"Country reports on human rights practices: Qatar," released by Bureau of Democracy, Human Rights and Labor, 4 March 2001, <http://www.state.gov/g/drl/rls/hrrpt/2001/nea/8292.htm>.

"Country reports on human rights practices: Qatar," released by Bureau of Democracy, Human Rights and Labor, 28 February 2005, <http://www.state.gov/g/drl/rls/hrrpt/2004/41730.htm>.

Cowell, Alan. "Bush spoke of attacking Arab news channel, British tabloid says." *The New York Times*, 23 November 2005. <http://www.nytimes.com/2005/11/23/international/europe/23britain.html>.

Da Lage, Olivier. "The politics of Al Jazeera or the diplomacy of Qatar." In *The Al Jazeera Phenomenon: Critical Perspectives on New Arab Media*, edited by Mohamed Zayani, pp. 49–65. London: Pluto Press, 2005

Davenport, Thomas H., and Laurence Prusak. *Working Knowledge: How Organizations Manage What They Know.* Boston: Harvard University Press, 1988.

"The decision affects the entire sub-tribe: 3500 people resort to Saudi Arabia after their Qatari citizenship was revoked." *Alarabiya.net*, 20 April 2005, <http://www.alarabiya.net/article.aspx?v=12355>.

Demick, Barbara. "The CNN of the Arab world, Al Jazeera, attracts big audiences and official ire." *Inquirer*, 5 March 2000.

"Director General for Al Jazeera Satellite Network appointed." Al Jazeera Press Release, 23 March 2006.

Djerejian, Edward. "Changing minds, winning peace: A new strategic direction for U.S. public diplomacy in the Arab and Muslim world." Report of the Advisory Group on Public Diplomacy for the Arab and Muslim World, 1 October 2003, <http://www.state.gov/documents/organziation/24882.pdf>.

Dobbs, Michael. "Qatar TV station: A clear channel to Middle East." *Washington Post*, 9 October 2001, p. C1.

Drummond, James. "Qatari broadcaster emerges as key channel of communication." *Financial Times*, 9 October 2001, p. 4.

Dyer, Evan. "Al Jazeera television." *CBC News Online*, 14 March 2003, <http://www.cbs.ca/news/iraq/players/aljazeera.html>.

Dyke, Greg. "Impact of global news channels on international relations." In *Arab Media in the Information Age*, pp. 399–416. Abu Dhabi: ECSSR, 2006.

El Nawawy, Mohammed. "U.S. public diplomacy in the Arab world: the news credibility of Radio Sawa and Television Al Hurra in five countries." *Global Media and Communication* Vol. 2, no. 2 (2006): 183–203.

El Nawawy, Mohammed, and Adel I. Farag. *Al Jazeera: How the Free Arab News Network Scooped the World and Changed the Middle East.* Boulder: Westview Press, 2002.

El Oifi, Mohammed. "L'Effet Al-Jazira." *Politique étrangère* 3 (2004): 649–60.

_____."Influence without power: Al Jazeera and the Arab public sphere." In *The Al Jazeera Phenomenon: Critical Perspectives on New Arab Media*, edited by Mohamed Zayani, pp. 66–79. London: Pluto Press, 2005.

_____. "L'Opinion publique arabe entre logiques éstatiques et solidarités transnationales." *Raisons Politiques* 19 (August–September 2005): 54–62.

El Sawy, Omar A. *Redesigning Enterprise Processes for e-Business.* Boston: McGraw-Hill, 2001, pp. 16–18.

Eriksen, Thomas Hylland. *Small Places, Large Issues: An Introduction to Social and Cultural Anthropology.* 2nd ed. London: Pluto Press, 2001.

Eves, B., and M. Olson. "User involvement and MIS success: A review research." *Management Science* 30, no. 5 (May 1984): pp. 586–603.

Fayed, Abdul Fattah. "Five billion dollars is the size of spending on advertising in the Gulf region for this year." *Al Hayat*, 22 March 2006, p. 12.

Feuilherade, Peter. "Al Jazeera debates its future." *BBC News*, 13 July 2004, <http://news.bbc.co.uk/go/pr/fr/-/1/hi/world/middle_east/3889551.stm>.

Fisk, Robert. "America increasing pressure on Al Jazeera TV." *The Independent*, 30 July 2003.

Forrester, Chris. "Al Jazeera's Adnan Sharif." October 2003, <http://www.worldscreen.com/interviewsarchive.php?filename=1003sharif.txt>

Gomez-Mejia, L.R., and T.M. Welbourne. "Compensation strategy: An overview and future steps." *Human Resource Planning* 11, no. 3 (1989): pp. 173–89.

Gouveia, Philip Fiske de. *An African Al Jazeera? Mass Media and the African Renaissance.* London: The Foreign Policy Center, 2005.

Greenberg, Jerald, and Robert A. Baron. *Behavior in Organizations: Understanding and Managing the Human Side of Work.* Upper Saddle River, NJ: Prentice Hall, 2000.

Guaaybess, Tourya. *Télévisions arabes sur orbite: Un système médiatique en mutation (1960–2004).* Paris: CNRS Éditions, 2005.

"Gulf neighbors hope to heal rift." *BBC News*, 11 June 2004, <http://news.bbc.co.uk/go/pr/fr/-/1/hi/world/middle_East/3797893.stm>.

Hafez, Kai. "Mass media in the Middle East: Patterns of political and societal change." In *Mass Media, Politics, and Society in the Middle East*, edited by Kai Hafez. Cresskill: Hampton Press, 2001.

Hardy, C., and S. Leiba-O'Sullivan. "The power behind empowerment: Implications for research and practice." *Human Relations* (April 1998): pp. 451–83.

Hatch, Mary Jo. *Organizational Theory: Modern, Symbolic and Postmodern Perspectives.* Oxford: Oxford UP, 1997.

Hirst, David. "Qatar calling: Al Jazeera, the Arab TV channel that dares to shock." *Le Monde Diplomatique*, 8 August 2001.

"Indiantelevision.com's interview with Al Jazeera MD Waddah Khanfar." 2 September 2004, <http://www.indiantelevision.com/interviews/y2k4/executive/wadah_khanfar.htm>.

"Iranian Foreign Ministry calls the Qatari ambassador to protest 'Al Jazeera's harmful statements' about Al Sistani." *Al Hayat*, 19 December 2005, p. 3.

"Jihad Ballout from Al Jazeera to Al Arabiya." *Al Bawaba*, <http://www.albawaba.com/en/countries/UAE/188184>.

"Jordanian becomes director of the Qatari Al Jazeera TV." *Jordan Times*, 26 October 2003.

Jorisch, Avi. *Beacon of Hatred: Inside Hizballah's Al Manar Television.* Washington, D.C.: Washington Institute for Near Eastern Studies, 2004.

Karimi, Nasser. "Tehran suspends Al Jazeera operations in Iran." Associated Press Worldstream, April 18, 2005.

Katzman, Kenneth. "The Persian Gulf states: Post-war issues for U.S. policy, 2003." Congressional Research Service Report for Congress, 14 July 2003, <http://fpc.state.gov/documents/organization/22873.pdf>.

Kazan, Fayad E. *Mass Media, Modernity and Development: Arab States of the Gulf.* Westport, CT: Praeger, 1993.

Khanfar, Waddah. "Credibility of specialized news channels: Competing for viewers." In *Arab Media in the Information Age*, pp. 391–397. Abu Dhabi: ECSSR, 2006.

_____. "The Future of Al Jazeera," *Transnational Broadcasting Studies* 12 (Spring 2004), <http://www.tbsjournl.com/khanfar.htm>.

_____. "Statement," World Electronic Media Forum in Geneva, 9–12 December 2003, <http://www.wemfmedia.org/documents/speech_khnafar.PDF>.

_____. "Why did you want to bomb me, Mr. Bush and Mr. Blair?" *The Guardian*, 1 December 2005, <http://www.guardian.co.uk/usa/story/0,12271,1654762,00.html>.

Kilmann, R.H. *Managing beyond the Quick Fix: A Completely Integrated Program for Creating and Maintaining Organizational Success.* San Francisco: Jossey-Bass, 1989.

Kraidy, Marwan. "Transnational television and asymmetrical interdependence in the Arab world: The growing influence of the Lebanese satellite broadcasters." *Transnational*

Broadcasting Studies, no. 5 (Fall/Winter 2000), <www.tbsjournal.com/Archives/Fall00/Kraidy.htm>.

Küng-Shankleman, Lucy. *Inside the BBC and CNN: Managing Media Organizations*. London: Routledge, 2000.

Lamloum, Olfa. *Al-Jazira, miroir rebelle et ambigu du monde arabe*. Paris: La Découverte, 2004.

_____. "De la nicivité des chaînes satellitaires arabes." In *Média, migrations et cultures transnationales*, edited by Tristan Mattelart, pp. 121–33. Bruxelles: De Boeck & Larcier, 2007.

Lavine, John M., and Daniel B. Wackman. *Managing Media Organizations: Effective Leadership of the Media*. New York: Longman, 1988.

Lawler III, E.E. "Strategic design of reward systems." In *Strategic Human Resource Management*, edited by N. Tichy, C. Formbrun, and M. Devanna. New York: John Wiley and Sons, 1983.

_____. *High Involvement Management: Participative Strategy for Improving Organizational Performance*. San Francisco: Jossey-Bass, 1994.

Leonard-Barton, Dorothy. *Wellsprings of Knowledge: Building and Sustaining the Sources of Innovation*. Boston: Harvard Business School Press, 1995.

Le Pottier, Gaëlle. "The emergence of a pan–Arab market in modern media industries." In *Transnational Connections and the Arab Gulf*, edited by Madawi Al-Rasheed, pp. 111–27. London: Routledge, 2005.

Lowesenstein, Antony. "Al Jazeera awakens the Arab world." 9 June 2004, <www.smh.com.au/articles.2004/06/09/1086749772562.html?oneclick+true#>

Lucas, James R. *The Passionate Organization: Igniting the Fire of Employee Commitment*. New York: AMACOM, 1999.

Lynch, Marc. *Voices of the New Arab Public: Iraq, Al Jazeera, and Middle East Politics Today*. New York: Columbia University Press, 2006.

_____. "Watching Al Jazeera." *The Wilson Quarterly* 24, no. 3 (Summer 2001): 36–45.

Manly, Lorne. "Translation: Is the whole world watching." *New York Times*, 26 March 2006.

Mansour, Ahmad. "Interview with Sheikh Hamad bin Jassim bin Jabr Al Thani." *More than One Opinion*, 22 June 2005, <http://www.aljazeera.net/NR/exeres/931FD653-1275-423E-BABA-84E59A1203D5.htm>.

"Mapping the Arab world: How curious world maps gave al Arabiya the edge." December 2004, <http://www.curious-software/userprofiles/alarabiya.html>.

Mariani, Ermete. "Youssef Al Qardawi: Pouvoir médiatique, économie et symbolique." In *Mondialisation et nouveaux médias dans l'espace Arabe*, edited by Franc Mermier, pp. 195–203. Paris: Maisonneuve & Larose, 2001.

Mernissi, Fatema. "How to seduce Arab minds." <http://www.mernissi.net/books/articles/cyber_islam_1.html>.

_____. "The satellite, the prince and Sheherazade: The rise of women as communicators in digital Islam." *Transnational Broadcasting Studies*, no. 12 (Spring 2004), <www.tbsjournal.com/mernissi.htm>.

"Middle East communications and internet via satellite." *Spotbeam Communications Ltd.* (October 2002), <http://www.mindbranch.com/page/catalog/product/2e6a73703f706172746e65723d31303326636f64653d523133312d303038.html>.

Miles, Hugh. *Al Jazeera: The Inside Story of the Arab News Channel that is Challenging the West*. New York: Grove Press, 2005

_____. "What the world thinks of Al Jazeera." *Transnational Broadcasting Journal* 14 (Spring 2004), <http://tbsjournal.com/miles.html>.

"New Al Jazeera International global news center to rely on Vizrt." *Primedia Business Magazines and Media*, 24 August 2005.

Ould Etfagha, Mohameden Baba. "Voyage à l'intérieur d'Al Jazira." *Outre-Terre* 14 (2006): 317–26.

Pearce, J.L. "Why merit pay doesn't work: Implications from organization theory." In *New Perspectives on Compensation*, edited by D.B. Balkin and L.R. Gomez-Mejia. Englewood Cliffs, NJ: Prentice Hall, 1987.

Pein, Corey. "Is Al Jazeera ready for prime time?" *Salon.com*, 20 April 2005, <http://www. salon.com/news/feature/2005/04/22/aljazeera/print.html>.

Peterson, J.E. "Qatar and the world: Branding for a micro-state." *Middle East Journal* 60, no. 4 (2006): 732–48.

Pfanner, Eric. "In shift, BBC to start Arabic TV channel." *International Herald Tribune*, 26 October 2005, <http://www.ift.com/articles/2005/10/25/news/bbc.php>.

Pollock, David. *The "Arab Street?" Public Opinion in the Arab World*. Washington, D.C.: The Washington Institute for Near East Policy, 1992.

"Power outage disrupts Al Jazeera." *The Jerusalem Post*, 2 December 2004.

"The Prospect/FP top 100 public intellectuals." *Foreign Policy* (September/October 2005), <http://foreignpolicy.com/story/cms.php?story_id=3249>.

"Qatar." *The World Fact Book*, <www.cia.gov/cia/publications/factbook/geos/qa.html>.

"Qatar: Al Jazeera to launch sport channel." *BBC Monitoring World Media*, 17 August 2005.

"Qatar is keen on selling Al Jazeera." *Al Hayat*, 31 January 2005, p. 4.

"Qatar pledges Al Jazeera review." *BBC News*, 30 April 2004, <http://news.bbc.co. uk/2/hi/middle_east/3674287.stm>.

"Qatar reshuffles Al Jazeera TV board." Associated Press, 22 November 2003, <http:// www.aljazeerah.info/News%20archives/2003%20News%20archives/Novem-ber/22%20n/Qatar%20Reshuffles%20Al-Jazeera%20TV%20Board.htm>.

"Qatar's Al Jazeera TV relaunches news format." *BBC Monitoring World Media*, 16 June 2005.

"A Qatari sub-tribe is collectively deprived of its citizenship for supporting the Emir's father." *Al Arabiya*.net, 30 March 2005, <http://www.alarabiya.net/article.aspx?v= 11736>.

Ramlall, Sunil J. "Measuring human resource management's effectiveness in improving performance." *Human Resource Planning* 26, no. 1 (2003): 51–63.

Reich, Robert B. "The Company of the future." *Fast Company* 19 (November 1988): pp. 124–29

"Report: Bush talked of bombing Al Jazeera." *The New York Times*, 22 November 2005, <http://www.nytimes.com/aponline/international/AP-Britain-Iraq.html>.

Richardson, Ian. "The failed dream that led to Al Jazeera." <http://www.richardson media.co.uk/al%20jazeera%200rigis.html>.

Robinson, Gordon R. "The rest of Arab television." Middle East Project Paper, USC Center on Public Diplomacy (June 2005), <http://uscpublicdiplomacy.com/pdfs/ Robinson_-_Rest_Of_Arab_Television_June05.pdf>.

_____. "Tasting Western journalism: Media training in the Middle East." Middle East Project Paper, USC Center on Public Diplomacy (May 2005), <http:www.uscpub licdiplomacy.com/pdfs/Robinson_Tasting_Western_Journalism_May05.pdf>.

Rugh, William A. *The Arab Press: News Media and Political Process in the Arab World*. Syracuse: Syracuse University Press, 1979.

Ryssdal, Kai, and Stephen Beard. "Al Jazeera forms partnership with British travel agency." *Market Place*, Minnesota Public Radio, 16 August 2005.

Saad, Lydia. "Al Jazeera: Arabs rate its objectivity." *Gallup Poll Tuesday Briefing*, 23 April 2002.

"Saddam's agents infiltrated Al Jazeera TV." *Sify.com*, 3 June 2003, <http://sify.com/news/international/fullstory.php?id=13163009>.

Saghieh, Hazem. "Al Jazeera: The world through Arab eyes." *The Muslim News*, 17 June 2004, <http://www.muslimnews.co.uk/pda/news.php?article=7600>.

Sakr, Naomi. "The impact of commercial interest in media content." In *Arab Media in the Information Age*, pp. 71–98. Abu Dhabi: ECSSR, 2006.

_____. "Maverick or model? Al Jazeera's impact on Arab satellite television." In *Transnational Television Worldwide: Towards a New Media Order,* edited by Jean K. Chalaby, pp. 66-95. London: I.B. Tauris, 2005.

_____. *Satellite Realms: Transnational Television, Globalization and the Middle East.* London: IB Tauris Publishers, 2001.

Schein, Edgar H. *Organizational Culture and Leadership.* 2nd ed. San Francisco: Jossey-Bass, 1992.

_____. "Sense and non-sense about culture and climate." In *Handbook of Organizational Culture and Climate,* edited by Neal M. Ashkanasy, Celeste P.M. Wilderom and Mark F. Peterson, pp. xxiii–xxx. London: Sage Publications, 2000.

Schermerhorn, John R., James G. Hunt, and Richard N. Osborn. *Organizational Behavior.* New York: John Wiley, 2000.

Schleifer, S. Abdallah, and Sarah Sullivan. "Interview with Mohammed Jassim Al Ali," *Transnational Broadcasting Studies* 7 (Fall/Winter 2001), <http://www.tbsjournal.com/Archives/Fall01/fal101.htmll>.

Schleifer, S. Abdallah. "A dialogue with Abdul Rahman Al Rashed." *Transnational Broadcasting Studies* 14 (Spring 2005), <http://www.tbsjournl.com/al-rasheddialogue.html>.

_____. "Al Jazeera update: More datelines from Doha and a code of ethics." *Transnational Broadcasting Studies* 13 (Fall 2004), <http://www.tbsjournl.com/aljazeera_schleifer.html>.

_____. "Interview with Mohammed Jassim Al Ali." *Transnational Broadcasting Studies* 10 (Spring 2003), <http://tbsjournal.com/Archives/Spring03/jasim.html>.

_____. "Interview with Yosri Fouda," *Transnational Broadcasting Studies* 11 (Fall-Winter 2003), <http://www/tbsjournal.com/Archives/Fall03/Yosri_Fouda.html>.

_____. "Stop press: Al Jazeera gets new manager." *Transnational Broadcasting* Studies 11 (Fall 2003), <http://www.tbsjournal.com/Archives/Fall03/stop_press.html>.

Schoemaker, Paul J.H. "How to link strategic vision to core capabilities." *Sloan Management Review* 34, no. 1 (Fall 1992): 67–81.

Scholtes, P., and H. Hacquebord. "Beginning the quality transformation." *Quality Progress* (July 1988): pp. 28–33.

Schwartz, Stephen. "Losing the hearts and Minds of Arabs," <http://www.islamicpluralism.org/articles/2005a/losingtheheart.htm>.

Shapiro, Samantha M. "The war inside the Arab newsroom." *New York Times*, 2 January 2005, <http://www.nytimes.com/2005/01/02/magazine/02ARAB.html?ex=1105725966&ei=1&en+da3e80ce3fdee22e>.

Sharp, Jeremy M. "The Al Jazeera News Network: Opportunity or challenge for U.S. foreign policy in the Middle East?" Congressional Research Service Report for Congress, 23 July 2003, <hhtp://fpc.state.gov/documents/organization/23002.pdf>.

_____. "The Middle East Television Network: An overview." Congressional Research Service Report for Congress, 9 February 2005, <http://www.usembassy.it/pdf/other/RS21565.pdf>.

_____. "Qatar: Background and U.S. relations." Congressional Research Service Report for Congress, 17 March 2004, <http://fpc.state.gov/documents/organization/33741.pdf>.

Siddiqi, Moin A. "Qatar economic report: the tiny emirate of Qatar is on track to become the Gulf's new super energy power." *Middle East,* no. 332 (March 2003): pp. 46–49.

Siefert, Denis. "Al Jazira: 'Une revanche sur l'agressivité de la narration occidentale' — un entretien avec Olfa Lamloum." *Idées,* 16 September 2004, <http://www.politis.fr/article1063.html>.

"Six years after its inception, Al Jazeera imposes itself on the Arab media scene." Organization Document (2002).

Snyder, Alvin. "Al Jazeera novelty wearing thin." *Middle East Times,* 25 January 2006, <http://metimes.com/articles/normal.php?StoryID=20060125-075509-5624r>.

Szewczak, Edward J., and Coral R. Snodgrass. *Managing the Human Side of Information Technology: Challenges and Solutions.* Hershey, PA: Idea Group Publishing & Information Science Publishing, 2002.

Szulanski, Gabriel. *Sticky Knowledge: Barriers to Knowing in the Firm.* London: Sage Publications, 2003.

Taheri, Amir. "News is not the only things on the agenda: Is Al Jazeera an independent news organization?" *Sunday Telegraph,* 26 December 2004.

Tait, P. and I. Vessey, "The effect of user involvement on system success: A contingency approach," *MIS Quarterly* 12, no.1 (March 1988): pp. 91–108.

Takhi Eddine, Rhanda. "Qatar Airways purchases 60 Airbus planes." *Al Hayat,* 11 September 2005, p. 11.

_____. "Qatar exports natural gas to consumers in the East and the West." *Al Hayat,* 27 April 2005, p. 11.

Tatham, Steve. *Losing Arab Hearts and Minds: The Coalition, Al Jazeera and Muslim public Opinion.* London: Hurst & Company, 2006.

Tayler, Jeffery. "The Faisal factor." *The Atlantic Monthly* (November 2004): 41–43.

Tremelett, Giles. "When a reporter got too close to the story." *The Guardian,* 3 October 2005, <http://media.guardian.co.uk/site/story/0,14173,1583259,00.html>.

Tumber, Howard, and Jerry Palmer. *Media at War: The Iraq Crisis.* London: Sage Publications, 2004.

Turban, Efraim, Ephraim McLean and James Wetherbe. *Information Technology for Management: Making Connections for Strategic Advantage.* New York, John Wiley and Sons, Inc, 1999.

"TV Beirut bureau chief on rationale behind Al Jazeera Live channel." *BBC Monitoring Middle East-political, BBC Worldwide Monitoring* (originally published in Arabic in *Al Safir,* 14 April 2005).

Wallis, William. "Qatar politics: Citizenship ordeal spotlights human rights record." *Financial Times,* Economist Intelligence Unit, EIU Views wire, 18 May 2005.

Weaver, Mary Ann. "Revolution from the top down." *National Geographic* 203, no. 3 (2004).

Weisman, Steven R. "Under pressure, Qatar may sell Al Jazeera station." *The New York Times,* 30 January, 2004.

Wheeler, Brian. "Al Jazeera's cash crisis." *BBC News,* 4 July 2003, <http://news.bbc.co.uk/go/pr/fr/-/1/hi/business/2908953.stm>.

"The world through their eyes." *Economist,* 26 July 2005.

Wright, Robin. "Al Jazeera puts reform into focus." *The Washington Post,* 8 May 2005, p. A1.

Zayani, Feiruz. "Al Jazeera Channel." *Kawalees*, 18 June 2005, <http://aljazeera.net/NR/exeres/2706A397-E5A8-46DA-853C-005C7E7316CD.htm>.

Zayani, Mohamed, ed. *The Al Jazeera Phenomenon: Critical Perspectives on New Arab Media*. London: Pluto Press, 2005.

Zayani, Mohamed. "Arab public opinion in the age of satellite television: The case of Al Jazeera." In *Muslims in the News Media* edited by Elizabeth Poole and John E. Richardson, pp. 176–187. London: I.B. Tauris, 2006.

_____. *Arab Satellite Channels and Politics in the Middle East*. Abu Dhabi: Emirates Center for Strategic Studies and Research, 2004.

Index

Index